THE STORY OF
Viewers FOR
Quality Television

The Television Series
Robert J. Thompson, Series Editor

THE STORY OF
Viewers FOR
Quality Television

From Grassroots to Prime Time

Dorothy Collins Swanson
With Forewords by Linda Ellerbee and Dana Delany

SYRACUSE UNIVERSITY PRESS

The paper used in this publication meets the minimum requirements of American National Standard for Information Sciences—Permanence of Paper for Printed Library Materials, ANSI Z39.48-1984. ∞

Library of Congress Cataloging-in-Publication Data

Swanson, Dorothy Collins.
     The story of Viewers for Quality Television : from grassroots
to prime time / Dorothy Collins Swanson.
        p. cm. — (The television series)
     Includes bibliographical references and index.
     ISBN 0-8156-0649-4 (alk. paper)
        1. Television viewers—United States—Attitudes. 2. Viewers for
Quality Television—History. I. Title. II. Series.

PN1992.55 .S93 2000
302.23'45'0973—dc21   00-029701

A television screen is just a piece of plate glass, but for decades it's been a brick wall, too. VQT represents a breakthrough into the throne rooms on the other side of the screen.

—Ed Bark, *Dallas Morning News*, Oct. 1, 1989

DOROTHY SWANSON cofounded and heads the fifteen-year-old grassroots consumer organization Viewers for Quality Television (VQT). VQT brings together TV watchers who may not have Nielsen boxes in their homes but are determined to have a voice in what the networks put on the air. Swanson has organized and led thirteen Conferences on Quality Television in Los Angeles that have hosted the network entertainment presidents, well-known television producers and writers, and actors. She can be reached at P.O. Box 195, Fairfax Station, Virginia 22039, or by E-mail at dswanson@his.com.

CONTENTS

ILLUSTRATIONS

FOREWORD
Linda Ellerbee

THERE is, in television, a certain arrogance that is hard to ignore. It goes like this: Most of the people who make television believe they are much smarter than most of the people who watch television. Obviously, most of the people who make television never met Dorothy Swanson and her crowd.

I met them back in 1987. Dorothy Swanson had decided to take on a very large network in an attempt to keep it from canceling a show I wrote and anchored. The name of the show was *Our World*. It was about recent American history, including much of the stuff that never seems to get in the history books, or takes years to get there. We who made the show loved the show. So did the approximately 12 million people who watched it each week.

But there was this tiny problem. *Our World* aired on ABC opposite *The Cosby Show* (the biggest hit in television history) on NBC. We were, it seemed, doomed.

Enter Dorothy.

Now, I want to be clear here. ABC *did* cancel *Our World*. But they did it in the face of a great deal of viewer protest, much of it generated by Dorothy Swanson and her group of committed citizens. Me, what I got was to go to Washington and, for the first time in twenty years of television, sit down with a group of television viewers to talk about television. It was a grand experience, and I came away knowing I was right; most viewers are much smarter than most of us who make television.

Of course, Dorothy already knew this.

We never did get *Our World* back on the air, although we tried (call me silly, but I still have hopes) and even to this day people stop me to ask where they can get tapes of the program. But I don't feel as if we lost. You see, we talked back to our TV. You never lose when you do that.

Frankly, I can't say enough about the importance of noisy viewers. Today, when the television universe is so much larger than it was even a dozen years ago, questions of quality come up daily. Sadly, people often tell me they would like to find some way to make their voice heard, but they just don't believe anyone at the top is listening.

I tell them they are wrong. I tell them that although it is true that some network executives cannot read, they can all count.

Then I tell them how to get in touch with Viewers for Quality Television. That way they can join other people, and although they can't necessarily make network honchos change their minds, those executives will sure know they've been in a fight.

It is a start.

A fine start, come to think of it.

After all, wasn't it Arlo Guthrie who said: "If there's one of us, they'll ignore us. If there's two of us, they'll call it a conspiracy. But if there's three of us, it's a movement!"

And I add, if there's a whole bunch of us, both on the outside and on the inside, all demanding better television, who knows what can happen?

Gee, we might even get better television one day.

And so it goes . . . I hope.

FOREWORD
Dana Delany

DOROTHY Swanson knew about quality television before I did.

When I was asked to audition for *China Beach* in 1987 I had no interest in being on television. I had just finished small roles in three films and I was going to be a "film actor." But I had a problem. The script for the pilot of *China Beach* scared me. The writing was great, and I honestly did not know if I was up to it. And I certainly did not want anyone else playing that part.

After a horrible audition process, I finally did get to play the role of Colleen McMurphy. I figured the show would not last past the pilot. It was too unusual. But I was wrong—we lasted three and a half wonderful seasons, and I had one of the best working experiences of my life. And I got to meet Dorothy Swanson and the members of VQT.

When I first heard about Viewers for Quality Television, I assumed they were part of the religious right. I expected them to dictate to us creatively; I first met Dorothy Swanson and Pat Murphy with wariness. I was wrong.

After our first season of *China Beach*, I had come to care passionately about television. I realized that we should not underestimate our audience, that people were craving shows of intelligence, depth, and emotion. It was a great time for television. On ABC alone we had *thirtysomething, Twin Peaks,* and *The Wonder Years,* all groundbreaking, innovative series that took chances. When I met Dorothy Swanson, I finally saw the face of our audience.

I don't think of Viewers for Quality Television as fans. I think of them as our conscience. They remind us to dig deeper and aim higher, because they notice and appreciate it. I also like to think of them as a thorn in the networks' sides that reminds them that not everyone wants mindless, numbing

"I-just-had-a-hard-day-at-work" television. Not everyone wants to be part of the lowest common denominator. Some people still like to think and feel.

I hope that Dorothy and VQT continue together for a long time, at least as long as I'm working in television. I think of them from time to time, and am reminded that it is important to get it right. Television is not about selling soap. It is about telling stories for our time. It makes me proud to be a television actor.

ACKNOWLEDGMENTS

W ITHOUT the ongoing encouragement, support, and friendship of Pat Murphy, this book could not have been written; indeed, there would be no story to tell.

I am grateful to Syracuse University professor Robert J. Thompson for suggesting, while interviewing me for his book *Television's Second Golden Age*, that I write the Viewers for Quality Television story. And I am grateful to friends Laurie Strollo and David Masterman for telling me in 1996 that it was time to do it.

Thanks to the members of VQT for urging me on, and to Mimi Kennedy for her inspiration and encouragement.

Thanks to Barney Rosenzweig for recognizing the potential in the idea of Viewers for Quality Television back in 1984—and, I guess, in me. Thanks also to Harry and Linda Bloodworth-Thomason, whose enthusiasm put VQT on the map.

Many others contributed to this book reaching the final stage; I want to single them out here: Pat Murphy for being there through it all; Arda Swift, Sue Chapman, and Heather Holt for proofreading—Sue and Arda for daring to criticize; Cindy Henderson and Norma Brown for helping prepare the index; Terri Corigliano (formerly of CBS) and Heidi Sanchez (of VQT) for their recollections that strengthened certain portions of the story.

Thank you especially to every VQT member who stayed, sustaining the organization. You have been my inspiration. Without you, there would have been no Viewers for Quality Television organization—and therefore, no story to tell.

Among the many VQT participants through the years who gave of their time and talent, some deserve special mention. Their ongoing support and encouragement were the reasons—along with my unflagging determination—that VQT survived all these years. Viewers for Quality Television *is* the people who believe in it, support it, and participate in it. They made this organization truly "grassroots." David Masterman and his wife, Laurie Strollo, live in Annandale, Virginia. Shortly after joining the group, David became VQT's attorney and was responsible for getting the organization incorporated in October 1988. Laurie joined the board of directors. They both became valued advisers and indispensable "front line" celebrity greeters at conventions.

Kathleen Harmon of New Jersey was instrumental in working with Masterman to secure VQT's 501(c)(3) status in December 1989. Nancy Lutzow, from Mountain View, California, helped us immensely with our first Los Angeles convention, an event we undertook absolutely clueless as to celebrity needs. Nancy's experience with the media and with entertainers, through her work as Joan Baez's personal assistant, was invaluable to us that year and other years thereafter. Strachan Pindar from Savannah, Georgia, enlisted as a "patron" as soon as she joined, and has remained so, by donating $500 every year. In addition, Strachan has served as a computer troubleshooter (can't have enough of those). Linda Crothers was for a while a volunteer from Virginia who helped with the early, massive campaigns. Sue and Don Chapman coordinated our conventions for a number of years. April Kost was always the first to sign up for our conventions, communicating to us that yes, we could confidently plan another one. Karen Hurst, a photography hobbyist from Torrance, California, lent her skills and took invaluable convention and production photos for us for many years. Tony and Rosie Ricciardi, two more indispensable volunteers, attended nearly every convention; Rosie eventually became a principal photographer and Tony videotaped most of our major events. Jean Hall from Washington, D.C., helped with numerous mailings and has been a board member from the corporation's inception. Ronald Wagner, professional computer troubleshooter and now an author, set me up in my early computer programs and continued to volunteer his expertise and time through the years. Tom Schwoegler from Naperville, Illinois, came to us late but made up for it big time by donating new computers, printers, scanner, and software—as well as providing ongoing computer support. Sandy Marshall, from Springfield, Virginia, didn't join us until 1999, but her expertise with computer programs proved to be invaluable. Mary Ellen Stroupe from Washington, D.C., helped with countless mailings and for several years handled our bookkeeping; Mark McClelland, a VQT board member from Baltimore attended every convention and worked the spotlight at many Quality

Awards banquets—learning as he worked. Ken Nielsen from Colonia, New Jersey, was a patron for many years and also covered the cost of printing two hundred Quality Awards banquet booklets annually. Volunteers Ken and Linda Herst and Janet Harding (another patron) prepared every newsletter for mailing starting in 1992. Heather Holt and Arda Swift took turns proofreading the newsletter starting in 1996. Jean Hall, then Chuck Sutton, compiled and analyzed the Nielsen ratings for us. So many others: Chuck and Barbara Adams; John and Rhea Baldino; Shan Stafford; Sharon Johns; Ann Keitz, who developed VQT's Web site (VQT.org) in 1996; Dawn Marie Geraghty, Ellen Gershman, Cathy Jackson, Kim Hehe, Mike Adams, Mike Pajaro, Judy Samelson, Diana Essert, Jane Marie Best, Carolyn Dennstedt, Ruth Schettenhelm, Linda McCaig, Debbie Lomberg, Mary Jane Richeimer, Mark Silverstein, Suzanne Simanaitis, Gail Miller, Joan Riedell, Julie Graziani, Cecile Hamermesh, Janice Young, Trish Elliott, Cindy Stabile, Nora Mandel, Lisa Sharp, Denise Treco, Jane Minoff, Kathleen Murphy. They can't all be named here, but they know who they are.

This is their story; this is Viewers for Quality Television's story; this is my story.

DOROTHY SWANSON
Fairfax, Virginia
July 1999

THE STORY OF
Viewers FOR
Quality Television

INTRODUCTION

THE envelope was addressed simply and arrived along with more than six hundred other letters to the Viewers for Quality Television post office box:

The TV Lady
Fairfax, VA

Because the post office box number and the zip code were both missing, and the actual mailing address is Fairfax Station, not Fairfax, it was no small feat that the letter found its way to me. I then realized that the organization I had founded and headed, Viewers for Quality Television—and I as the "TV lady"—had achieved a certain notoriety.

This happened in 1988, in the middle of VQT's national campaign to save CBS's charming comedy *Frank's Place*, starring Tim Reid. VQT was a mere three years old, not yet incorporated and not yet claiming 501(c)3 nonprofit status.

To get to this place we must return to the beginning—how I as an individual viewer began an advocacy for one show that ultimately developed into a national organization that championed many worthwhile television series. *Frank's Place* is a prime example. Critically acclaimed and endorsed by Viewers for Quality Television, *Frank's Place* was one of VQT's biggest campaigns. To this day, some refer to "the curse of *Frank's Place*" on CBS.

All crusades have a beginning. Mine was a personal war to save *Cagney & Lacey* in 1983.

CAGNEY & LACEY & ME

The Campaign

ALL I wanted was to see more episodes of *Cagney & Lacey,* the CBS drama about two police officers who were friends as well as coworkers. But CBS canceled the show in May 1983 after one and one-half seasons and marginal ratings. This cancellation set off a reaction in me that profoundly changed my life, and, if my press clippings are to be believed (always dangerous when you believe those), changed the course of network television. *I wanted to save that show.* Christine Cagney, as played by Sharon Gless, and Mary Beth Lacey, as played by Tyne Daly, were the most fully realized characters I had ever discovered on television, and I couldn't let their stories end. So I set out to save the show. An activist was born.

There were many *Cagney & Lacey* fans around the country who petitioned CBS that summer of 1983, so I'm told. According to people connected with the show at the time, I was the most ardent and determined.

The "campaign" started late that winter as journalists began predicting which series would be renewed and which would be canceled. My first letter to the show was to writer/producer Steve Brown, then partnered with Terry Louise Fisher (who went on to cocreate *L.A. Law* with Steven Bochco). I also wrote a letter to Sharon Gless. Steve wrote back on March 3, 1983, giving me my first real indication of what was looming by telling me the show was borderline for renewal. Barney Rosenzweig, the show's executive producer and driving force, wrote on March 7, thanking me for my letter. "We are in some trouble, so if you are so inclined, a similar missive to Bud Grant couldn't hurt." (Bud Grant was the CBS Entertainment president.)

Emboldened by the personal contact, I eventually called the *Cagney & Lacey* production office to see what else might be done. I told Barney's assistant that I was a fan from Michigan (where I lived at that time). He said, "You must be Dorothy." That's when I started sending the producers a copy of every one of my multitude of letters.

Dear Mr. Grant: Your network will soon make a statement regarding its attitude towards women in non-traditional roles by either renewing or canceling *Cagney & Lacey*. At the same time, you have an opportunity to commit yourself to quality by renewing this outstanding series.

Speaking as a woman in a *traditional* role, I find *Cagney & Lacey* to be refreshing, thought-provoking, challenging, and inspiring, as well as entertaining.

I know ratings are important. But viewers trust you to bring us excellence, uniqueness, sensitivity and intelligence in your programming. You have all of the above in *Cagney & Lacey*. I trust that you will give *Cagney & Lacey* the special consideration it so richly deserves and thoughtfully review all your options before making this important decision. (Written and signed by me on April 25, 1983.)

Barney wrote encouraging, motivating notes on stationery strips with the *Cagney & Lacey* logo on them; I assume he did this with other fans as well, although Julie D'Acci wrote in *Defining Women: Television and the Case of Cagney & Lacey* in 1994 that "by May and June, as the mail continued to come in, Rosenzweig developed a form-letter response."[1] D'Acci reprinted the form letter that told fans what they could do. But I never received a form letter.

In May 1983 Barney wrote me: "You've done more than any of us have the right to ask," and went on to say how critical the May 2 and 9 episodes would be, and that I might let my local television critic know that "the idea of a national 'election' on May 2 may appeal to him or her." For me, those critics were Mike Duffy and Bettelou Peterson of the *Detroit Free Press*. They began to hear from me, and more than once printed my entreaties on behalf of *Cagney & Lacey*.

On May 10, 1983, Barney called me from New York, where he learned the network's decision. He identified himself and said, "You're our biggest fan, but I'm afraid I don't have very good news for you. We're not on the schedule." I was amazed that he would take the time to call. He didn't want me to read it in the newspaper or hear it on TV. I vehemently protested, "No! It's *not* over!" That night Bud Grant said on *Entertainment Tonight*, responding to the media outcry, "We don't cancel shows, we just don't renew them." Subtle difference. Battle lines were drawn—and for me, Hillsdale, Michigan, was ground zero.

From my recollections of that summer and from my correspondence with those associated with the show at that time, none approached or sustained the effort of appealing to CBS for *Cagney*'s resurrection with the insane dedication that I did. None wrote as many letters that demonstrated such familiarity and emotional involvement with the show. There were, for me, five hundred different ways of expressing to CBS executives the value of *Cagney & Lacey*—and I did. I saved many of those five hundred letters I wrote that summer for others to sign and (I confess now) even signed myself, using names from my college alumnae directory and mailed from Indiana and Ohio as well as Michigan. I averaged about a half-dozen letters a day all summer long. It's how I spent my summer vacation. Each letter was unique. I used different typewriters with various fonts, and assorted stationery. Some were handwritten, but most were typed. They poured into CBS. I wrote them as if I were the only one doing so. I did not realize then that this fervor was being echoed all over the country.

> Dear Mr. Grant: As an educated professional woman, I wish to reaffirm some feelings about an unusually fine program, *Cagney & Lacey*. I feel it consistently offered a quality of excellence found too rarely on television; it was intelligent, sensitive and real; it said something that women were eager to hear and identify with, and it said it eloquently and profoundly. It portrayed something else quite rare on television: women doing something worthwhile with their lives. Tyne Daly and Sharon Gless portrayed those women with perfection.
>
> I commend you for your judgment in presenting this outstanding series; however, now I must withdraw that commendation. I truly wonder what has happened to CBS's principles. I will miss this program very much and will hold some small hope that you reconsider your choice and offer it once again. (Written by college sorority sister Bobbie Pankratz, June 1, 1983.)

I recruited "lieutenants" in many states who mailed letters I sent to them for appropriate postmarks. I sent a letter on behalf of everybody I had ever known in my life who might not object, especially those who might not even find out. Two close friends were particularly helpful; after writing their own letters, they enlisted *their* friends, family, and coworkers to sign letters: Marian Herriman of Jackson, Michigan, and Norma Brown of Port Richey, Florida.

> Dear Mr. Grant: Some of the ordinary moments on *Cagney & Lacey* outshone the so-called great moments on other shows. Something notable happened in every episode. I wasn't looking for it. It just struck me as I was watching that *this* was a special moment. It is the greatness of the small moments that make a show memorable, Mr. Grant. Who cares who is stranded in a fire on *Dynasty* or who drowned in the pool in *Dallas?* I'd rather wonder if Mary Beth can keep it together while trying to run a house and hold down a demanding job, or if Chris ever found a man worthy of her. Fully realizing, sadly, that we'll never learn the answers. (Written by me and signed by Gladys Herriman, mother-in-law of "lieutenant" Marian Herriman, June 16, 1983.)

Barney continued to send me notes of thanks and encouragement. He was inspiring. One said: "You're doing a great job." Another: "The letters do count." He would also get discouraged, and wrote, partly in response to my admission that I had resorted to signing other peoples' names to my letters, "Although all's fair in war, I think forging fan letters (especially in this case) is—at the very least—unnecessary. It is sweet of you to continue your campaign. I think there is little or no chance of success with the network. Still— you never know." I did not consider this forgery. Rather, I rationalized that I was writing on behalf of others who did not take the time.

But viewer letters weren't the only things *Cagney* had going for it that summer. The show benefited from the combination of a savvy producer and outraged television critics. As a result of this triple advocacy, the public took another look at the show. It gradually and steadily—and amazingly—rose weekly in the Nielsen ratings. I could *feel* the tension and the hope building week after week, through the long months of that very focused summer. (These were the days when networks reran their canceled shows during the summer.) The week ending June 19, 1983, *Cagney* placed number 5; the week ending June 26 it ranked number 11; July 3, as well as 12, it placed number 2; it ranked number 6 the week of July 18–24; number 8 August 1–7. Then, the week of August 15–21 *Cagney* reached number 1 with a 19.9 rating, reaching 16.5 million households. What more could CBS want? The show was a winner! I wrote a batch of letters that all basically said, "See!?" And then, as if more proof were necessary to force CBS to change its mind, the show and both of its stars received Emmy nominations.

Dear Mr. Grant: As a proud, excited, enthusiastic *Cagney & Lacey* fan, do I have any reason to hope that your network will now reconsider its unfortunate (for television, for CBS, for viewers) decision to cancel it because it has received recognition from the Academy for its excellence? And for finally achieving the kind of ratings CBS apparently insisted upon?

I protest its cancellation. I re-affirm its unparalleled excellence, and I strongly request its return. (Written by me and signed by Sandra Wesley of Boca Raton, Florida, a Detroit neighborhood friend since we were both six years old.)

Dear Mr. Grant: Recognition, validation, acclaim, top 10, unsurpassed quality, superb acting, incredible writing, sensitive directing. Have I omitted anything? I speak of *Cagney & Lacey,* perhaps the best series your network has ever offered and will offer no more. Television will not be appealing to me after *Cagney & Lacey's* last rerun.

The purpose of this letter is to ask, in view of its quality and recent award nominations and ratings, that you restore this fine series to television sometime soon. (Written by me and signed by my sister, Marilyn Davey, on August 16, 1983.)

Heartened and further inspired, I wrote a poem called "Chris Laughed" and sent it to Barney. He wrote back, "I'm trying to get 'Chris Laughed' published. I think it is that good." I was over the top. *Way* over the top. My brother, Bill Collins, called my efforts and involvement "an immense act of will."

Why? What was it about *Cagney & Lacey?* What was it about *me* that made me respond to it and made me vulnerable to its message? I've tried to articulate that in countless interviews over the years. Time, distance, and maturity have lent a deeper perspective and allowed more substantive analysis—much better for my self-image than admitting that I was nuts.

The show spoke to me. It reached me on an emotional level. The characters drew me in and made me care. They heightened the compelling stories about homelessness, date rape, father-daughter relationships, drug use, spousal abuse, and working mothers (and this in only the first season). *Cagney & Lacey* took women's issues and put them in a male-dominated workplace. Never before had we seen two women heroes, flawed ones at that, lead a dramatic television series. We felt like we were there as they worked together, talked together, agreed, argued, fought, supported each other, disappointed each other, loved each other—always with convincing and intriguing chemistry. It was absolutely brilliant, thrilling, and of course, *interesting.* Quite simply, the show and its characters were seductive. Whether unintentional or by design, the result was the same—I was seduced.

On July 4, 1983, Sharon Gless began to call me. I say "began," because she would call many times that summer. She wanted to thank me for everything, especially for watching the show so carefully. (I had drawn attention to the fact that every time Cagney looked at her watch she wound it, something Sharon had not been aware of doing.) She said she had been meaning to call for a long time. We talked about *Cagney* and about her work. Sharon Gless did not call other fans that day, or even that week. (I asked her years later.) My letters had gotten through to her because her assistant at the time, a complex, soft-spoken, formidable woman named Beverley Faverty, decided that they should. Sharon's mail was handled for her by Beverley, and her photos signed by Beverley. Sharon was too busy bringing Cagney to life to autograph photos and answer fan mail. Talk about being motivated. A call from Sharon Gless? Onward with more letters.

Sometime that August I wrote Sharon that I would celebrate the final episode ever of *Cagney & Lacey* on network television (September 19, 1983) with a bottle of champagne. On September 19 I received a very special delivery—a bottle of Piper Heidsick champagne with a note that said: "This one is on Christine. She and I will be with you in spirit. Sharon." Soon after, another delivery came, a New York Yankees baseball jacket like the one Chris wore in so many scenes. They were spoiling me with attention, and pulling me closer. I went along easily.

When I would meet Sharon Gless the following March, I would ask her why she kept calling back. She would reply with a sweet smile, "You always seemed so excited to hear from me." Indeed.

The Victory

In late September, soon after my champagne celebration, I was watching *Entertainment Tonight* when Bud Grant announced that there would be "room" for *Cagney & Lacey* on its schedule. I literally fell back onto the carpet of my family room in a relieved heap, where my husband found me. I told him, "CBS renewed *Cagney & Lacey!*" He wasn't surprised. His response was, "Of course they did." Programming vice president Harvey Shephard added that it was the "emotional content" of the letters that convinced them. Yes! I had won. Viewers had, as my brother wrote me, "triumphed over the arbitrary mandates of corporate entertainment."

Television journalists went wild with the story. *The Hollywood Reporter* wrote, "Rosenzweig saluted the press for its part in the resurrection. Still, he

noted that it was the many letters written by fans of the series—many dupli-
cated and sent to several producers and executives—which made the difference in the mind of Harvey Shephard, CBS senior vice president of programs."[2]

Barney Rosenzweig told the *Los Angeles Times* news service, "I tell you, it
[the revival of the series] comes directly from the public and the press."[3]

The Associated Press quoted Barney: "CBS said they're doing this because
of the avalanche of mail and because the press would not let the show go."[4]

By December 1987, however, Barney was less inclined to share the credit.
To Beverly M. Payton for *Emmy* magazine he acknowledged, "There is no way
Cagney & Lacey would have been picked up if I [hadn't been] leading the
cheers. Without that producer fighting for his show, it'll never happen. But
that's not to say every producer should fight for every show. You have to pick
your shots."[5] Exactly.

Ecstatic and still on an adrenaline high, I commissioned a mug to be
designed by an artist in Hillsdale that had "Cagney" engraved on it in a
scrawl. Sharon liked it so much she decided to keep it on Cagney's desk for
pencils—on camera—throughout the run of the series. I told her that there
was a legend about that mug—that if she kept it on her desk, the show would
not be canceled. Every time I saw it there, on camera, through the next five
seasons, I marveled at the wonder of it; it felt as if a part of me were there in
the "squad room."

Sometime that spring Sharon and Tyne appeared on Gary Collins's *Hour
Magazine*. They talked about the viewer letters and they mentioned my name
as an example of a fan who noticed the small details of their work. It just kept
getting better and better. I heard from Tyne Daly on February 8, 1984. She
wrote of valuing my support and expressed that she was in my debt, both in
spirit and in letter. The bond seemed complete now.

Throughout that fall and into the winter, my long-distance relationships
with the people at *Cagney* continued to accelerate. I became acquainted with
two new staffers, Lisa Mason and Niki Marvin. And Sharon continued to call,
not often, but always a surprise, and never taken for granted. A friend said
one day, "You're going to be invited out there." It hadn't been voiced yet, by
me or by them, but now I got to thinking how logical that would be. One day
on the phone Niki said, "You'll have to come and visit us." Ready, I said simply, "I could do that." It was mentioned to Barney. He approved. I should
spend a week with them, meet everybody, watch them shoot. Lisa and I
agreed that the last week of filming would be a good time, because then I
could attend the "wrap party" at the end of the week. Sounded good to me!
When word got out, Sharon called and said, "There's no one I'd rather have

here than you." She added that she felt as if we'd already met and told me not to be nervous; "we'll take good care of you." I should add that I paid for my trip and all of my expenses.

I made arrangements for my family; my husband and three children (then ages 11, 14, and 17) would have to manage for a while on their own. I was going on Dorothy's incredible journey. My husband was wonderful about it; his only concern, and that of my parents, was that I might be disappointed or hurt. I had absolute trust that neither would happen. On the night of March 17, 1984, I flew to Los Angeles, where I was met by Lisa Mason, whom I stayed with in Redondo Beach until the following night, when I checked into the Glendale Holiday Inn.

The Visit

As promised, Lisa picked me up that incredible Monday morning, March 19, and took me immediately to the facilities at Lacy Street in downtown Los Angeles, where the show filmed and where the production offices were located. It was just an old converted warehouse, but it was the home of *Cagney & Lacey* to me. After I met Niki, Lisa took me on a tour. I sat in the squad room, stood at the sign-in board (which years later would have a place in my home), the holding cell, the locker room, and ladies' room where Chris and Mary Beth conducted so many of their often-heated discussions. The highlight was being in Cagney's loft, which looked precisely as I thought it would; all the details were there, exactly where I expected them to be. It was more than just a set to me; it was Chris Cagney's home, and I was in it. I felt indescribably elated and very privileged to be there.

On this tour I met Peter Lefcourt, who had written one of my favorite episodes, "Jane Doe #37." He said, "The famous Dorothy Swanson" and made me believe it.

Then I met the man himself, Barney Rosenzweig. He greeted me with a warm hug and a kiss, and showed me around his office. He told me that if he ever got around to writing his book on *Cagney & Lacey,* I would be in it. (He later wrote it, but it was not published.) Barney explained protocol and procedure to me. I was to take my signals from Sharon's assistant, Beverley Faverty, and I would have a driver every day. Then he instructed Lisa to take me to the location set, which was a downtown Greyhound bus terminal. It was a beautiful, sunny day, quite warm, so I left my jacket in Lisa's car. On the set, Lisa pointed to where they were filming. I saw Tyne Daly first, because she was off-camera watching. There she was, in Mary Beth's gray winter coat, her hair shining and brown in the California sunshine. I thought she was so *pretty*. Then I saw Sharon Gless in the distance, in character as Cagney, all ticked off at Brian Dennehy in a gas station scene from "The Bounty Hunter." She was wearing Chris's New York Yankees jacket. I was really here. Surprisingly, after more than a month's nervous anticipation, I was now absolutely calm. I felt like I belonged there.

While Sharon filmed the pickup scene for "The Bounty Hunter" ("Choices" would start filming the next day), Beverley Faverty seemed to come out of nowhere and was introduced by Lisa as Sharon's assistant. Her smile was warm and welcoming, her eyes penetrating. I would discover during that week that Bev was not just Sharon's assistant; they had been best friends for years. Bev anticipated Sharon's every need on the set and sometimes off, pumping her up when, as Bev would say, her tires needed inflating, seeing to her emotional and physical well-being. Sharon's best interest was Beverley's mission.

Sharon had known the moment I arrived because Beverley had told her. At a break in the filming she peered around the camera and waved, and with a signal indicated that she would be right over. I saw her start my way, a smile lighting her face. My first impression was how small she looked. She came to me unhesitatingly and gathered me into a tight hug, which I returned in kind. She felt hot; she was wearing a long-sleeved shirt, sweater, and that jacket. This was supposed to be New York, after all. I took her wrist and examined the watch I had seen Cagney wind so many times. I mussed her hair as if I had a right to do that. We took each other in, these two not-quite-strangers who had bonded over a summer and fall of phone conversations. It was as if Sharon Gless and Chris Cagney were melded into one, and I was meeting both in the same moment. She was absolutely drop-dead gorgeous. Chris Cagney vanished as Sharon Gless seemed to go shy. Then Tyne was standing beside her, and another hug was shared. It couldn't get any better than this! Could it?

Both actresses were called back to the scene, and I was put in as an extra by assistant director Stewart Lyons. They wanted me to look "New York," so Lisa ran back to the car for my blazer. Sharon was leaping with delight at my being in the scene with them. I can be seen near the end of "The Bounty Hunter" waiting in line for the bus as Chris and Mary Beth chase the perp; I turn and look surprised as they run by. They would put me in another scene later in the week, at the bar in "Choices."

Tyne Daly has a very specific way of using language; they called it "Tyne-speak." We had an opportunity to talk for a few minutes that afternoon. She said, "So say about you." It was important to her that my husband felt okay about my being there with them. I told her that he had been wonderful, and the times he hadn't totally understood he was at least patient, and added, "He's no Harvey Lacey." Tyne said, "No one is."

I met more cast and crew members that afternoon. Everybody welcomed me. I had entered nirvana.

When filming ended, I was invited into Sharon's trailer, which would be my daytime home for the next week. The only rule was that I knock before entering, even if I knew she wasn't inside. She sat beside me on the small sofa in her trailer and said excitedly, "I can't believe you're really here." She smiled a lot. I smiled a lot. Piper Heidsick champagne was brought in; we toasted the moment. I think they were all relieved that I had turned out to be "normal." They had taken a chance on me. The show had been, like most, a closed set.

Sharon promised she would see me tomorrow and explained that she had been up very early to do a spot on CBS's morning program to promote the show's premiere that night. She sent me off with Barney to a dubbing session of the episode titled "A Killer's Dozen." Barney and I had a long, easy, familiar talk in the car in rush-hour traffic to the studio. The dubbing session was fascinating, the screen as huge as in a movie theater. I met yet more people associated with the show.

Upon returning to my motel room that night, I found a beautiful floral arrangement and a card with the message, "To Dorothy, our No. 1 fan, Love, Sharon and Chris." I don't think I slept.

Tuesday morning, March 20, found us again on location, this time for that week's episode, "Choices." How fascinating, and educational, to watch the company rehearse and then film. I was surprised by all the "down" time as lighting and blocking was done. During this down time the actresses would perfect their lines, and sometimes they would conduct an impromptu rehearsal off in a corner. Hector Figueroa, the cinematographer and, at the time, Sharon's beau (her term), took photos for me using my camera. Sharon acknowledged me with waves and smiles.

Word spread that Barney was on his way out to the location and that the Nielsen overnights had been terrific, or why else would he come. When he arrived, he gathered everybody together and announced that he usually didn't take much stock in overnight ratings, but this time he just had to share them. I stood nearby as Barney announced the overnights, city by city. "Detroit, 42." My city. Cast and crew were jubilant, embracing each other, some weeping. They were ecstatic and proud. Sharon made me feel a part of the celebrating by saying, "How fitting that you should be here for this."

The fact was that the show had to perform in the ratings or it would be canceled again. Even after all this, that was the bottom line. It still is.

Filming switched to Lacy Street that afternoon. Bev and I rode back in Sharon's trailer. Shooting that day would last well into the evening, not an unusual occurrence. It was a slow, exacting process. The lighting had to be perfect, the sound had to be recorded without any unintended background noise, lines had to be said just right. Many times a scene was shot and reshot before the director (Karen Arthur that week) was satisfied with it. Sometime that week Sharon confided in me her secret of how she knew when an emotional scene was successful. Smiling mischievously, she told me, "My nipples get erect." It was impossible to dismiss that image through the following years as dynamic scenes unfolded between the two actresses on my television screen.

On the way out that night, I glanced into Barney's office and recognized Barbara Corday, cocreator of *Cagney & Lacey* and Barney's wife. He invited me in to meet her. We immediately connected, and continue to keep in touch sporadically.

When the nationals (the more complete Nielsen ratings) came in the next day at Lacy Street, Barney again interrupted shooting. While hoping for a 29 share, they'd managed a 38! The excitement in that room was palpable. Somebody pointed to me and said, "There's the person who helped bring this about." It was hard not to believe it.

I saw everything there was to see that week. I watched Sharon and Tyne in makeup. I sat nearby as they rehearsed together and then filmed. I watched editing in progress and saw how the show was put together. I watched dailies, the raw footage from the day's shooting before editing, in Barney's office. This is where I saw the mug I had given Sharon used on camera for the first time. A scene opened on a close-up of it; then the camera slowly pulled back. I rewound the tape and watched again, thrilled. When I mentioned to Sharon later that I had seen it, she said, "Oh, no! You weren't supposed to see that yet, it was going to be a surprise." It just got more and more extraordinary.

More than once a crew member would come up to me and say, "Are you Dorothy Swanson?" Each would thank me for all I did. I think, to them, I represented all the fans. They couldn't thank them all individually, but they could thank me, because I was there.

It was as thrilling meeting the writers I admired as it was the actors. Meeting Terry Louise Fisher and Steve Brown was particularly rewarding, because together they had written many of the more memorable episodes.

There is a little-known story about the last scene of the last episode ("Choices") of *Cagney* that season. I don't think there is any harm in telling it now, sixteen years later. The scene called for Chris and Mary Beth to be in a bar together, drunk, easing some of the stress of the week. Sharon and Tyne decided that to prepare for that scene, they would imbibe together in Tyne's trailer as they practiced their lines and rehearsed. I was intrigued by this. Beverley was not intrigued, nor was she amused. I don't know how they said their lines, for when they appeared for the scene, it was apparent to me that they had fully and in every sense of the word prepared for this scene. How much was acting and how much was real? Watch the final scene in "Choices" and determine for yourself. For the opening shot of that scene, as Barney Rosenzweig walks in with Tyne's double on his arm, an extra himself, I can be seen at the bar, my back to the camera.

The wrap party was that Friday night after the final scene of the season. They had completed the seven episodes for their short 1984 season. A crew member told me, "This is the first *Cagney & Lacey* wrap where we know it isn't the end." It was a celebration.

Throughout the week, Tyne and I had discovered that we had something in common—an appreciation of quotes from novels and poetry. Upstairs in the warehouse, I was waiting for Sharon's last scene to begin filming when Tyne came over to me, placed her palm on my cheek and said, "I know you think we're different, but we're not, because we both love quotes." I missed Sharon filming that last scene to have this special time with Tyne, which she had generously offered. She thanked me for being so patient all week, and told me that she'd found me to be totally unintrusive. (Well, those were the rules.) She also thanked me for allowing her to "warm up" in her own time, and told me that "you have the [right] instincts, or you wouldn't be here." Through the next year, Tyne would surprise me with an occasional poem or quote. Each remains a treasure.

The wrap party itself was another unique experience, where I had an opportunity to tell them as a group how much I appreciated having been welcomed into their fold. Even Karen Arthur had jotted in my notebook, "Dorothy, you will always be right there along side of us."

It could have ended there, but it had been planned all along that I would stay through Saturday night to visit Sharon in her home Saturday evening. Barney's limo driver took me to her small bungalow in Studio City. We sat on the floor in front of a glowing fireplace and talked, watched some of Sharon's tapes in her cozy den, talked some more on her sofa, drank too much, ordered Chinese in, and talked some more on the floor. Well after midnight, she drove me back to Glendale to the Holiday Inn in her green Datsun, then called to tell me she had arrived home safely. It had been a perfect week—exciting, satisfying, emotional, magical. It was time to go home.

The Aftermath

What does one *do* with that? Where was I to put such an experience? In what file folder in my brain? In what corner of my heart? That energy. That passion. What in life could compare to what I had just been through? I was apparently at some kind of crossroads anyway; why else had *Cagney & Lacey* spoken to me in that tone of voice? It just seemed natural to continue to advocate. *Cagney* was still on the air, and would likely be for some time. Why not be ready, in case this happened again, either with *Cagney & Lacey* or with another quality show? I was already watching *Hill Street Blues* and *St. Elsewhere* with similar attention. Life went on. But life was changing.

HUMBLE BEGINNINGS

IN mid-1984 I read a letter from Donna Deen of Plano, Texas, in TV critic Mike Duffy's column in the *Detroit Free Press*. Deen, a champion of the NBC series *St. Elsewhere,* had written an open letter to Nielsen viewers urging them to watch the low-rated hospital drama to increase its ratings. She called her efforts the "Viewers' Campaign for *St. Elsewhere.*" Her address was given in the column; I wrote to her as one quality television advocate to another, and sent her a copy of an article about my *Cagney & Lacey* experience that had appeared in the *Jackson Citizen Patriot.*[1] Entertainment writer Jo Griffin would later win first prize in the 1985 Michigan Press Women Communications Contest for that article.

Donna wrote back, and in the ensuing months, in correspondence and on the telephone, we formulated the idea for Viewers for Quality Television. We envisioned a positive organization that would band together like-minded viewers, who would encourage the networks to keep their quality series on the air. The only question—a fundamental question to this day—seemed to be how to get the word out.

Enter Barney Rosenzweig. I wrote him about our idea, Viewers for Quality Television, in December 1984, nine months after my *Cagney & Lacey* visit. As Barney would explain to me later, he was making his annual Christmas season calls to television journalists and happened to mention me, Donna, and our "idea." I don't know how many critics he alerted, but Michael Duggan of the *San Francisco Examiner* was one who was (in his words in a column a year later) "tipped off." He called both Donna and me to ask us more about VQT. On December 18, 1984, he became "midwife" (his word) to VQT when he wrote an article entitled "Viewers of the World, Unite."[2] It told his readers that "Deen and Swanson are forming an organization called Viewers for

Quality Television. They know which shows have quality—the ones they like." Deen was quoted as saying, "These are shows that really get to people. People talk about the characters. The dialogue is believable. They sound like real people."[3] I was quoted as saying, "[Deen and I] discovered there is an audience out there that is discerning and chooses the same types of shows. We want to band these people together and see if there isn't something we can do to make a difference. We're appealing to those people for whom the TV set is a little more than entertainment."[4] Duggan invited his readers to "enlist" and gave both our addresses. First we heard from viewers in San Francisco who wanted to join our efforts. Then Duggan's column went over the wires, was printed around the nation, and we heard from even more viewers. Suddenly, without consciously trying, we had an organization and five hundred "members." It was now necessary to *do* something with them; so we began to involve them. We mailed our first poll, created an endorsed list of quality shows, and published our first newsletter in February 1985—a two-pager that we typed, copied, and mailed.

VQT was never a deliberate "plan"; it did not have a prospectus, or a budget, or long-range goals. It simply *evolved,* keeping up with the circumstances, responding to the need. There was no institution after which to pattern ourselves. We were the first of our kind, a group of concordant television viewers who wanted to be specifically heard.

The year 1985 brought more interested journalists, some as a result of the Duggan article, others as a result of Barney Rosenzweig's helpful new assistant, Carole Smith. She gave me names of columnists and critics to contact who had been supporters of *Cagney & Lacey* and who might be interested in knowing about a viewer group that had sprung up as a result of the now-infamous campaign. Two of her suggestions, Joan Hanauer of UPI and Judy Mann of the *Washington Post,* proved instrumental in March 1985 in increasing VQT's visibility with the media and with viewers. The address was always given so that readers could contact the group. Judy Mann wrote,

> They have never met, but Dorothy Swanson of Hillsdale, Michigan, and Donna Deen of Plano, Texas, have joined forces to organize a movement that they hope will liberate America from the tyranny of the Nielsen television ratings. Energized by the success they had in helping keep two shows on the air, the women have formed Viewers for Quality Television, which could become the lobbying force for the television viewer who is sick and tired of intelligent, sophisticated shows going off the air because of low ratings.[5]

My address was printed and I received close to five hundred letters from the Washington, D.C., area during the next few weeks, all to my mailbox in front of my home.

Several of those responding to the *Post* column would become longtime VQT members and valuable volunteers, including Tom Galioto of Arlington, Virginia, and Jean Hall of Washington, D.C. Also responding was Patricia Murphy of Fairfax, Virginia, who would become vital to the future direction and success of VQT.

As a result of Mann's column, Donna and I finally met, that same month, in Washington, D.C., for Carol Randolph's "Morning Break" talk show. We appeared along with David Poltrack of CBS and Jack Curry, then TV critic for *USA Today.* The night of our arrival, *Entertainment Tonight* profiled the new viewer organization and showed taped interviews with its cofounders. It was very exciting for Donna and me to watch that together. On "Morning Break" the next day, Poltrack said, just as the live show ended, "People don't want to see themselves on TV, they want to escape." With no time left on the air to challenge that statement, I argued with him off mike that indeed they did want to see their lives reflected on television. It's called identifying.

On January 3, 1985, I received a reply from Barney Rosenzweig to my inquiry about how much or how little I should mention my association with *Cagney & Lacey* to journalists. It seemed wise to downplay that close connection. Barney agreed, and congratulated me on VQT. "Sounds exciting—good luck with it all and thanks for keeping me informed. I guess that it is probably better to not mention our personal contact if you can help it, lest every follower of this show expects that kind of attention."

Numerous other journalists contributed to VQT's growth and credibility that first year, including Mike Duffy of the *Detroit Free Press,* Rick Shefchik of the *St. Paul Dispatch,* Keith Watson of the *Houston Post,* and Ray Richmond of the *Los Angeles Daily News.*

Within this time frame, we announced our first annual Quality Awards; this gave journalists another reason to mention our work. These writers included Jerry Buck of the Associated Press, David Bianculli of Knight-Ridder, Sally Vallongo of the *Toledo Blade,* Michael Duggan again, and Peter Farrell of the *Portland Oregonian.* Donna and I had appeared together on that city's *Talk Back to TV* "Town Hall" TV show. Kathleen Merriman of the *News Tribune* in Tacoma, wrote an article on July 19; Greg Dawson of the *Orlando Sentinel* in early July; Joan Hanauer of UPI contributed to VQT's growth in October; Mark Lorando of the *New Orleans Times-Picayune* called VQT "America's first and only consumer watchdog representing network TV viewers."[6] Lorando reported a letter I had received from NBC programmer Brandon Tartikoff congratulating VQT for becoming "a new force in the industry."[7] Walt Belcher of the *Tampa Tribune-Times* wrote about the group on July 14. VQT member and skilled writer Cheri Jenkins of Houston submitted an article about VQT to *Emmy* magazine; it was printed in their July/August 1985 issue. They gave Cheri three columns and printed our addresses. On December 10 of that year, Michael Duggan wrote a one-year follow-up, calling us "feisty ladies" and telling his readers that "in [the] VQT [newsletter], bright people are writing intelligent things to each other on the topic of television."[8] He also quoted from the newsletter. "One of the primary goals of VQT is to ensure that no 'quality' show be canceled because of low Nielsen ratings." Fifteen years later, that still remains our lofty goal.

In March 1985 ABC flew me to New York to tape a one-minute segment for *Good Morning America*'s series "What Makes Me Mad." On camera I complained about the Nielsen families and their influence over network programming, of course.

Throughout the summer of 1985, with VQT not a year old, Donna and I brainstormed by mail about VQT's course. She confided in me that her *St. Elsewhere* campaign had been frustrating and unsatisfying, and attributed it to her reluctance to write the producers from her heart and tell them how much the show meant to her. She believed that her failure to establish a rapport with the producers kept them from bonding with her, just the opposite of my *Cagney & Lacey* experience. She told me about a few TV critics who mentioned her campaign, including Mike Duffy in Detroit, which is how I learned of her.

That summer Donna was offering terrific suggestions for VQT and various ways to implement them. But she suggested that I handle it because she was working outside the home, and VQT *was* my work, which was certainly true.

By October, Donna was losing enthusiasm and expressed to me that she felt her tenure would be brief and that she doubted she could ever feel enough fire to help another TV show. I got the impression from her letters that her zeal was limited, her vision shortsighted, and that she felt VQT would be short-lived. At my insistence, we kept going, because I refused to accept that what had seemed like such a good idea should end so prematurely.

By coincidence, as VQT was beginning, my twenty-three year marriage was ending. In early 1986 I left Michigan and moved to Virginia, where I had spent the early part of my childhood, to be with friends, making new ones among the large VQT enclave that had grown in the Washington, D.C., area as a result of the Judy Mann article.

Adding to the problems that Donna and I were experiencing was the fact that Donna had a severe hearing loss. She got along well in the hearing world and did not use sign language, rather read lips skillfully. In fact, she graduated Phi Beta Kappa from Baylor University. With in-person interviews, such as "Morning Break" and the one in Portland, Donna was marvelous. The telephone, however, was a different story. I never understood why her family did not attach an amplifier for her on the family phone. On radio talk shows we did jointly, I would have to answer questions she could not hear. Sensitive about her disability, she resented this. But silence in radio is dead time, and interviewers don't like it. As we tried to keep VQT alive, Donna and I did not have the means to convey our ideas and plans clearly and quickly over the phone to each other. This was before E-mail and faxes.

We continued to write the newsletter together, and Houston member Cheri Jenkins produced it on her Commodore computer. It wasn't the most efficient way to operate, but neither Donna nor I had a computer. We were discovering that VQT ran on the energy, the skills, and the talents of its willing volunteers around the country.

In the beginning, there were no dues or subscription fees. People would send us stamps, envelopes, and dollars; but mostly we were out-of-pocket and drawing no salary. Once we started charging $15 per year to meet expenses, I kept a separate bank account for VQT's meager monetary assets. Unfortunately, once we instituted this fee, some people dropped out.

Then things got exciting. I had only been a Virginia resident for two weeks when an NBC publicity person called to invite Donna and me to participate in NBC's "Tuned In to America" series of thiry-second messages in which well-known Americans were to offer their observations and ideas about television. Participants in this first group in February 1986, besides Donna and myself, included Steve Allen, Ralph Nader, former astronaut James Irwin, PTA president Ann Kahn, and William R. Hutton, executive director of the National Council of Senior Citizens. We felt honored to be in such company, but knew we had definite ideas to contribute on what we wanted to see on television. One of my comments used on the air was "When the quality isn't there, television can be mind-numbing. When the quality *is* there, it can be breathtaking." Tom Shales quoted that comment in the *Washington Post* on June 11, 1986. Pat Murphy, my friend and eventual VQT, Inc. vice president, had given me sound bites to memorize before leaving for Los Angeles. That was one of them.

On this trip to Los Angeles, I had time for a second visit to the *Cagney & Lacey* set. There to meet me at the door at Lacy Street was new writer Patricia Green, who would go on to write and produce *China Beach, L.A. Law,* and

Chicago Hope. It was wonderful being there again. Toni Graphia was my "guide" that day. Toni was a new production assistant and an aspiring writer who would eventually write for *China Beach, Cop Rock,* and *Dr. Quinn, Medicine Woman,* and create and produce the short-lived series *Orleans* with John Sacret Young (of *China Beach* fame) for the 1997 midseason. The *Cagney & Lacey* cast and crew looked at me through new eyes this visit. Not only had I taken my zeal for *Cagney* and turned it into a positive venture that had captured the interest of the media and now a network, but I also had made a drastic change in my life.

Later that night at the Bel Age Hotel, Donna and I shared our day's experiences. I was ecstatic and she was disheartened. Donna had attempted what sadly turned out to be an unproductive visit to *St. Elsewhere*. The *St. Elsewhere* people hadn't even been expecting her and were not particularly welcoming. So I downplayed my exhilaration at my reception at *Cagney*. We went to the NBC studio carrying those respective moods.

By now Pat Murphy and I were producing the newsletter using a printer who showed us how to paste up copy in columns. I had my own Commodore computer now, on which I also kept the first VQT database. VQT also finally had a post office box—195—in Fairfax Station, a few miles from my home in Fairfax.

Sometime in the summer of 1986, at the suggestion of Pat Murphy, Donna visited me in Virginia so we could talk about VQT and work together face-to-face. Donna paid her own airfare; VQT paid her hotel room. Vacillating about VQT, she was trying to decide whether to move to the D.C. area and assume a larger role, fully acknowledging that there needed to be one headquarters, not two. We discussed whether to incorporate, whether to be for profit or nonprofit, and how that might be accomplished. And we wondered how we would continue to run the organization together with so much geographical and philosophical distance between us. It wasn't a fruitful visit. I found Donna unwilling or unable to make decisions regarding VQT's future. She still seemed to lack a vision for VQT, and her indecisiveness was stifling any forward movement the organization needed to make.

I also realized at this time that our writing styles were vastly different. Every time we tried to collaborate on an editorial for the newsletter, it didn't work. We were not "one voice." We couldn't communicate on a creative level.

On December 29, 1986, Matt Roush (then reporter, later critic) for *USA Today* wrote about VQT and included our pictures, calling the article "The Push to Improve What's on the Tube." A photo of Sharon Gless and Tyne Daly as Cagney and Lacey was the centerpiece. This happened many times, and always made me smile because it linked VQT and *Cagney & Lacey* and strengthened the connection between the two. Matt printed our tips on writing an effective letter to a network, tips that are used by advocates to this day: address the letter to a specific person, usually the entertainment president; type or write clearly; keep it short; don't send a form letter; be specific, note what impressed you about the show. He quoted me saying that "I like a show that provokes thought, that will challenge me." Donna Deen said, "Dorothy and I would like to make a career out of this. We think there's a market for us, but we haven't hit our stride yet." When I read that, I wondered if Donna and I were at cross-purposes. I wanted VQT to survive so that quality shows such as *Cagney & Lacey* would have a better chance. Donna (as would become clearer shortly) wanted to "make a career out of this." Bud Grant, still CBS entertainment president, was quoted as saying, "We pay attention to the mail, because these people are our customers. If there is a spontaneous and grass-roots letter-writing campaign for a show, we pay a lot of attention to that." As a result of this article, in which the VQT address was given, VQT grew to a thousand members.

VICTORY AT CBS
THE RESCUE OF *DESIGNING WOMEN*

The Hook

BACK in September 1986, when Julia Sugarbaker lectured Ray Don for assuming that she and the other women with her in the sushi restaurant would surely be honored if he joined them at their table, I knew I had discovered another quality show. On cursory glance, it was a sitcom about four women who happened to be interior designers in Atlanta. But, unique in television comedy at that time, these women *talked* to one another—frankly, honestly, and humorously—about men, women, family, friendship, about everything about which women talk to one another, and struck a familiar chord in viewers, men and women alike. It was funny, innovative, smartly written, and featured characters the likes of which we had not seen on television before, played by highly believable, endearing actresses. This show inspired the VQT definition of a quality comedy: it touched our hearts as well as our funny bones. The highly publicized viewer campaign to save *Designing Women* would put producer Harry Thomason and the voice of *Designing Women,* Linda Bloodworth-Thomason, *and* Viewers for Quality Television on the map. A bond was created, a "partnership" that we all assumed would never break. Harry Thomason said of me and of a fan in the *Los Angeles Times,* "If I were a candidate for president, I'd consider getting those two women on board."[1]

I started hearing from VQT members, being the outspoken lot they are, with *Women*'s premiere. Yet, with the first VQT ballot of that fall, the show did not reach full endorsement status. Were VQT members being too picky? Why were they so tentative? I felt it was important that the show be acknowledged for its quality, so at the suggestion of numerous members, Donna and I created a second tier of supported shows that we called "tentative support." *Women* immediately and easily qualified for this category. I wrote Harry Thomason, and told him how much I loved the show.

The Campaign

That November, in a typical network move, CBS took this fragile new show from its successful berth on Monday night and put it on Thursday opposite the popular *Night Court*. In weeks it was obvious that the move had hurt *Designing Women*. It plunged from number 16 to number 65 in the Nielsens. *Women* was just too new to succeed opposite an established hit on NBC's biggest night.

I was in my basement home office one evening in mid-December when the phone rang and Harry Thomason introduced himself. He said he had my letter in front of him and he had some troubling news: CBS was placing the show on hiatus. What should he do? *He* was asking *me*. Together, right there on the spot, we devised a plan. I would notify VQT members of the situation, and I would appeal to TV critics who were raving about *Women* to urge their readers to get in touch with VQT so we could empower them. In the meantime, Harry would continue to encourage Phyllis Hall, a Los Angeles-area receptionist and part-time actress who was president of a *Designing Women* fan club. Hall was working with Thomason's friend, actress Bobbie Ferguson. I contacted Donna Deen right away. She did not share my excitement and expressed concern about campaigning for a show that wasn't "fully endorsed." I told her that her instincts were wrong, that this campaign was necessary for the present and future state of quality television, and that action had to be taken *immediately*. She insisted that it was not the right thing to do. I was annoyed with her for her reticence. I talked to Pat Murphy and to other local VQT members; all urged me to go forward with the enthusiasm I felt and was receiving from others. The consistent advice I received was to follow my instincts. Yet, I felt so hindered by Donna's position that my initial press release to the television media, printed by several publications, explained that VQT would not spearhead the Save-the-Women campaign, but would guide fans on how to make their voices heard. That caution soon vanished when viewers wrote me of their unabashed support

for the show and their passionate desire to save it. I went forward uncondi-
tionally and with full confidence.

I wrote a "Dear TV Critic" letter on December 16, 1986, saying that "I call
a foul" on CBS's treatment of the show, and mailed copies to journalists. I
wrote, "The amazing thing about *Designing Women* is that it's a sitcom, yet
we have 22 minutes of dialogue." Across the country, journalists mentioned
VQT's campaign to their readers and gave our address. To every viewer who
wrote me asking what to do, I sent a letter outlining exactly what steps to
take. The last step I noted was to send a copy of their letter to Harry Thomason
and to VQT so that we would have evidence of the support. Once again, passion proved to be the key.

An example of that passion is contained in a comment from Sue Anderson, then a college student in Blacksburg, Virginia, published in our February
1987 newsletter:

> The characters are real and well-developed, each with particular quali-
> ties that any woman can recognize and relate to. Julia's suffer-the-fools
> attitude laced with humorous sarcasm, Suzanne's breezy vanity and
> equally windswept mind, Mary Jo's halting optimism in the face of any
> disaster and Charlene's honesty and enthusiasm are vital, interesting,
> understandable traits. In every episode, deeper layers of character are
> exposed.

And this from a male viewer, published in the same issue: "Losing contact
with the characters on that show is like losing contact with all my friends
from a favorite job, or all my friends from college. The characters on *Designing
Women* seem so real to me that I'd swear I'd met, worked with, maybe even
had lunch with, every single one of them."

Donna was not happy. VQT was rushing down the track at breakneck
speed and she was not on the train. She called and told me she wanted to be
a part of this, so I made every effort to include her, putting her in touch with
the show and with the press. In David Zurawik's December 23, 1986, column
in the *Dallas Times Herald,* I am quoted: "After a solid Nielsen showing, CBS
moves *Designing Women* to Thursdays—and two weeks later axes it because it
can't destroy the powerful NBC lineup. This does not make sense. You don't
take a show that is just getting off the ground and expect it to anchor a night
like Thursday, and then only give it two outings." Donna was now on the
bandwagon, saying to Zurawik, "We plan to continue the effort, keep writing,
to keep the pressure on. The show should not have been moved." Zurawik

provided the VQT address and hundreds more letters poured into VQT, and then into CBS as we mobilized these outraged viewers.

More and more journalists joined in the outcry. The Gannett News Service wrote on December 16, 1986, "*Women* shows signs of becoming this year's *Cagney & Lacey*—that is, a show that grass-roots fans will band together to save."[2] Liz Smith even joined the fray, urging fans to "do whatever they did to get *Cagney & Lacey* reinstated and back on the air," and listed VQT's address.[3] It is impossible to remember every journalist who was actively involved, or how many letters VQT received or can claim responsibility for being sent to CBS. In the end, though, CBS admitted to receiving fifty thousand letters.

Barbara Corday, cocreator of *Cagney & Lacey* (with the late Barbara Avedon), was now head of Columbia Pictures Television, which made *Designing Women*. As she and I were both quoted in various news stories, we were once again linked.

On January 9 the *New York Post* reported that CBS's Bud Grant told Phyllis Hall and Delta Burke in a meeting that "women should go back to the kitchens and leave me alone. I don't like being told how to run my network. And I resent all these letters coming in."[4] Barbara Corday was reported to have responded, "I'm surprised at his attitude which he has never expressed before. What is on the airwaves is the business of the people. People should fight for what they see and don't want to see. The networks are custodians of the airwaves. They don't own it."[5] This became known as the CBS kitchen war and only heightened the fervor to save the show.

Pat Murphy ran the day-to-day *Women* campaign with me, helping me write copy, suggesting sound bites for interviews, supporting me, working all hours opening and responding to the mail. She had the instincts—she was visionary—and her writing was brilliant. We found that we were "one voice."

The *Designing Women* campaign was brief and intense, lasting less than a month. On January 8 the *New York Post* reported that the show would resume production immediately with no announced airdate. Then, on January 9, Matt Roush reported that the show would return on Sunday, February 1, at 9 P.M., and that Bud Grant told the show's staff and stars that "the network received an unprecedented amount of mail in favor of the show."[6] Both George Maksian of the *New York Daily News* and Roush reported a few days later that Bud Grant had in fact hoisted a white flag on the CBS building in Los Angeles. Roush said that "Hollywood is calling it Grant's surrender."[7] Maksian reported that Grant hadn't meant the women-in-the-kitchen remarks, that "it was all a put-on to grab some headlines and attention for the returning show."[8] Maksian quoted Grant as saying, "It was all a huge publicity stunt."[9] Annie Potts told Maksian, "Whether it was a publicity stunt or not doesn't matter. Grant admitted he was wrong in moving the show. It was a bold step. And we accept the gesture with a hearty thank you."[10] Donna Deen called it a "victory for viewers" in the *Dallas Times Herald*.[11]

Mike Duffy of the *Detroit Free Press* wrote in February 1987 that David Poltrack, vice president of research for CBS, admitted that the letters were "a factor."[12] Poltrack also admitted to Duffy that "the fact that there was a hue and cry and the fact that there was a letter writing campaign did present CBS with some promotional opportunities. It may have resulted in bringing the show back quicker."[13] I proclaimed to Duffy for the same article, "The days of passive television consumerism are over."[14] (This was when I still believed that viewers were the consumers of television. Linda Ellerbee would set straight that myth a year later.)

Despite the victory and the celebration, and despite her own involvement, Donna Deen reverted to her previous stance. She told me that because *Women* was not endorsed, she felt it was inappropriate for me to have used VQT to help a series I personally liked or to have paid for this campaign with VQT money. She also let me know that she felt it was not appropriate for me to write to the critics as VQT cofounder on VQT stationery. She was disgusted with herself for getting involved and for not opposing me more strongly. She thought that *Women* had promise, but that it wasn't that wonderful.

The reader can judge us both.

I was visiting family in Hillsdale, Michigan, in mid-January, when Georgette Deveney, *Women* publicist from Columbia Television, called to invite me to Los Angeles for the taping of the return episode in just one week. Columbia publicity would pick up the costs. I immediately accepted the generous invitation and asked that Pat Murphy be included as well because she had been so actively and critically involved. Within minutes, it was confirmed. I did not attempt to include Donna for obvious reasons. I flew out of Detroit to Dulles International Airport on the heels of one of the worst winter storms in the history of the nation's capital. It was a white-knuckle reentry; a small private plane had skidded off one of the two runways and was blocking it. Because we couldn't land, the plane had to circle. The pilot announced that if we did not get clearance to land within thirty minutes, we would have to return to Detroit, which somehow would require less fuel than circling. That wouldn't do; our flight to Los Angeles was the very next morning. I was having a panic attack.

The plane did eventually land, and Pat Murphy met me, clutching the Los

Angeles airline tickets in her hand. I unpacked and repacked in the same night. My third Los Angeles adventure in less than three years was about to begin.

The Reward

Columbia/Mozark Productions had a limo meet us at the airport and take us to the famed Chateau Marmont Hotel. After a quick snack another limo arrived to take us to the studio where *Women* taped. We were met there by David Horowitz, publicist for the Thomasons and for the show. Still feeling like I was circling above Dulles airport, Horowitz escorted me to a *People* magazine reporter who was writing a story about the show's return. I was asked what it was about the show that had invoked such passion in viewers. A grounder.

Pat and I were introduced to numerous people associated with the show, but Horowitz wouldn't let us near any of the women themselves, or Harry Thomason and Linda Bloodworth-Thomason. He made it clear that he wanted to "save that" for the photographers. As we went from place to place, we saw Delta Burke making moves toward us, bringing her arms together in a hug. She said more than once, "Let me at them." It was frustrating and artificial to keep us apart, just waiting for the right "staged" moment. When it finally did come, it was brief and hurried. At a break in taping, Pat and I were told to hurry onstage where we joined Linda and the women for a photo op and spoke briefly. Then they had to tape again. But Harry had brought Linda to us in the audience earlier, just before the taping began. She was very cute and very sweet, reminding me of Sally Field. She greeted us exuberantly, focused on us, stayed with us a while, and thanked us for loving her writing. Linda didn't leave us in our seats for long; she brought us down onto the stage to be with her where we became completely enchanted by her charm and sincerity. Here we first noticed Linda's ability to concentrate on more than one thing at a time. She could be deep in conversation with us and still notice that a cast member said a line differently from how she had intended it to be said; after dealing directly with that, she would return to the conversation without missing a beat.

When we posed with the women and Linda for a group photo, Linda said to her stars, "These women know your characters better than you do." Oooooooh. I don't think so. Neither did they.

Pat had asked me earlier, "What will I say when I meet them?" I advised her to "say something they've never heard before, so they will remember you." So Pat said to Dixie Carter moments before the camera flashed, "The highlight tonight is watching your husband in the audience watching *you*."

"Oh," Dixie responded, taking Pat's hands. "Really?" Pat had meant it. Hal Holbrook was in the audience that night (as he usually was when Dixie taped), and obviously totally captivated by his wife's performance. "Just say something they've never heard before." This became a challenge for us both through the years.

It had been thrilling to meet them all on that very special occasion; we would have numerous other times to be together through the years—at a *Designing Women* party at the Pacific Design Center, at script read-throughs, at tapings, in offices. Each moment with Dixie, Annie, Delta, or Jean, as well as with Linda and Harry, was treasured. I have to say that we became best acquainted with Dixie, and found Delta and Annie to be endearing. Jean never really connected with us.

It wasn't over, though. Ratings on Sunday night were so-so. Harry Thomason lobbied for the show to return to Monday nights where it had been successful. But Bud Grant had given that time slot to *The Cavanaughs*. Viewers sent another burst of letters telling CBS they almost had it right. Eventually, *The Cavanaughs* faltered and *Designing Women* reclaimed its 9:30 Monday night slot where it remained for six more successful seasons. *Designing Women* maintained its quality until the year it lost three of its women all at once: Delta Burke, Jean Smart, *and* Linda Bloodworth-Thomason.

Donna Deen continued to fight things that I felt were in the best interest of Viewers for Quality Television. In March 1987 she told me that she felt VQT should discontinue its awards (which we had only just begun), because we existed only to give support to quality shows. I was exasperated with her because I believed that in bestowing the Quality Award, we *were* giving support and bringing attention to quality shows.

The Aftermath

The year 1987 continued to be eventful for VQT. Barbara Miller, a *Los Angeles Times* "Calendar" intern, wrote an article on April 4 that chronicled what was being interpreted as my somewhat personal successes with *Cagney & Lacey* and *Designing Women*. Because of those two accomplishments, people from other shows were now contacting me, shows that VQT had not singled out for their quality content. Miller suggested that "they don't necessarily get it,"[15] and quoted Linda Bloodworth-Thomason, "[Dorothy's] not just some public relations service." Linda quipped, "If Dorothy had been around during the Normandy invasion, it would've ended much earlier."[16] Bud Grant wasn't giving us too much credit. "The general public, represented by the Nielsens, is really the determining factor. As a national network, the TV medium serves many different populations, so it's important for us and the advertisers to reach a large number of people. That's why it's *broad*casting, not narrowcasting. But groups like VQT do make a contribution, and I'm fully in favor of and support their goals."[17] Donna was mentioned in a few places in the article, now referred to as an assistant manager of an antiques store in Plano (earlier, I had read that she was a freelance writer): "It's difficult running an organization half a country apart." She attributed the triumph to "the three P's—the press, the people and the producers."[18] But Miller added that although *Women* and *Cagney* had those things, they also "had Swanson." Yes, indeed, they had. With *Women,* despite Donna's opposition.

I have a large poster of *Designing Women* on my office wall that Harry Thomason sent me; all four of the actresses signed it. It reminds me daily that it *can* be done. On the poster Jean Smart wrote, "Dear Dorothy, With *much* gratitude! Jean Smart." Delta wrote, "To Dorothy, what would we ever do without you? Thanks so very much for your help and support. Love, Delta Burke." Dixie wrote in her bold scrawl, "Dear Dorothy, *You did it,* and we'll never forget it. Love, Dixie!" And Annie Potts wrote beneath her perfect caricature, "To Dorothy, Could never thank you enough. Love, Annie Potts."

A turning point for VQT occurred that spring of 1987. The *Women* campaign had given Donna the impetus she needed to finally leave VQT. Since her vacillation about *Women,* I hadn't trusted her instincts. She told me it was time for her to quit, and in our June 1987 newsletter she wrote a farewell to VQT. In part, she said, "The physical distance [of attempting to head VQT while living a half a country apart], along with differences in philosophy, makes it necessary for me to leave VQT to pursue other projects—hopefully in the television industry." She wanted our readers to believe that she had not actively participated in or condoned the *Women* campaign and reiterated, despite the historic achievement, her view that VQT should not have spearheaded the campaign. She conceded that "while Dorothy and I are unable to reconcile our differences in this and other matters of principle, we do agree that VQT serves a vital purpose for both viewers and those in the television industry." She urged us to keep up our "good work."

In private, it wasn't so congenial. Although in December Donna agreed in writing to release VQT, its agents, directors, and me from any and all interests or rights to past, present, or future income, profits, reimbursements, wages, salaries—and VQT and I released Donna from any manner of action or responsibility for VQT's debts—she acquired a "legal advisor" to whom she referred in much of her correspondence that spring. She mentioned a Texas partnership law. I asserted that we weren't partners in anything, rather we cofounded something that wasn't even a legal entity. She wanted me to buy out her share. I told her that if anything was to be shared, it would be *expenses*, not nonexistent profit. I reminded her that there had been no initial capital investment and that I had assumed the accountability because I filed VQT's taxes as a sole proprietorship. I also pointed out that the funds that existed as of the date of her resignation ($1,364.87) were used for printing and mailing of the newsletter.

She spoke of "ownership" and insisted that we had not dissolved our "partnership" in a way that would be recognized in a court. I suggested that because I had been responsible for VQT with the IRS, I owned it. Donna was consuming a lot of my energy. She still wanted to be included in any interviews that came my way. I had to tell her that it was up to journalists to include her or not.

It seemed to me at this point that she was as angry with me as she had been at the *St. Elsewhere* people for not giving her the attention she felt was her due.

This matter was still unresolved in May, when she informed me that she would let me or my attorney know whether she felt the terms of an agreement I suggested were acceptable to her.

In June, the *Los Angeles Daily News* ran the news of Donna's resignation in an article in which the increase in letter-writing campaigns to networks was also reported.[19] In the article I expressed well-founded concern that the increase could diminish the impact of each campaign, and said, "It's getting to the point where every fan of every show that has ever been canceled thinks all they have to do is sit down and write a letter and it'll be back."[20] Of Donna, the *Times* said: "Citing long-standing differences with co-founder Dorothy Swanson, Deen served notice in the group's current newsletter that she is quitting." Donna had responded to the reporter, "We're trying to work something out, hopefully without lawyers."[21] Donna again cited the *Designing Women* campaign as being the catalyst for her departure, stating that she felt I had not made "enough of a distinction between" my "personal support and that of VQT as a group." Donna specifically said, "I felt it was inappropriate for her to use VQT and her status as co-founder to support the show. She could have written on her own, instead of using VQT stationery."[22] I am quoted as countering that I did not understand why Donna "decided this was wrong after participating in it." Really. The writer added that "Deen is currently looking for work in the television industry, 'maybe in public relations.'"[23] I already knew this. A letter had come for Donna to the VQT post office box from a public-relations firm in Los Angeles. I had accidentally opened it along with all the other mail that day. So I read with interest the rejection to Donna's application for a job as a publicist in the television industry. It had come to the official post office box because Donna had used VQT stationery, which at the time contained both our names. She had berated me for having used this exact stationery during the campaign. I used VQT to try to save a quality show; Donna used VQT to try to get a job as a publicist.

Donna's "legal advisor" had written a twelve-page rambling letter to my attorney, in which she made spurious accusations and insinuations, demanding full disclosure. There was nothing "full" to disclose. Donna had received regular accountings of VQT's meager bank statements.

In November, Donna sent me a copy of a letter she sent to her legal advisor essentially relieving her of any further concern in the matter. She asked me to stay in touch, and told me she was still hoping to write or work in public relations. Donna wanted to continue to receive VQT newsletters. She would even occasionally contribute to them—once with an interview with none other than Tom Fontana (a producer of Donna's beloved *St. Elsewhere*).

In April 1988, VQT's big break would come, a feature article in *Parade* magazine. Donna's part in VQT (that I always related and always tell to this day) was edited out by *Parade*. She wrote me a sarcastic letter about her surprise at my new version of how VQT was formed—without her. She was very angry, and instructed me *not* to offer any explanation. So I couldn't tell her that it was the editor or writer, not me, who simplified, for the sake of space, the story of VQT's founding. (In truth, Donna had nothing to do with the founding of the corporation known since 1988 as Viewers for Quality Television Inc.) Then—to finally end the Donna Deen chapter—on October 22, 1988, after VQT's first enormously successful Los Angeles convention that enjoyed the in-person participation of the Thomasons, Barney Rosenzweig, Sharon Gless, Annie Potts, Dixie Carter, Ron Perlman, Meshach Taylor, Alice Ghostley, Larry Drake, Susan Ruttan, Julia Duffy, Tim Reid, Daphne Maxwell Reid, and others, Donna handwrote a simple final message that instructed me to remove her name from the VQT mailing list.

OUR WORLD
Not in This World

VQT was still struggling to reach its stride in the early part of 1987. My goal was to make VQT a force so strong, with so many viewers banded together, that no network would dare cancel a show bearing our quality imprimatur. I felt we needed at least ten thousand people to accomplish this. (Thirteen years later, I still believe it.)

The group was floundering financially and searching for quality viewers who would lend their voices and their support to the group. I still was not taking a salary, so I returned to my former career as a teacher, substituting in the Fairfax County school system. I would rather have given my full attention to VQT. I was totally committed to its cause and potential, and believed that the organization had a finger on the pulse of the disenfranchised viewers who knew what good television was, as exemplified by *St. Elsewhere, Cagney & Lacey, Hill Street Blues, Family Ties,* and other shows of that caliber.

By the spring of 1987 I was wondering, What next? and knew that, for VQT to survive, something dramatic had to happen.

Enter a program of nostalgic charm, brilliantly researched and written. Enter Linda Ellerbee; enter cohost Ray Gandolf. ABC's *Our World* was the catalyst for VQT's next phase.

> We will not require that the network news division become a significant profit contributor to justify its continued operations. It is not insignificant that since the merger we have added to the network schedule the highly acclaimed *Our World* primetime program. There are two things that will not change—first, our company's commitment to quality, and

second, the editorial independence of ABC news. Quality is the bench-
mark against which we judge our performance. If our years in broadcasting and publishing have taught us anything, it is that success in the
long term is built on a quality product.[1]

Fifteen days after citing *Our World* as evidence of his commitment to quality news programming, and just one week after VQT's official endorsement,
ABC announced the cancellation. According to John Carmody of the *Washington Post,* Linda Ellerbee and the staff learned of the cancellation by watching *Entertainment Tonight.* "Nobody from the ABC news division bothered to
say a word to them," wrote Carmody.[2] Unlike others abruptly canceled, Ellerbee and Gandolf had a unique forum in which to address this development:
their own live stage. That's how most viewers learned the news—from the
cohosts themselves in a matter-of-fact but impassioned farewell on the last
live show. *Our World*'s loyal viewers were stunned. Gandolf said, "We apparently fell down and broke our crown on the bottom line. You have been faithful and eloquent supporters of *Our World.* Thank you. You deserve better. I
hope you get it." Linda told her viewers, "Our flaw was we didn't have enough
audience. But just because we won't be here next year, that doesn't mean we
weren't here this year. *Our World* was about history. Now it's about to become
history. Nothing is always. Thank you for watching." Viewers were aghast.

Our World had consistently placed at the bottom of the ratings against
number 1 *The Cosby Show,* part of NBC's Thursday night blockbuster schedule
that also included *Family Ties.* But *Our World* was designed to be an inexpensive alternative to the NBC hits, and it made money for ABC despite low advertising rates and a small audience. It cost only about $350,000 to produce each
week, compared with an entertainment hour cost of $800,000 to $1 million.

VQT members embraced *Our World.* We weren't particularly targeting this
type of show; rather we were focusing our discussions and interest toward
drama and comedy. But "this type of show" didn't exist before *Our World,* and
it so captured the essence of quality that VQT endorsed it—just in time to
have a campaign for it.

What was *Our World,* other than a nostalgic look at a date in history
through music and film clips from that time, with commentary by Ellerbee
and Gandolf? The show's opening said it all: "When we remember a time, we
remember moments, a kaleidoscope of the sights, the sounds, the emotions
that remind us of the way we were."

As Mark Schwed of UPI wrote that September, "Linda Ellerbee and Ray
Gandolf co-hosted *Our World,* which informed and entertained by taking
viewers back in time to a place or period, reliving it through the eyes of people

who were there, and accenting it with their own wit and wisdom."[3] He added, "It told us about the present and the future—by looking at the past. It educated, but it was not school. It entertained, but it was not mindless. It was quality—television's noblest service."[4]

Gandolf said to journalist David Freedman of the *Philadelphia Daily News* on May 28, "We enabled viewers to go back in time, to remember what their lives were like then and to see how much those lives have changed in the years since because of those events. For those who weren't alive during the period we were talking about on a particular show, our hope was to re-create the mood and, in so doing, create some interest on the part of those viewers in that period."[5]

VQT members wrote me frequently and eloquently about *Our World*.

"I would hate to see this show defeated by *The Cosby Show*. I taped [*Our World's*] 'Gone With the Wind' episode and watched Cosby. I don't remember Cosby, but I saw and learned things about 'Gone With the Wind' that I never knew!" wrote Barbara Adams of Springfield, Virginia. Sharon Brown of West Haven, Connecticut, wrote, "The show is presented with just the right balance of tongue-in-cheek humor and seriousness."

So what went wrong? Schwed wrote that "to ABC Entertainment President Brandon Stoddard, *Our World* was a sacrificial lamb, a cheap way to fill the hour opposite the most popular program in the history of television, *The Cosby Show*."[6] But it placed 104th out of 104 network shows and had "only" 9 million viewers, with a 6.5 rating and 10 share. *The Cosby Show* attracted 63 million, a feat never again repeated by a network series. And it wasn't *Our World's* fault. Linda Ellerbee would tell me later that *Our World* had unfortunately and simply become caught between the entertainment division and the news division of the network.

The Campaign

There was no questioning the wisdom of a full-blown *Our World* campaign, even though VQT had few resources and embarrassingly little money. But again, passion—mine, television journalists' and viewers', especially Linda Ellerbee's legion of fans—would propel this machine of public opinion forward.

I notified television journalists that VQT would organize a letter-writing campaign to save *Our World*. Critical response to *Our World* was strong in the journalism community, as was the reaction to a cancellation that seemed unnecessary. I heard from Linda Ellerbee, who wanted to know what she could do to help. Right after the cancellation she went on a scheduled book tour promoting the paperback version of her book *And So It Goes.* She assumed she would be asked about *Our World,* and she was right. To every inquiry, she would tell the person to get in touch with VQT.

ABC received so many calls that they began referring *Our World* protests to me. The irony of the network referring callers to the organization that was protesting against it did not seem to occur to ABC. The very entity that had canceled the show was blindly referring calls to VQT, and ABC was giving out our address. Affiliate stations, radio stations, and newspapers also referred callers to me. By July, ABC was admitting to fourteen thousand letters. I told the *Cincinnati Enquirer's* John Kiesewetter on July 9 that "if ABC says they've got 14,000 letters, you have to double that. That's not enough."[7] I knew that, based on *my* mail. I was averaging four hundred letters a day and had received about five thousand copies of letters sent to ABC executives. I added to Kiesewetter, "ABC has tapped into very articulate, educated, informed, upscale viewers who are usually tuned to PBS, and who were surprised to find something like *Our World* on the air. And ABC is going to throw these viewers away."[8] Which they certainly did. Nine million disposable viewers.

During that summer, I could always tell which city Linda was in by the calls and letters. I told TV critic Don Freeman of the *San Diego Union* on July 12 that "I am hearing from educators, doctors, attorneys, judges, parents, grandparents, senior citizens, children. There is no age group unrepresented."[9] I added that there were interesting subthemes in these letters: "(1) Most of the people have never written to protest the cancellation of a TV show before; (2) Most of them do not ordinarily watch network television, preferring instead PBS or cable."[10] Freeman injected, "That ABC knowingly tapped into the PBS audience may or may not be good."[11] It would turn out to be positive. My list of subthemes continued in his column. "(3) Most are aware that *Our World* was an inexpensive show to produce and argue that in their letters; (4) Most are fed up with network television and consider the cancellation of *Our World* the final insult; (5) All recognize that *Our World* was in last place according to Nielsen but argue that it is time that the networks recognize and have the courage to support a low-rated quality show; (6) This is both an intellectual and an emotional outburst from viewers."[12]

Three times that summer, I sent multiple pages of quotes from viewer letters to journalists to demonstrate the passion for this show. Many of them printed comments from my mailings.

The $15 participation fee from VQTers barely allowed me to keep pace with the cost of processing and answering three hundred to four hundred letters a day. I poured $1,000 of my own money into the campaign. I believed that unless VQT made noise here, it would no longer exist as a viable organization. I gathered another $1,000 in donations from *Our World* viewers to help pay for postage. The campaign continued on a dollar and a prayer.

A VQTer and *Our World* fan with two small children made my acquaintance and arrived daily to take a box of mail home and open it. The next day, she would bring that box back to me and pick up a new one. It is not an easy or quick task to open four hundred letters day after day. Susan Bailey's reward was meeting Linda Ellerbee three months later at VQT's first convention and being singled out as the one who had opened all the mail. Susan, of Oakton, Virginia, became one of my best friends.

Every inquiry was read and responded to, giving the network address, journalists' addresses, and tips on writing an effective letter. There was a postcard from a seven-year-old, handwritten notes from grandmothers, typed letters from professional people. Most were not short notes, but were long, eloquent missives about *Our World*'s value. By September, ABC admitted to twenty thousand letters but remained unimpressed. In a *Los Angeles Times* article, however, ABC audience relations coordinator Sue Levkoff admitted, "It's the largest response we've ever gotten for a news show that we know of."[13] In his June 25 column in the *San Francisco Chronicle,* TV critic John Carman printed ABC's form letter postcard to *Our World* viewers: "We have received your letter concerning *Our World* and we appreciate your thoughtful comments. Since our audience is an integral part of the news process and its input is carefully considered, it is always helpful to have the opinion and suggestions of our viewers. Thank you for taking the time to share your opinions with us."[14] Sure.

In the August 1987 VQT newsletter, I published excerpts from some of the nearly seven thousand letters VQT had received thus far—heartfelt entreaties in which viewers poured out the anguish and outrage in their souls at the loss of the program that had touched them and made them believe in the potential of commercial network television again. This was a grassroots response at its essence. ABC just didn't get it. It could have taken advantage of a great public-relations opportunity. And it ultimately tried to, according to UPI: "Sometime after he canceled *Our World*, [Brandon Stoddard] realized he had an hour slot to fill in January. He had an idea. Bring back *Our World*. He called ABC Network President John Sias and asked that it be done. Sias called ABC News President Roone Arledge to find out if it could be done, but Arledge told him that half the staff of *Our World* had been let go, the other half had been reassigned, and Ellerbee was halfway out the door."[15] Mark Schwed was right when he said that the networks just don't get it. Only the viewers "got it."

Excerpts from letters printed in the VQT August 1987 newsletter prove it.

I used this fine program as a teaching device. I would record the show; then we would view it together, many times, pausing to discuss certain areas. I am *not* a teacher. These were my children. (Mrs. Edie McDermott, Beacon, New York)

It was sly and good-humored and sad and sharp and wistful and well-written and shocking and important and fun. It was a marvelous instrument of instruction. (Barbara Youngs, El Cerrito, California)

Our World represents the blood, sweat, and tears of our nation. Bill Cosby is fun, but *Our World* is important. (Janice Bauer, Melrose Park, Pennsylvania)

To paraphrase General Patton when rushing to the rescue of McAuliff[e] at Bastogne: "People that eloquent must be saved!" (E. Tim Friel, Philadelphia, Pennsylvania)

I am a confirmed cable and PBS viewer who was lured to a network program by the high quality of this show. I would have thought that any network would strive to achieve the viewer/cost equation that this show obviously achieved. (Gwendolyn Russo, Trenton, New Jersey)

My greatest surprise was coming home on a Thursday evening to my son (14 years) who was alone and finding him watching *Our World*. "Hurry up," he said, "it's about 1963. You've only missed 10 minutes." (Cathie Goehler, Holland, Pennsylvania)

I was born in 1937. My mother had all of *Life* magazine bound. When my children return to her home (one is in his second year at Georgetown Law School and the other is a third year student at London University), they still race to the library to read them. I tape *Our World* each week, and hope that our future grandchildren will have the same privilege. (Julia Biggs, Upper St. Clair, Pennsylvania)

Our World is ourselves and what we were, who we were, and what we became. (Doris Harris, Pomona, California)

History and a sense of vision is what *Our World* offers. *Our World* stimulates conversation, promotes thought, and deserves a second chance. (Pam Levy, San Jose, California)

Our World is about our life. It is current although its topics are not. It is worth watching because it reminds. I don't have to watch television, but I do want to be able to continue to watch *Our World*. I *do* deserve better! (Robert J. Ramsey III, San Francisco, California)

Our World's numbers were small by television standards, but those numbers should carry an asterisk. First, because the numbers are growing as word of *Our World*'s quality spreads; second, the numbers that the show did achieve ought to be of interest to a select group of advertisers. We're bright, we're selective, and we do spend money—on quality consumer goods, on vacations, on electronic audio/visual equipment, on automobiles. We are a market that can, and should, be reached by television. I think we ought to be "sold" that way. (Joseph G. Biscontini, Lansdowne, Pennsylvania)

Please don't get the idea that without *Our World* my son will grow to manhood uneducated as to our past, but the series did assist in this process. Note only that when he reaches manhood he can have an effect on how *Webster*'s defines ABC entertainment. (L. L. Bert Hofer Jr., Austin, Texas)

The Victory

Then the dramatic happened. On a routine day in late July (which consisted of processing hundreds of pieces of mail), I received a call from Dr. William Baker, president of PBS's WNET in New York. His first words were "Do you realize what you've done?" I didn't know what he was talking about; he explained. All the publicity from VQT's campaign had captured his interest. PBS wanted *Our World*. As he would say in the *Wall Street Journal* on August 4, "The excitement [of the campaign] galvanized me into doing something. She [Swanson] stirred this huge national pot of electronic media. It's amazingly wonderful."[16] Bob Davis called me "a television flop's best friend" and said, "It looks as though she has helped raise another one from the dead. WNET-TV, a New York public-broadcasting station, plans to announce soon that it will launch a new version of *Our World*, a nostalgia news program that ABC-

NOT IN THIS WORLD

TV cancelled and Ms. Swanson battled to save."[17] Davis observed something that I hope holds true today, that "[Swanson's] mission is to preserve the few good shows on television—especially ones that portray characters or controversies in a fresh light." Ellerbee commented for the article, "I couldn't have done better if I was sitting with a mimeograph machine in my basement."[18] The catch was, Davis wrote, that Ellerbee had to be released from her ABC contract *and* Baker had to raise $5 million from corporate sponsors and other public stations *and* he had to negotiate with ABC over rights to the name of the show. Seemed like tough "ands."

But I was ecstatic, as were VQT volunteer staffers and all who had badgered ABC. Another victory! It felt marvelous. Not powerful, but as if it were supposed to happen this way if you cared that much. I contacted Linda and asked her to attend VQT's first convention that September, to be held at the Ramada Inn in McLean, Virginia. There would be about sixty VQT members from across the country in attendance. She said yes, that she wanted "to shake hands with every person in the room." The TV critic for *USA Today* at the time, Monica Collins, told me when I ran into her at a *Designing Women* party later that despite what Linda had promised, "You'll never get her." Although this comment was somewhat disturbing to me, I trusted that Linda would appear. I had listed her as a convention participant in print. So, of course, that meant she would come, didn't it?

For our August newsletter, Bill Baker gave me the following statement, which appeared on our front page after the headline "AND SO IT GOES—TO PBS."

> If it weren't for VQT, *Our World* would be relegated to the museum of broadcasting and *not* part of television's future. The public attention generated by VQT over Linda and *Our World* is unique in the annals of communications history in this country—and I'm delighted that we at WNET-13 can be part of that.

For the same front page, Linda gave me the following statement:

> It's quite clear that Viewers for Quality Television made the difference. The message is also clear: you *can so* talk back to your TV and be heard. WNET has taken you at your word. Now, together, we will find the corporate sponsors to fund the program. If, when you turn on your television set and see the first new edition of the show, you will be right to say, "That's my show." Maybe that's another reason they call it public TV. I look forward to seeing as many of you as possible in September at

VQT's first convention. You've made a liar out of me. This time when I
said "And so it goes," I was wrong. Thank you.

Linda indeed came to that first convention in September 1987. Word of
her progress preceded her, thanks to a friend of hers who was traveling with
her. As we all waited in that small hotel suite living room—Harry Thomason,
Matt Roush of *USA Today,* Bill Allen (then head of MTM Enterprises), Carole
Smith (still Barney Rosenzweig's assistant at *Cagney & Lacey*), Ray Gandolf and
Entertainment Tonight—the calls came. "Linda just arrived at Union Station."
"Linda just checked in to the hotel." "Linda is now coming down the hall-
way." I was being interviewed by *Entertainment Tonight* the moment she
entered, so I could only distractedly watch in fascination as Linda Ellerbee
swept into that room and proceeded to own it. We were dazzled by her. She
truly did shake hands with everybody and patiently signed countless autographs (we *are* fans, after all). Linda also was interviewed for *Entertainment
Tonight,* and told the world how viewers saved *Our World.* She was indefatiga-
ble. All of us in that room were riding the crest of the wave of victory.

While addressing the VQT group that next morning, Linda officially
announced that PBS had picked up *Our World,* that she was free of her ABC contract, and that title rights with ABC had been resolved (the show would probably be called *Your World*). She was informative and flattering, giving VQT credit.

> Everybody who worked on *Our World* thanks you. This organization
> got to its typewriters, its computers and its pencils and its pens and its
> postcards, and now ABC admits to getting 20,000 letters, more than it
> has gotten on anything, ever. It wasn't enough, however, for ABC. But
> my company [Lucky Duck] and WNET in New York are going to put on
> a program next spring that you might be familiar with. And if it's not
> called *Our World,* you better believe it's *your* world. PBS paid attention
> to what you did, you really are the mouse that roared, and may your
> tribe only increase.

Here Linda revealed to us—and it was a revelation to me—how the networks perceive viewers—in a sense, who the viewer is: "The product is not
the program. The product is the audience. The consumer is not the audience;
the consumer is the advertiser. The product is simply the thing that they
want. They want *you.* What the show is supposed to do is build an audience.
If it doesn't build an audience, there is no product."

She also said we had a right to complain about how we, as products, were
being delivered. To me, then and since, this was an epiphany. I had never

understood this to be the case. I have never forgotten Linda's words, and her insight has guided me in leading VQT.

That night, after our first awards banquet, a humble affair without any major award winners present except Harry Thomason, Linda held court for Pat Murphy and me in her hotel suite. She lounged in a chair opposite us and gave us the benefit of her wisdom and experience for us to apply to VQT's present and future—all the while slowly but thoroughly ripping and shredding her pantyhose from her legs in apparent nervous energy. I did not take notes, and could not have applied any more concentration than I did. Linda basically counseled us to be very cautious about accepting any money from anyone connected to the TV industry—whether networks, advertisers, or individuals—so as not to create any possible appearance of a conflict of interest. She was particularly concerned about any First Amendment conflict. Because VQT was unique, we had to be above any real or perceived influence. She talked prolifically, fast, and brilliantly; it was more a mood that she set than any quotables I can share. It was advice that shaped the organization. She gave us her greatest gift, her time. We heeded that advice, and VQT remains poor but honorable to this day. Thank you, Linda Ellerbee.

The Disappointment

Our World, or whatever it would have been called on PBS, never came to be. The search for funding was not successful. I do not know what other factors might have contributed to the lack of follow-through. No formal announcement by PBS or Ellerbee was ever made that I know of. The promise that was *Our World* just faded away, as did the excitement its reprieve had generated. I do know that most of the *Our World* viewers, at least the ones I heard from—and we can assume they were a representative sample—never returned to network television. If they had, I would have heard from them. But to the networks, that's a loss of "only" nine million people. They were among the most outspoken, the most outraged, the most articulate, the most intelligent group of viewers I have ever heard from. For the network, they never counted anyway. Now network television does not count with them.

Our World was unique then and remains unique now. Nothing has replaced it that comes close to capturing its sentiment or its intellectual and emotional appeal to viewers wanting to engage their minds while being entertained. As David Bianculli wrote in 1992, "They [*Our World*] did in a network prime-time TV series what TV can also do in the classroom: they taught history in a way that made it come alive, and made you want to learn more."[19]

The Aftermath

The *Our World* "victory" did have an exciting outcome. Michael Ryan, a writer for *Parade* magazine, read the front page story about me and the *Our World* campaign in the *Wall Street Journal* and was interested. After a telephone interview, his interest grew and he arranged to come to Virginia to interview me for an article to appear in *Parade* the following April. Pat Murphy and I met Ryan at a Tysons Corner (in northern Virginia) restaurant for lunch and gave him the seeds of his story that would run on April 17, 1988, complete with my photo and the VQT address for the benefit of readers who might want to participate in the organization. The *Parade* editors even included what was then our set participation fee, $15.

Pat and I couldn't be sure the address would run. We had stressed the importance of it to Ryan, and he had passed it along to his editors. But until we saw it in print, we couldn't count on it. That one act by *Parade*, along with the published participation fee, not to mention Michael's insightful article, brought us enough new members and immediate revenue that we were able to declare ourselves solvent for the first time in our history.

In the article, Ryan struck a nerve with viewers who had experienced the frustration of having their favorite quality show canceled. He began: "It has happened to every one of us. A new television season starts, and you discover a program that you fall in love with. The acting is first-rate, the writing is crisp, the plots are intelligent. The whole show not only entertains you, it also makes you think. Then, suddenly, the show disappears."[20] He said of me, "The substitute teacher from Fairfax, Virginia, almost singlehandedly organized campaigns that put two of her favorite shows back on the air, and she is hoping to transfer a third from a commercial network to public broadcasting."[21] Ryan even explained how VQT's purpose was not necessarily to save TV shows. "Swanson is determined to see that VQT does not simply become a vehicle for saving endangered shows. She wants to give viewers a voice that will let the networks know what programs they consider good—before cancellation decisions are made."[22] Readers identified, and the response was overwhelming. We had to shut down normal operations while we processed all five thousand new participants. Because we felt an immediate need to get them on our mailing list, I purchased a second Commodore computer for $800 instead of trying to transfer the existing database from Commodore to PC format. That would not be an easy or quick task, but would be accomplished later by Minneapolis volunteer Steve Lenius. Susan Bailey pitched in again. She and I entered the names on the two computers, using floppy disks;

the Commodore had no hard drive. Pat Murphy and a Washington, D.C., volunteer, Jean Hall, opened the mail and processed the checks. I don't remember how long this took; it was probably several weeks of almost constant labor.

Some of our most valued, active, and loyal members joined VQT as a result of the *Parade* article. They changed the course of the organization and taught me the meaning of true volunteerism. Many new volunteers from the northern Virginia area came to us at this time, as well as many from around the country. They were people who wanted to do what Michael Ryan had suggested: "If we do our job, and the networks pay attention, we'll never have to campaign again. That is our goal."[23] There were also those who misunderstood the thrust of the article and thought that VQT's purpose was to "clean up" television and to get "offensive" material off the air. They soon grew disappointed with VQT's positive agenda and angered by the organization's endorsements of cutting-edge, adult programs. They ultimately left.

QUALITY TELEVISION—
AN OXYMORON?

W HEN challenged by skeptics with *"Quality* television? Isn't that a contradiction in terms?" I would defend and explain.

Linda Bloodworth-Thomason told a VQT audience once that there are good television programs just as there are good books. You can walk into any library and pick up a boring book, just as you can also find a classic; you just need to know where to look and take the time to choose wisely. Linda said that television is like that; on any given night you can find a worthless program and you can find a worthwhile one. Just as you don't read everything on a library shelf, you don't watch everything on television. She expressed her amazement when people proudly declare that they don't watch television. To her, that was like admitting they don't read books because they aren't smart enough to pick out the good ones.

TV critic David Bianculli argued in *Teleliteracy: Taking Television Seriously* that "the best of TV is very good indeed, and the idea of indiscriminately ridiculing or avoiding the medium of television displays no more intelligence than denouncing all movies as fluff or holding a 'Don't Open a Book Day.'"[1] Admitting that 90 percent of television is "crap," Bianculli makes a case for the other 10 percent and states that "TV deserves more respect than it's getting."[2]

At our 1989 convention (our second in Los Angeles), the three network entertainment presidents offered their definitions of quality television. NBC's Brandon Tartikoff felt that "a quality show is one in which the people who are crafting it are really working at the height of their powers. Their intention is not to do what has been done before, but to try to establish some new territory, a new horizon for whatever kind of show that they're doing." ABC's Robert Iger said that "quality programs deal with the human experience in a responsible manner. That can be through humor or through drama."

John Ritter responded during a panel discussion in September 1989 that quality television contained "things that [a]ffect me deeply, things that make me think, things that seem to make a difference, as opposed to the kind of thing where it doesn't make any difference whether you're awake or asleep. Quality television is something that has a density to it."

Ever a barometer of what defines quality, Matt Roush, wrote in 1997 that "if network TV is in a golden age of anything, it's the adult crime drama, a dark genre launched by *Hill Street Blues* that continues to deepen and disturb, exploring the human condition through unsettling brushes with the inhumane."[3]

The *Los Angeles Times* assembled a group of TV writers in 1997 who talked about the issue of current creative merit on network television. Brian Lowry reported it on April 13. Allan Burns, who produced *The Mary Tyler Moore Show* and *Lou Grant,* said something viewers already know and appreciate: "I've always felt the best shows have one writer, or a team, working the whole thing from beginning to end. A lot of what makes comedy successful is not the jokes, it's the people. If you base a show on jokes, you're dead."[4]

But how does the *audience* define "quality television"? Viewers for Quality Television formed as a grassroots organization. Its newsletter is the forum in which viewers nationwide share their insightful feelings about the programs that affect their lives. VQT member comments on quality demonstrate an intelligence for which television executives do not give their audience credit.

First a quality program must be *interesting*. If a drama, it is compelling; you can't turn away from it. Even though it aired on Friday nights, *Picket Fences* was a "watercooler" show—fans still discussed it Monday morning.

As *Picket Fences* did so brilliantly, a quality series often challenges our point of view. In its first two years, *Picket Fences* continually caused viewers to rethink issues about which they thought they had already formed solid opinions. A quality series, then, provokes thought. It does not always tie up the loose ends, for life is not like that. It moves us, delights us, or thrills us. It dares to take risks. It is honest. It illuminates the human condition. It requires more concentration and attention than other programs. It is unpredictable. It is usually character driven. (An exception is NBC's *Law & Order,* a story-driven Dick Wolf production that has survived cast changes for every major character and most minor ones.)

If a quality comedy, it *usually* (but it's not a rule) touches the heart as well as the funny bone. VQTer Mary Platt from Costa Mesa, California, said that "quality comedies not only reflect our lives and mirror our reactions to events in our lives, but they also, at base, have a *heart*. There is a human lesson— sometimes gentle, sometimes wise and thoughtful, sometimes even sobering— at the center of quality comedy."[5] But not always. *Cheers* was a quality comedy, as was *Seinfeld,* yet neither touched the heart. But the quality of each was indisputable. The quality writing in both of those shows assumed the intelligence of the audience. *Frank's Place,* however, as well as *Frasier* and *Everybody Loves Raymond,* possessed that heart and often touched us as they made us laugh.

Viewer Dara Monahan wrote for VQT's December 1987 newsletter that "the essential difference between ordinary sitcoms and 'qualcoms' is the source of the humor. Ordinary situation comedies most often rely upon the situations themselves to elicit laughs—the more outrageous, the better. The humor in these situations often has little to do with the characters involved." In citing *Designing Women* as an example of a "qualcom," Dara pointed out that "the humor comes from our knowledge of these women—their attributes and foibles. When rich characters are developed, there is not a great need to create unusual situations for them." One of the longest laughs ever on *Designing Women* occurred when about a hundred Viewers for Quality Television members were guests at a taping. This was an audience that *knew* these characters. Linda Bloodworth-Thomason had her women ruminating about how they would spend a $3,000 inheritance. Each—Mary Jo, Charlene, Julia—had grandiose ideas. But the biggest laugh came when Delta Burke's character, Suzanne Sugarbaker, said, "I'd buy a blouse." Our laughter stopped the show. It was so typical of Suzanne, so true to that character that it was hysterical. Backstage afterward, Delta commented that the thunder of laughter over that line shocked her. And invigorated her. Not only did the writers know her character, the audience did.

In the *Everybody Loves Raymond* episode that aired October 19, 1998, two full years since its debut, a quality moment occurred that was a payoff for viewers who had followed these characters all that time. In the story, Raymond's wife, Debra, is enduring a visit by her somewhat aloof mother. Raymond's mother, Marie, drops in, welcome or not, every day. (Raymond's parents live across the street.) Marie's intrusions are a constant source of comic friction between Raymond and Debra. The payoff moment occurred when Debra, frustrated and disappointed that her mother was not as involving with the kids as Raymond's meddling mother, tries to describe how she wishes her mother could be. Finally, she points across the room to Marie, and shouts in exasperation, "Like *her*!" Debra's admission, and Marie's reaction (played in almost slow motion by Doris Roberts) to finally getting this recognition, is the quality moment.

Characters on quality series are often flawed, multidimensional, and layered. They tend to endear themselves to us. We know about "the clothes they wear, the food they eat, their politics, prejudices, weaknesses and strengths. Immediate and vivid images are evoked simply by thinking their names."[6] Characters on quality shows are "admirable and sometimes deplorable, and sometimes they're both at the same time. They hold up a mirror, and in their responses to their lives we see something of ourselves in ways that alternately please us, anger us, shock us, make us feel good, make us laugh."[7] Characters on quality shows *are* us.

Rick DuBrow of the *Los Angeles Times* based his December 1, 1992, column on an editorial by Pat Murphy in VQT's November 1992 newsletter. She had criticized that fall season's shows.[8] DuBrow's subheading was "Viewers for Quality Television resents racy prime-time plots that aren't given enough development time to make relationships believable."[9] Murphy had criticized the gratuitous displays of sex in the current crop of shows, reminding readers (and hopefully producers and networks) of how sex could be portrayed intelligently and maturely, making the point that before we care about sex between two people on television, we have to care about the people who are engaging in the sex. DuBrow quoted from Pat's editorial: "This season lacks foreplay, it lacks seduction. The viewer is confronted with characters involved in situations and experiencing a pitch of excitement that the viewer does not identify with or believe that the characters are feeling."[10] Murphy also wrote that there seemed to be little connection between the characters, only disjointed sex. DuBrow reported that "VQT cites with admiration the intimate, adult relationship of the characters played by Daniel J. Travanti and Veronica Hamel in *Hill Street Blues*," and "there is warmth and sexiness among the couples on *Evening Shade*. There are funny situations of an adult nature on *Cheers*, but we've been allowed the time to get to know these characters."[11] DuBrow noted that Murphy criticized the Thomasons' *Hearts Afire* for putting John Ritter and Markie Post in a bathtub together long before the viewer felt any fire or even warmth between the two, and that in Diane English's *Love & War* the two characters were discussing the need for safe sex long before the viewer felt any urgency between them. DuBrow quoted Murphy: "What this season is emphasizing is sexual situations between characters who are not emotionally connected to each other and not yet emotionally connected to the audience."[12] In the newsletter, Murphy had also said,

"If we don't know who [these people] are, how can we understand
what they see in one another? By not involving the audience with the
characters, by not taking the time or the care for the equivalent of
viewer foreplay or afterplay, the audience is treated without respect,
just like a one-night stand. Eventually the quality audience will lose
interest and treat the show the same way—as a one-night stand, not as
a long-term relationship."[13]

VQT was not just a cheerleader for network television. Appreciated or not,
we did not hesitate to point out what was *not* quality.

Examples of quality series are *China Beach, St. Elsewhere, Hill Street Blues,
Cagney & Lacey, Frank's Place, Homefront, Designing Women, Murphy Brown, L.A.
Law, Northern Exposure, I'll Fly Away, Brooklyn Bridge, Homicide: Life on the Street,
Picket Fences, The Wonder Years, Seinfeld, ER, Law & Order, NYPD Blue, The X-
Files, The Practice, Everybody Loves Raymond, Ally McBeal, The Sopranos*. These
are programs whose characters became familiar; programs that we made an
appointment to watch. Sometimes they were just too good for network television, too complex for the viewing public who made up the decision-making
Nielsen households. Now, as network television panders more and more to
the lowest common denominator, we get not more quality, but the dumbing
down of television.

When asked to explain why they might vote to endorse a show as quality, VQT members offered varying reasons in the December 1994 newsletter.

The plot is complex with human emotions and meaningful issues. The
characters are real, mature and distinct. I care about them. The show
makes me think and feel.[14]

It has the guts to tackle the hard issues with dialogue that resonates
realistically. The dialogue is intelligently provocative and delivered in
impeccable keeping with the character. You forget you are a passive
viewer; you are interactively involved and you clamor for more.[15]

Has complex subjects that are not resolved in an hour.[16]

Identifying a quality series in 1997, Tom and Cheryl Della Sala of Schenectady, New York, reminded VQT participants that a quality show is not
predictable with moralistic themes.[17] They maintained that "what viewers
want are shows that are so well written that they *aren't* predictable and in
which the morals are a naturally evolved conclusion of the plot, not messages
that are pounded into one's head."[18] John Christensen of Charlotte, Michigan, told us of his frustration, as an "appointment" television viewer, with

an industry "simplifying storylines, creating cardboard characters and making every show for the masses. When complex characters deal with hard-hit-
ting issues, you believe it and feel the emotions. When will the networks learn
that there are many of us who like to be challenged?"[19]

Through the years VQT members did not merely identify a show as quality, they articulated *why* in the pages of our newsletter, to one another and to
the television industry. Why *St. Elsewhere?* What distinguished *Designing
Women?* Why is *Law & Order* so enduring? Why do viewers still miss *China
Beach?* Why did *ER* succeed? What is the secret of *NYPD Blue?* What differ-
entiates *Frasier* from other sitcoms? Was is so endearing about *Everybody Loves
Raymond?* Why did *Cagney & Lacey*'s messages reach so many on such an emotional level? Why was *Northern Exposure* so appealing? What explains the
charm of *Picket Fences?*

Why *Designing Women?*

Can there be more to say beyond the groundswell of affection that saved it?
VQT members would think so. Viewers found it to be one of the most refreshing and stimulating shows ever. They discovered "delightful adult comedy,
insightful glimpses into women's minds and devastating repartee. It was innovative in that the women verbalized a stream of consciousness that before
remained silent for women in TV comedies."[20]

Valerie Deckard of Bloomington, Indiana, wrote in a 1987 newsletter, "For
every point the writers make, they provide an equal or greater number of
laughs in getting us there." Carol Callaway of Turnersville, New Jersey, commented, "This show celebrates an open mind and the thinking woman."

Throughout the years, VQT members have had three requirements of a
show to be championed as quality: be consistent, don't talk down to us, don't
get lazy. *Designing Women* was not excused from this "rule," and as the years
of enjoyment passed, viewers insisted that the writers remain true to the
premise and characters of the show, and would speak out when they did not.
When it veered from the conversations that were its trademark, and followed
ill-conceived attempts at physical comedy (remember when Julia got her head
stuck in the stairway rail?), Cindy Thompson from Pittsburgh, Pennsylvania,
complained: "*Designing Women* should never, ever do physical comedy. *Never!*
As soon as the ladies start thinking they're Lucy and Ethel and Laverne and
Shirley, they embarrass themselves and us. The show was conceived in the
design studio, as intelligent conversations among four very different, very
bright women. When they hold to that format, the program is superlative;
when they don't, it's not worth watching."[21]

Designing Women was a perfect example of how extraordinary a quality show can be when in the capable hands of its originator (Linda Bloodworth-Thomason) and how it can deteriorate when delegated to somebody incapable of following the creator's vision. What other comedy of that time dealt with such issues as AIDS, women in the ministry, race, and women as friends rather than competitors in a consistently funny and enlightening way? Linda Bloodworth-Thomason wrote sixty-six episodes in a row, and left a magnificent body of work. When Linda backed away, *Designing Women* suffered. But what she had created changed television comedy.

Why *St. Elsewhere?*

If there were two shows that defined Viewers for Quality Television in the beginning, they were *Cagney & Lacey* and *St. Elsewhere*. TV critics praised *St. Elsewhere* often and lavishly. But why did viewers relish it so?

Pat Murphy expressed why *St. Elsewhere* was a quality show in VQT's April/May 1988 newsletter when she wrote, "The brilliance, the pain and the poignancy of *St. Elsewhere* is summed up for me in one scene: Morrison listening to the beat of his dead wife's transplanted heart in Eve Leighton's chest. It left me in stunned silence, and it is still with me." Lydia Moon wrote in the same issue, "I laughed, cried, mourned and celebrated with the staff of St. Eligius Hospital the last six years. These people became my friends, and I learned from them. For that one hour a week, St. Eligius was a real place with real people."

Acknowledging the creative force behind the show, Gary McCloy of Palm Springs, California, wrote, "The writers on *St. Elsewhere* are national treasures. I feel truly blessed that they chose to see viewers as intelligent, complex, sensitive, sophisticated and involved."

As *St. Elsewhere* producer Tom Fontana explained in VQT's February 1988 newsletter,

> We decided to take more chances—to go much further with the comedy in order to balance out the specter of death. And we only killed people whom the audience had gotten to know and care about, so that when they died, the viewers felt something. The truth is, we thought we were going to be canceled and we realized we had nothing to lose. And that sense of imminent cancellation, of "kamikaze" television, has remained with us ever since.

Of how he and John Masius worked together, Fontana explained, "If Masius and I had a system, it would have to be called the Haphazard Method. No patterns, no formulas, just one of us at a desk writing longhand while the other paces the room doing bad impressions of Norman Lloyd." He told us that the series was in a constant state of evolution. "We never think about topping ourselves, just stretching ourselves as writers. We tinker with the series, try to perfect stories, themes, characters. Once we start to play it safe, to repeat ourselves, we move on." Will any *St. Elsewhere* fan ever forget the image of the ever-complaining Mrs. Huffnagle squashed in her hospital bed, Dr. Mary Woodley (played by Karen Austin) placing the stuffed animal with the baby's body in the morgue, the poignant story of "Cora and Arnie," or Dr. Craig (played by William Daniels) reading aloud Dr. Seuss's "Green Eggs and Ham" after learning of his son's death? Quality scenes and memories linger long after the show ends.

Why *Cagney & Lacey?*

Although critics have explained it, and I attempted to do so in a previous chapter, one viewer's analysis of this show is particularly revealing. VQT member Tom Galioto from Arlington, Virginia, paid tribute to *Cagney & Lacey* in VQT's August/September 1988 newsletter and perhaps summed up its allure to men and women alike. These are the words of a viewer, not a critic or a media professor. Quality programs inspire eloquent responses, and this is a sample:

> *Cagney & Lacey* wrote a continuing essay on the eternal warfare
> between reason and emotion, conflicts cast in terms of duty versus
> conscience, or morality versus legality. The problems that challenged
> Chris and Mary Beth changed them and drew them into humanity.
> They questioned priorities and alternatives, choices and consequences.
> Mary Beth and Christine had to sort through their own experiences,
> come to a more critical evaluation of themselves and a fuller under-
> standing of their partner. What Mary Beth and Christine shared had
> meaning because they experienced the human condition. They were
> partners in life. Characterization was detailed, multidimensional and
> consistent. Dialogue, in which *Cagney & Lacey* excelled, demanded
> attention. Humor evened out intense dramatic peaks. A humanistic
> bias prevailed, better suited for an investigation into life than crime.
> Programs were beautifully assembled with skill, care and purpose, yet
> in acting resided the true substance of the series.
>   Tyne Daly gave us compelling reasons for the battery of principles
> Mary Beth carried along in her ordered world. Mary Beth's strengths

were self evident, but Tyne Daly also grasped Mary Beth's insecurities, hopes, prejudices and fears. These she molded into a comprehensive study of a sincere, intelligent, highly motivated woman struggling with an inability to integrate her vision of life with her experience of it. Family defined, but never limited, Mary Beth Lacey. However much she sought to distance herself, crime represented a personal antipathy, a repudiation of all her fundamental beliefs, and this private battleground was a fertile source for Tyne Daly's artistic efforts. Tyne Daly's serious scenes were stunning and disturbing in their severity. Her incomparable dramatic reach was at times, simply overpowering. But some of her most moving scenes were quiet, tender moods when alone or with one of her children, or sharing a magic moment with Christine. Then a special communication reached out to the audience to touch sympathetic chords.

Sharon Gless was animate and radiant, captivating with the unexpected. Much of her appeal came from an inexhaustible store of creativity in coordinating the bundle of contradictions that made up Chris Cagney. Over the years Sharon Gless explored Christine, sometimes with careless, brilliant fluency, other times with methodical, searching introspection. She could muster enough emotional commitment to instill the most embittered passions, engender images of anguish or flashes of hidden steel. Yet her rhythmic comedic sense was never far away, bridging those intense dramatic gulfs with a certain ingenuous eccentricity or with mercilessly directed sarcasm. A supremely subtle artist, she mastered a silent language to convey feelings behind words. Chris was an extremely complex character, and Sharon Gless's interpretation had to run the gamut of color and atmosphere to develop her fully. Sometimes when Cagney thought herself about to be challenged, a reflex reaction in the form of a preemptive visual retort set in, pugnacious and quick. It stung and silenced. It could be grim and frightening. But it could also speak softly and tenderly and was especially eloquent when traversing the frailty of dependence or the bonds of love. Sharon Gless penetrated Cagney's mantle of assertiveness to illuminate a character rich in enigma. Her portrayals reached levels of profound intimacy with a kinetic style exciting and unforgettable. Tyne Daly and Sharon Gless performed surpassingly in blending individual talents or working singly. Each could easily carry an episode solo; together they were unmatchable.

VQT members did not merely enjoy *Cagney & Lacey*. They devoured it.

Why *Frank's Place?*

Although a more detailed analysis of why *Frank's Place* captured the hearts of viewers can be found in "Growing Campaigns," some mention of the phenomenon belongs here.

Created by Hugh Wilson and coexecutive produced by Wilson and Tim Reid (Wilson had created *WKRP in Cincinnati* and Reid had costarred in it), the concept of a college professor returning home to run his father's restaurant in New Orleans was pitched to them by CBS programming vice president Kim LeMasters.[22] Wilson and Reid decided to run with LeMasters's idea, and never did present their own idea about a ballplayer who buys a restaurant in Atlanta.[23] After researching in New Orleans, they came up with a plot about a Massachusetts college professor who inherits a New Orleans restaurant (Chez Louisane) from a father he barely knew. It was a classic fish-out-of-water story, which Frank Parrish then had to adapt to a different lifestyle in New Orleans. The cast was headed by Reid, his wife, Daphne Maxwell Reid (playing mortician Hannah Griffin), and an unfamiliar but strong cast of supporting characters. There was a proud cook who didn't want to be called a "chef" and a feisty "waitress emeritus" who wouldn't wait on anyone who hadn't been a customer for at least twenty years. It didn't resemble a sitcom. Its humor was often bittersweet.

Reid was insistent that his show was a comedy, not a drama, even though many episodes contained pathos and poignancy. He told the *Los Angeles Daily News,* "What makes our show different from the standard sitcom is the fact that we will rely on subtleties. We will spend a minute and a half in a room with the fan going foof, foof, foof, without a word being spoken. That's what makes people think it's a drama, but it isn't. It is a sharing of the moment."[24] The *New York Daily News* TV critic, David Rosenthal, said in his review, "It builds slowly, drawing its humor from its rich characters instead of cheap one-liners. It's a gentle show that grows on you with a lilting rhythm seldom seen on television."[25] David Gritten, television critic for the *Los Angeles Herald,* agreed: "Wilson has drawn such fine characters here that action becomes secondary."[26]

In VQT's February 1988 newsletter, Pat Murphy responded to NBC Entertainment president Brandon Tartikoff's comments that years from now people won't remember episodes of *Frank's Place.*[27] Murphy wrote, *"Frank's Place* assumes that its audience will know when to laugh, be able to follow a multicharacter premise and comprehend a layered storyline," and cited "moments that will be remembered for years to come." She mentioned the episode about the old woman breaking down in tears as she explains her husband's suicide to Bubba; the conversation between Frank and the bum—the bum that Frank wanted to get rid of and then missed when he was gone; the "nine-to-five" conversation; Frank's uncle continuing to fabricate enviable life stories and going home to his real life as a postman; the soul-searching conversation between Hannah and her mother before Hannah's wedding, daughter challenging mother to define love in marriage and marriage without love; and Cool Charles's reparation for his misdeeds by pouring money through the mail slot in the door of his childhood orphanage. Murphy ended, "Frank's Place involves me. It tantalizes the mind, it pleases the ears. It is sensual with the mixtures of the stories, the rhythm of the jazz, the aroma of the cooking. I will remember it tomorrow, in four years and beyond."

Critics lauded the rich characters who seemed true to the region that the show depicted. "Their presence gives the program a depth and texture uncommon in the comedy format."[28] Robert P. Laurence said it was "rich in characters. And in character."[29]

According to its executive producer and star, Tim Reid, Frank's Place was "about family—the extended family. It's about the neighborhood—friendship. It's about people who, despite racial and economic differences, all have a common goal and that is to live a quality life, to get the most out of life and help where they can and take their lumps with a smile."[30]

Of all the network shows that VQT fought for and lost, Frank's Place remains perhaps the most mourned. It could have succeeded with a little more faith, trust, and time. As black leaders criticize the television industry, perceiving that blacks are under represented and under portrayed, one wonders what a difference Frank's Place would have made given that it transcended race and raised the level of comedy and pathos in a series with black leads. We'll never know because CBS said "No."

Why *China Beach?*

Produced by William Broyles Jr. and John Sacret Young, China Beach began its network life with a run of six episodes on ABC in the spring of 1988. It came as close as any series I can think of to a textured novel, conceived on a epic scale, peopled with fascinatingly real characters. It was a series that achieved greatness at a time when mediocrity was considered good enough. It made the viewer live the characters' lives, think their thoughts, and feel their emotions each week. It touched the viewer on all levels as it explored the Vietnam War through the experiences of the women who served there. The appeal of its lead, Dana Delany, cannot be overemphasized. She created an intimacy with viewers that drew them to her and kept them there. Critic Ruth Butler called her the "show's anchor, the one who keeps things focused for the rest of us, the nurse whose stoic exterior belies the suffering she has seen during her tour."[31] Executive producer John Sacret Young raved to critic David Gritten about Delany. "There's something about her ability to evoke things without words."[32] Creator William Broyles agreed. "She moves in silence. When you write for her, you cut out dialogue."[33]

Viewer Pat Strahle of Robbinsville, New Jersey, commented in the June/July 1989 newsletter, "It's the 60s again and our friends are in 'Nam. You're so drawn in by the story you can't turn away. Yet, when you know someone is going to die, or feel pain, you want to turn away, or turn it off. But you can't, and you continue to watch, feeling that pain." Cindy Stabile of Hayward, California, felt that "it always challenges my convictions and presents different points of view with respect for all of them."[34] Rob Killian of West Jordan, Utah, commented, "It is poetic and honest. It is a show about healing."[35] Lori Ploeser of Corona, California, said, "It engulfs the spirit of war while not glorifying war. It takes me to a place I know nothing about and shows me a lifestyle I know nothing about."[36]

Trish Elliott of Oakland, California, wrote, "It doesn't shirk the emotionality of its constant involvement with fear and death. It doesn't attempt to justify war or their presence there. Irony is king here, and so is futility. This show displays such a depth of sensitivity it takes my breath away."[37]

Pat Murphy and I had the pleasure of visiting the set of *China Beach* a number of times. Through our advocacy, we worked closely with the show's Warner Bros. publicist, Heidi Trotta, and had the privilege of making the acquaintance of John Sacret Young, Dana Delany, and other cast members. Being on the set of a drama show can be boring; filming goes very slowly and there is much downtime. However, we never experienced tedium on the set of *China Beach*. The quality was evident even in observing the production. Everything was done with great care.

Heidi took us to the location where the show did most of its shooting, nestled between mountains and looking amazingly close to the real thing. (Some of the interiors were shot on the Warner Bros. lot.) The first visit was to the location set. As Pat and I walked onto the outdoor set, a shower scene was being readied for shooting; cast and crew were going about their assigned tasks. A woman with a script in her hands turned to Pat and gave her a headset so she could hear the dialogue. She then said, "I'm the writer." It was Carol Flint, who would go on to be an executive producer of *ER*.

During this visit we first met Dana and the rest of the cast. Over the years, we have found Dana Delany to be most genuine and natural, interesting and—we didn't find this too often in Hollywood—*interested* in the people around her.

The highlight of this visit was eating lunch from the catering trucks along with the cast and crew. We sat at a picnic table across from Dana, Bob Picardo (who played Dr. Richard), and Marg Helgenberger (who played K. C.). They interacted with each other with a familiarity and camaraderie that explained the chemistry and intimacy between the characters on-screen. Dana leaned back-to-back with Marg while picking food off Bob's plate.

We discovered that if Dana is comfortable with people, she possesses an openness that leaves her somewhat unguarded. She stands close when she talks to you; what might be perceived as an invasion of personal space becomes an accepted intimacy as she connects without the need of barriers. It is disarming and altogether charming.

There is a Delany anecdote that has a place here. On one visit, late in the show's network run, Heidi took Pat and me to Dana's trailer on the Warner Bros. lot where she was being made up for the episode where McMurphy would advance to her forties. When she emerged from her trailer, the four of us stood in the hot sun and talked. It was strange seeing her made up to look ten years older than she was. Dana mentioned that McMurphy was supposed to be in her early forties in this episode; Pat said, "That's my age." Well, Dana stepped close to Pat and peered at her face, studying every minute detail. Dana decided that Pat looked younger than McMurphy was being made to appear, and that maybe she would mention it to the makeup people. At some point Bob Picardo joined us. After talking a while, he stepped up to us and kissed us each on the mouth, as he usually did when parting. We always looked forward to being with him because, besides being a nice person to talk to, Bob is also a great kisser. Pat commented on this fact. I saw a glint form in Dana's eye. Once Bob left, she said to us, "I won't be outdone by Bob." I was too startled to prepare as she, too, stepped forward and spontaneously kissed me—right on my lips. Pat watched it happen and was prepared for Dana's playfulness. We were amused and flattered that she felt comfortable enough with us to be so daring and unguarded. She not only liked us, she also trusted us.

Speaking for the quality of *China Beach,* viewer Susan Hawkins of St. Louis appreciated that "*China Beach* seems not to editorialize but rather to fairly present the joys and sorrows of the war." Valerie Deckard of Bloomington, Indiana, thought it was "nothing flashy, just interesting, well-told stories about human behavior and the rational (and irrational) ways of coping with life in an incredibly stressful situation." It made viewer Claudette Keller from Rohnert Park, California, "see Vietnam personally for the first time." Sylvia Cooper from Houston, Texas, found it to be an "incredibly powerful show. Characters are explored from many angles and allowed to grow. Dana Delany and Marg

Helgenberger portray McMurphy and KC with thoughtfulness and under-standing of their strengths and vulnerabilities, sometimes so achingly real you are forced to cry out." Catherine Windsor from Medford, Oregon, told us in the April/May 1989 newsletter that the show "provides us with a vehicle to experience Vietnam through the character of Colleen McMurphy and the other characters who act as our guides on a journey not willingly taken by many who would just as soon forget the Vietnam experience totally. We become no longer spectators, but vicarious participants shouldering our share of their sufferings and wondrous joys." In the August/September 1989 newslet-ter, Barb Mangels of Bloomingdale, Illinois, wrote, "The show has opened its audience to a whole new range of feeling about a once unsympathetic sub-ject." Margaret Verble of Lexington, Kentucky, thought that "there is an in-depth investigation into these characters and the issues confronted by them."

In his beautiful eulogy of *China Beach* in the *Wall Street Journal*, Robert Goldberg raised the show to a new level in television entertainment: "In a time of escapist entertainment, *China Beach* didn't give its viewers much in the way of escape. It took them into the morgue of Vietnam, and stuck their noses right in among the body bags. Rich, powerful and deeply felt, it throt-tled its viewers, but every once in a while—a rare and wonderful thing on television—also offered some kind of catharsis, too."[38]

Playing by enough of television's rules to allow it to break a few,[39] *China Beach* forced the audience to overcome a natural reluctance to confront unpleasantness and made us want to follow its poignant stories. It accom-plished that through endearing and interesting characters, truthful writing, and a feeling that watching it was as important as making it.

Dana Delany remains one of the *real people* we have met. Knowing her has enriched my life.

Why *The Wonder Years?*

A television critic once shared with me the reaction of a group of television critics after viewing the pilot of *The Wonder Years* at a press gathering in Los Angeles. "What was that?" they all commented after watching the episode in virtual silence. It was immediately tagged as special and recommended to the viewing audience that way. The final scene of the pilot was a true quality moment: preteen Kevin Arnold finds his childhood friend Winnie alone in the woods, sitting on a rock, mourning the death of her adored older brother in Vietnam. He wordlessly joins her on the rock and sits with her silently as the song "When a Man Loves a Woman" begins to play in the background.

Kevin places his arm around Winnie's shoulders in friendship and sympathy. In silence, he understands what Winnie is going through. And through Kevin, the viewer understands, too. Then, very sweetly, in a moment of sparkling tenderness, the two childhood friends kiss. It was a magic moment that propelled this unusual series toward success. Viewers fell in love with Kevin, Winnie, and Paul, and grew close to the other characters as they unfolded through Kevin's eyes.

Viewer Cindy Henderson of Bluefield, Virginia, summed up the show's appeal in VQT's January 1991 newsletter. "Visually, emotionally, and intellectually stimulating. A flawlessly tender, yet realistic artwork that fully captures the complexities of a simpler time. Touches long buried memories with a sweet understanding that eases the hurts and heightens the joys."

Fred Savage was as endearing as the character he played. VQT members voted him Best Actor in a Quality Comedy two years in a row. The second year he attended the Quality Awards banquet with his parents and thanked us in person. Poised at the microphone, he told us, "What makes this award so special is that I'm being acknowledged for being part of a quality television show."

My favorite Fred Savage memory occurred when Pat and I visited the set in Culver City where *The Wonder Years* filmed. We had honored Fred the year before as Best Actor in a Quality Drama, but he had been unable to attend. We met Bob Brush, Ken Topolsky, and the other producers, then were taken downstairs to meet Fred's mother. There were child extras and actors waiting to audition in the "cafeteria." Mrs. Savage was friendly and warm, and took us right to Fred's dressing room, where this eleven-year-old exuded poise and social graces beyond his years. As his mother would tell me later about Fred's outgoing personality as a toddler, "I just thought all children were like this. I didn't know he was different."

Fred showed us his VQT award from the previous year, a plaque, hanging on the wall of his dressing room. His mother praised VQT for often recognizing quality talent before the industry did. After getting Fred dressed for an upcoming scene, the wardrobe person changed her mind about the shirt Fred should wear and brought him a different one. Unmindful of our presence, he removed his shirt, unzipped his trousers to tuck in his new shirt and put on the new one. Then he remembered we were there. Thoroughly unflustered, his pants askew, he said without a pause, "I just feel so comfortable with you both." We told him that we both had sons, and took away a very endearing memory of this appealing young actor. Another unguarded moment with an actor very comfortable with himself and his surroundings.

In paying tribute to *The Wonder Years* in our August 1993 newsletter, Dojelo Russell in Hot Springs, Arkansas, wrote, "The power and glory of this show was its ability to take a pre-teen youngster growing up about 30 years ago and to make his growing, learning, self-discovery and pain real to us all. That is what gave the show such impact: our ability to see ourselves in such situations and thus to re-live and even re-learn from them." As for the so-called wonder years, those years from twelve to sixteen, Russell felt that "they've been totally ignored except by silly comedies. This show treated them with the dignity they deserved and gave us splendid writing, caring direction, beautiful acting, and deeply poignant moments."

In October 1997, *Nick at Nite* on the Nickelodeon channel ran marathon episodes of *The Wonder Years*, reminding viewers, lest they had forgotten, why they were not watching as much network television anymore. When compared with just about any comedy on the air at the time, *The Wonder Years*, by stark contrast, diminished all other situation comedies.

Why *Northern Exposure?*

It premiered in midsummer of 1990, catching viewers eager for something new, and captivating them with its beautiful landscapes, unique stories, fascinating characters, and intelligent writing. Critical reaction, acceptable ratings, and a belief in the potential of the series earned it a place on CBS's schedule the following spring, and soon after, VQT's endorsement.

One VQT member called it a "wonderful bedtime story for adults."[40] It educated and it enchanted in ways not done before. Patricia Hickson of Atlanta, Georgia, wrote us that she could "almost sense the clean, crisp fragrance of the firs in the cool vista. The characters are believable, fun, humorous, interesting, easy to embrace and indeed, eagerly anticipated each week."[41] Cindy Thompson of Pittsburgh, Pennsylvania, loved it because it was "like nothing we've seen before. A realistic fantasy, a Magical Wilderness Tour. It delights us and piques our interest and cleverly instructs us. It meanders through legends and folklore and myths, introducing us to a philosophy and a lifestyle as foreign to us as if Joel Fleishman had gone to practice medicine on Atlantis."[42] She added in another newsletter, "It is relaxing and soothing, and encourages us [to believe] that a world without danger and tension and relentless ambition could possibly exist, if only in our Monday night imagination."[43] Miriam Ford of Birmingham, Alabama, who had labeled it a "bedtime story for adults," explained why when she added, "It contains the amazing, the original, the unique and the fanciful. Master storytellers are at work here. The show covers broad themes such as the meaning of life, concern for the environment, and respect for religious and ethnic differences. Every Monday night I can go to sleep secure in the knowledge that, at least in Cicely, Alaska, all is right with the world."[44] Heather Holt of Salt Lake City, Utah, commented that *Northern Exposure* "is a reminder of how beautifully television can tell stories with creativity and dignity. When it is utilized as it is in *Northern Exposure,* television is truly an art form."[45] Cecile Hamermesh of Baltimore appreciated the "tapestry on display. Unexpected richness characterizes this show by the galaxy of its assembly and the luminosity of its characters. It engages the observer's critical thinking skills. It is an hour of gentle but provoking organic mind play."[46] Jamie Greco of Riverdale, Illinois, appreciated that "virtually everyone on *Northern Exposure* is treated with respect, including the viewer."[47]

Viewers cherished the show because it left them with ideas to reflect upon and it involved and demanded that their imagination remain active. It had heart. It was also literary. The town's disc jockey, Chris, read from the classics. Cindy Thompson of Pittsburgh wrote, "Where but in Cicely would there be a radio personality who reads to his audience from Proust one week and from a children's book the next, and finds equal wisdom in both?"[48] As careful a watcher as any in VQT, Cindy did raise the question "Are there children in Cicely? I would guess that there has never been a child with a speaking part in this series."[49]

As with too many quality series that enjoyed a long run, *Northern Exposure* eventually encountered new writers, new visions, and new directions. Fans were reluctant to accept any storyline that they felt betrayed the original premise of the show, or any character who did not seem to "fit." When Rob Morrow left the series during its last season, and CBS changed the time slot, that was it. CBS can be partly blamed for the show's demise by changing the time slot, but so can a decline in script quality and the defection of the primary character. As VQT member Carolyn Wilberger of Corvallis, Oregon, said in our March 1995 newsletter, "*Northern Exposure* has many lovable characters and interesting story possibilities, and it could have survived without Rob Morrow. But it will *not* survive these scripts." Viewers rejected the writers' attempts to interest them in a new doctor hanging his shingle in Cicely. They clung to the "reality" that Joel Fleishman, as played by Rob Morrow, *was* the premise of *Northern Exposure.* The show just did not work without him.

Why *Law & Order?*

Dick Wolf told a VQT audience in September 1991, after *Law & Order* had survived a rocky first season, that the show did not necessarily fit our quality definition because it was story driven, not character driven. "We can't twist the law to give us the resolution we want all the time. It's not so much research by the writers [as it is] careful attention to the storyline by a battery of research people."[50]

Wolf told us how VQT's survey results may have saved the show in its first six months. *Law & Order* had been fraught with network interference because it had the highest advertiser pullout on television.[51] The standards department people made frequent calls to him. "Then your rating came out [VQT Viewer Survey results] in January 1991, where *Law & Order* was the number 1 quality show for that week. All the calls stopped. I cannot overemphasize what your ratings mean to the networks. We haven't had problems since. It's a totally different atmosphere. The imprimatur of this organization has tremendous respect."[52]

Cindy Thompson of Pittsburgh called *Law & Order* "a very straightforward, hypnotically compelling program. We trust the characters to take care of whatever matter is at hand. This series always knows what it wants to say and says it with perfect clarity."[53] Sylvia Cooper of Houston, Texas, added that "there is nothing extraneous. It is tightly put together and finely drawn."[54]

Trish Elliott of Oakland, California, stated, "No glitz, no frills, no substory, just a complete and thorough exploration of one case. There are no manipulations; they manage to hold my attention throughout and surprise me at the end."[55] "It's exciting to see a show in which the story is the star," added Mary Jane Bigley from Wilkinsburg, Pennsylvania.

As Dick Wolf stated during the 1991 panel discussion, VQT named *Law & Order* the number 1 quality network show in our January 1991 viewer survey. In February NBC used that information in its on-air promotion for the show. I reiterated to members in our April 1991 newsletter that the VQT Viewer Survey is the way in which we present our collective voices to the people who make the television programs we watch. It was exciting to have our efforts noticed.

The praises for *Law & Order* continued. In May 1991, Lacey Wood of Canaan, Connecticut, reminded her fellow VQT members that *Law & Order* stood out because of its unique treatment of the genre and the attention to detail in the stories. "The characters are not the main focus here; instead, the system, the process and the actions take center stage."[56] Pat Strahle of Robbinsville, New Jersey, commented that "following the crime along the criminal justice system has never been presented with such realism. The cast, with the help of great scripts, does this with grit and depth while never losing our interest in an arena that could easily lose our attention or bore us."[57] Susan Sachs of Ft. Lauderdale, Florida, appreciated that "it makes you think all the time. There are no black and white issues, only shades of grey. The good guys don't always win, and sometimes there's not just one right answer."[58] Tom Speicher of Williamsport, Pennsylvania, commented in 1993, "Whether the outcome of a case satisfies me or frustrates me, the series always forces me to re-examine our problem-ridden society. Obviously, that examination is not always pleasant, but its impetus is television at its best."[59] Sue Chapman of Johnson City, Tennessee, reminded VQTers in the May 1995 newsletter that "probably more than any show in memory, *Law & Order* has proven itself to be a starring vehicle for the writers and the topical stories rather than the actors."

The *New York Times*'s TV critic, Bill Carter, said of the show in February 1997, "Nothing has ever been what it seems on *Law & Order*. Murderers turn out to be victims, victims to be accomplices. The show's regular characters are often fallible, misguided or just plain wrong."[60] Carter added, "With intricate, challenging plot lines, [it] breaks the rules of conventional television storytelling."[61] The group that defined a quality show as one that was character driven fully embraced and appreciated to the fullest a show where the story was the center.

Law & Order goes on and on, like the Energizer Bunny, prevailing over cast changes and maintaining its quality. Dick Wolf told us during a panel discussion at our 1996 Conference on Quality Television that he likes to keep good writers locked up in a room for eight years. He doesn't want them to move on.[62] It should also be noted that Dick Wolf has stayed with the show in a hands-on way, not relinquishing control of his creation to somebody else, thus contributing largely to maintaining the integrity of this quality program.

Why *Picket Fences?*

"*Picket Fences* raises our consciousness, lowers our defenses, challenges our intellect, affirms our humanity, touches our hearts, tickles our funny bones, and takes us to a new place inside ourselves," wrote Joan Considine in VQT's August 1993 newsletter. It wasn't just quirky, it could be bizarre. Relegated to Friday nights by CBS, it was not "must-see TV,"[63] it was "must discuss" TV. It was unpredictable. It stimulated the mind, touched the heart, and challenged solidly held views by exploring serious issues through the characters of a fictional town called Rome, Wisconsin. Premiering on CBS in the fall of 1992, it was populated with eccentric, fascinating characters whom viewers grew to care about as they responded to the issues that swirled around them. It was David E. Kelley at his most creative. He wrote or cowrote nearly every episode in its first three seasons.[64] Until Kelley turned over the control—and the vision—of the show to Jeff Melvoin in the fall of 1995, *Picket Fences* truly bore "the stamp of a single artist."[65]

VQT was proud to honor *Picket Fences* with eight Quality Awards over three years, including two for Kathy Baker and one for the show itself. In thanking us for her Quality Award in 1994, Kathy Baker conveyed a sentiment from David E. Kelley, who could not attend that year. Kathy told us that David wanted her to "just let them [VQT] know that we know that they were here for us first."[66] (We had named *Picket Fences* Best New Drama the fall it premiered.)

VQT members were vocal about the quality of this show. Chuck Sutton from Grand Rapids, Michigan, wrote early in the first season, "David Kelley has created a wonderful drama that successfully melds different genres. It can be a murder mystery or cop show. It can be a heartwarming family show about a dying teacher. The opportunities seem endless."[67] Janis Navikas of Cambridge, Massachusetts, noted that "it is the one show with true originality. The crazy crimes are fascinating and the characters always hold my attention. It's funny, touching, shocking, and suspenseful."[68] Beverly Scott of Plaistow, New Hampshire, commented in our February 1993 newsletter, "Just when you think it's all over and has made its point, it hits with a zinger. It happens every week." Suzanne Mather of Sebastian, Florida, found it "always thought-provoking, often inspirational, sometimes disturbing; an examination of both the essence and purpose of the law and of the moral and ethical values that the law upholds. There are no grand heroes nor monstrous villains; there are no smug, self-righteous answers. For them, as for us, there is only the struggle day by day to remember who we are. Week after week, *Picket Fences* is there to remind us. It should be considered a public service."[69] Bonnie Beeferman of Hilton Head, South Carolina, noted that each episode said something important about life's issues, but made them go down easily with humor and compassion.[70] Beeferman reiterated in August 1994, "Each week the show tackles an issue and draws me into the swirl of various viewpoints without preaching or taking sides. Several times I have been forced to reassess my own values and opinions. To me this is television at its finest—entertaining, educational, and eye-opening." Laura Manthey of San Jose, California, said in June 1993 that the show "makes you stop in your tracks to think." In the same issue, George McAdams shared that "by the time an episode is over, not only do I understand an issue better, but in many instances I am able to understand, even empathize, with points of view I don't necessarily support." In August 1994, Jeffrey Knight of Hollywood, Florida, commented that "any show that addresses the issues of the day (elder care, workplace love affairs, gun control, euthanasia, religion, fetishism, alternative lifestyles) with a balanced yet slightly giddy view of the situation deserves to be watched and appreciated." Heather Holt of Salt Lake City, Utah, reaffirmed in 1995 that *Picket Fences* "continues to challenge, provoke, anger, soothe, captivate, and amuse the viewer by addressing fundamental social and personal issues. Each episode resonates with emotional honesty and confronts the audience with compelling ethical dilemmas about which we should all take a strong stand."[71] Kathy Kahnke of Redwood Falls, Minnesota, believed *Picket Fences* to be intense, delving and honest, that "no one writes a better scene between a husband and wife than David Kelley."[72] Genia Shipman, of Studio City, California, loved the way "the smaller, personal stories that spin off from the larger stories take the focus. Jill and Jimmy's relationship is far more important than who killed the masseur."

Contributors to VQT's newsletter consistently noted that the characters were fully developed from the beginning, and made us care about them. So it was disconcerting to learn, in the summer of 1995, that Kelley was turning over the reins of the show to Jeff Melvoin (*Northern Exposure*) to follow Melvoin's, not Kelley's, vision.[73] Melvoin told an audience of VQT members that September that he wanted to make the show "character-driven" instead of issue-driven. He hoped "one of the repercussions is that we are more accessible and we draw a bigger audience."[74] The actual repercussion was that new viewers did not come, and long-standing, loyal viewers were indignant about the changes and stopped watching. I wrote to producer Alice West after just a few puzzling episodes asking if my opinion might be valuable. There was no response so I did not press the issue. A group of VQTers (myself included) got into a heated weeks-long argument with one of the new *Picket Fences* writers on an Internet bulletin board. He had asked how we felt about the new season, and we told him. Instead of respecting our opinion, or at least considering it, he defended the direction of the show and had harsh words for our outspokenness. I finally relayed the exchanges to Alice West, who had attended our Quality Awards Banquet when *Picket* had won. She hadn't been aware of the situation. The exchanges stopped. In retrospect, I suppose it was arrogant to claim that we knew the characters better than the current writers did and insist that they would never behave the way they were being depicted. But I firmly believe that we, the small, loyal, and very involved *Picket Fences* audience, had intimate and insightful knowledge of these characters. However, it was my impression that the efforts of VQT members to constructively criticize were resented by the producers.

For VQT's newsletter forum, Nora Mandel of Forest Hills, New York, wrote in October 1995 that "an innovative, daring drama has been turned into a heartwarming soap opera." It was generally felt that although it was fine to devote more time to exploration of character, these characters were no longer being explored in a compelling way, that the characters had become trivialized as the stories became more ordinary. Miriam Cooper of Cheshire, Connecticut, questioned the direction by saying that "this program was once a lovely, intricate weave of issues *and* characters; I can't understand why it suddenly had to be either/or."[75] Cheryl Bond of Phoenix, Arizona, agreed, mentioning in the same issue, "I'm a big fan of character studies, but the unique ability to combine relevant issues *with* character examinations is what made *Picket Fences* so special."

Television journalists also decried the change in the show, all but begging the writers to reverse course. David Bianculli was particularly astute: "The series and its characters took a drastically different turn. It was so drastic, in fact, that *Picket Fences* may be unable to regain its former luster or momentum. Melvoin and company tried, and succeeded in writing with a different sensibility. The trouble is, it was too different, and happened too quickly, and now that *Picket Fences* is at the end of a season, even a mended fence may no longer do the job."[76] It was too late; the ship had left the harbor and could not be turned around quickly. A beloved show had diminished in quality because its creator had stepped back from his vision.

Why *Frasier?*

"*Frasier* puts an intellectual edge to the traditional sitcom format." VQT's Michael Smolinski of Grand Rapids, Michigan, said it in one of our newsletters, pointing out that a sitcom could be intellectual and still be funny. It didn't have to be vacuous, it didn't have to be silly, it didn't have to be populated with stereotypical characters. *Frasier* redefines the situation comedy, and many think it defines the quality comedy. Of course, it has impeccable credentials—cocreators David Lee, Peter Casey, and Peter Angell had worked on *Cheers* and Frasier Crane already existed in the minds of viewers. Add what turned out to be brilliant casting (David Hyde Pierce, Jane Leeves, John Mahoney, and Peri Gilpin), a pool of writers who know their characters and remain true to them, cocreators who remain involved with the show, and you have critical and Nielsen success.

Mary Platt of Costa Mesa, California, told fellow VQT members that *Frasier* is "witty, urbane, and just laugh-out- loud hilarious. It punctures the pomposity of its very human characters with the finest comedy writing on

TV."[77] Paul Webb of Huntsville, Alabama, called it "the funniest and most literate show on television," which refuses to talk down to its audience, "never sacrificing its intelligence or that of its characters to find a quick and easy laugh."[78] Janey Graves of Osawatomie, Kansas, thought it treated its audience "as intelligent, presenting witty situations grounded in truth."[79] Lou Ann Griman of Troy, Ohio, found it "hilariously funny while still connecting with the audience on an emotional level."[80] Cecile Hamermesh of Baltimore, Maryland, called *Frasier* "the small-screen American heir to Noel Coward's dazzlingly sophisticated drawing-room comedies" and said that "the dialogue becomes a character itself."[81]

Cocreator David Lee told a VQT audience in September 1994 that he felt sitcoms were getting "too frenetic" with "too much peppy music" jumping from one joke to the next. He cited an episode of *Frasier* called "My Coffee with Niles" and explained how it had come to be. He told us that he had wondered, Is there any way we can have our two main characters sit down in real time, twenty-two minutes, just discuss whether or not they're happy? He said that all you have to do is decide to do it and you can. And added, "It still gives me a warm feeling in a warm place."

It is also nice to know that an endearing character can be portrayed by an endearing actor. David Hyde Pierce has been charming and approachable at each of the four Quality Awards banquets he attended; in person he is as funny as Niles Crane. After viewing a clip and going to the podium to receive his award in 1994, he thanked us and said, "I've eaten a great meal, talked almost exclusively about myself, and then watched myself on a giant television. It's as if you talked to my friends and asked, 'What would David's idea of a perfect evening be?'" *E! Entertainment* aired the quip.

Frasier's quality faltered during the 1998–99 season when its creators and some of its writers and producers focused on a new, ill-fated sitcom (*Encore! Encore!*). It is unclear whether or not it will regain its former luster as perhaps time and familiarity begin to take their toll.

Why *NYPD Blue*?

"It progressed the art of television. It pushed the envelope and expanded the borders and limits of what television drama can accomplish. It helped us mature as an audience." VQT's quality barometer, Michael Smolinski of Grand Rapids, Michigan, expressed it in our August/September 1994 newsletter. Sandra Hopwood of Vienna, Virginia, commented in the same issue that "it is a fascinating, shadowy, adult, highly moral program that presents decent human beings wrestling with the ambiguities of duty, ethics, and questions of right and wrong."

Jefferson Graham, *USA Today* television columnist, pondered *Blue*'s success "when so many hourlong dramas from recent seasons—*Going to Extremes,
The Young Indiana Jones Chronicles, Bodies of Evidence* and *I'll Fly Away,* for
example—have come and gone?"[82] Leslie Moonves, at the time president of
Warner Bros. TV, answered Graham: "Bochco created a quality show that is
accessible, something you really can't say for some of the quality dramas of
the past. The Rev. [Donald] Wildmon's campaign [see "Growing Campaigns"]
got a great deal of attention, but Bochco delivered with a great show."[83]

The one across-the-board criticism was its underuse and underwriting of
female characters. VQT's male participants seemed most outspoken about the
poor use of the female cast members. Viewer Karl Wickerd of Grand Terrace,
California, called it "a series that continues to cheat its female characters" in
August 1995.[84] Sam Manbeck of York, Pennsylvania, wanted to "see the
women doing their jobs, displaying the skills that made them detectives in
the first place."[85]

We found Dennis Franz to be one of the most accommodating and per-
sonable actors we ever encountered. At our Quality Awards banquets in 1994,
1996, and 1998, he stood up after being seated at his table and shook the
hand of every VQT member there. When accepting his first Quality Award in
September 1994, he told the audience of industry people and VQTers, "I
would like to thank the Viewers for Quality Television for honoring my contribution to [*NYPD Blue*] with this prestigious award. I'd like to thank them
for not just hearing the four-letter words, but for feeling the emotions sur-
rounding those words. You have all confirmed my belief that I can continue
to hold my head up high and be proud of all the work that we do."

More on the quality of *NYPD Blue* can be found in "Growing Campaigns."

Why *Homicide: Life on the Street?*

Brought to TV by film director Barry Levinson and *St. Elsewhere* producer Tom
Fontana, with Henry Bromell (*I'll Fly Away*) as capable show-runner through
the 1995–96 season, *Homicide* captured TV critics immediately. Once VQT
members adjusted to the "swishing and slamming camera moves and the jar-
ring jump cuts,"[86] they too embraced this show that explored the way crime
affects the police officers who fight it.

As usual, VQT's newsletters spotlighted the excellence. What quality-seek-
ing viewers seemed to appreciate most were the edgy relationships and intelligent dialogue. The city in which the show was filmed and that it was about,
Baltimore, was like another character. Michael Adams in Glendora, California, called the show "an exhilarating trip into the fictitious squad room of

the Baltimore Police Department; it's well-written, well-acted and gripping."[87] Nora Mandel in Forest Hills, New York, said it was "like watching literature. The writing is breathtaking."[88] Sue Scolaro of Smyrna, New York, believed that "good television is made up of small, powerful moments that are the threads that link the bigger, action-filled scenes together. Every scene in *Homicide* counts. The small moments are as essential as the larger ones. Each reveals something about these fascinating characters; each tells us something that helps us to know who these people are."[89]

One of the problems early in the show's history may have been characters that weren't instantly likable. A viewer had to be patient enough to wait for the character to unfold, flaws and all. As Barbara Adams said in our February 1995 newsletter, "I've heard it said that the characters are not developed enough for the viewer to care about them. These characters are finely honed, and the interaction between them is outstanding."

Homicide collected several Quality Awards—a Founder's Award in 1995, Best Quality Drama in 1996, and Andre Braugher as Best Actor in a Quality Drama in 1995.

Why *ER?*

It isn't very often that the number one show with Nielsen households is also the number one show with Viewers for Quality Television. But *ER* not only topped the Nielsen charts in 1996 and 1997, it also consistently ranked in VQT's top five for quality level and most-watched series. VQT members liked its vividness and tension and the fact that the characters were engaging and involving. Prof. Robert J. Thompson wrote in 1996 that "*ER* brought quality into the mainstream. Its hit status was greatly helped by its hyperkinetic pacing. *ER* was perfectly designed for the remote-controlled cable era: it moved so fast, you didn't need to change the channel because it kept doing it for you."[90] VQTer Lou Ann Griman in Troy, Ohio, agreed, but took exception to the frenetic pace in January 1995 when she commented, "It's like they are trying too hard never to lose the viewer's attention and end up jumping from one situation to another at an exhausting pace. I'd prefer it if they would slow down a bit." Perhaps planned, perhaps not, they did. With each episode through each season, the show took more time to explore its wealth of rich characters; viewers still did not zap away.

VQT members generally liked the high energy level with many overlapping storylines. John Christensen of Charlotte, Michigan, found it "*St. Elsewhere*–esque" and liked the humor and drama and unresolved issues.[91] Jeffrey Knight of Hollywood, Florida, appreciated that it presented the normal and the eccentric with an uncritical eye, and was fast-paced, soundly written, ponderous one moment and silly the next.[92] Maria Nott from Kent, Ohio, thought the show had it all—hand-wringing suspense, compelling storylines, heartfelt emotion and realistic characters."[93] Celeste Ellis of Brooklyn, New York, felt the show took her through "a roller coaster of emotions, up, down and sideways."[94] George McAdams in Yuma, Arizona, thought that ER "provides a weekly lesson in sociology. That it occurs in the emergency room of a hospital is incidental to the story, and perhaps, its greatest strength because it shows that life, as a commodity that doctors deal with on a day-to-day basis, goes beyond the heartbeat of a doctor."[95]

Reaction wasn't 100 percent positive at first, however. VQTers continued to constructively criticize. A nurse, Barbara Novak from Naperville, Illinois, pointed out after an early episode that a baby given a lumbar tap and picked up vertically right afterward would have had a screaming headache. "Major no-no."[96] Nora Mandel in Forest Hills, New York, criticized that a medical student would not be asked to identify a DOA. "That's a police matter."[97]

Praises from viewers continued as ER's popularity—and quality—grew. Lou Ann Griman of Troy, Ohio, who had criticized it earlier, wrote for our June 1995 newsletter, "It isn't the pace, the technical jargon or medical situations that impress me about this show—it is the way the individual staff members confront the varying crises going on in their lives. I can relate to human situations far more than medical ones, and for me that's what turns a good show into a really great one. When I can feel their heartache, their compassion, their joy and their fear—that's what does it for me." In the same issue, Elaine Davis of Fairfield, Connecticut, told us that "my heart races and I'm on an emotional roller coaster ride for one hour a week. The engaging and engrossing plots, strong acting, writing and plot development truly exemplify quality television at its best."

Unfortunately, ER's quality waned during the 1998–99 season. It did not receive a VQT Quality Award nomination that year. In 1999 it slipped to qualified support. There seemed to be multiple causes: show-runner John Wells stepped back to focus on new projects; storylines grew tired and at times stretched; its major star, George Clooney, left. Uninteresting and undevelpoed characters were added. In VQT's newsletters, viewers called the show mundane and accused it of trying too hard. NBC resorted to declaring an episode "breathtaking" in an on-air promo. As Pat Murphy wrote in the April 1999 newsletter, "There was a time when nearly every episode of ER was 'breathtaking.' Now NBC promos tell us ahead of time that it will be 'breathtaking.' If you have to tell me, then it probably isn't [breathtaking]. Let the show speak for itself; let the viewer decide if it is 'breathtaking.'"

Why *The X-Files?*

"Is there a more atmospheric show on television?" asked VQT member Beth Gehman of Quakertown, Pennsylvania, in one of VQT's newsletters. "I always feel like I'm transported to another time and place as I watch this show. The surrealism of the stories only adds to my disorientation. What's real? What's not? What should we believe? Who should we trust? It's like reading a well-crafted horror novel, and every bit as fun." Diana Essert from Sacramento liked that the show "is guaranteed to always glue you to your chair and make you peer between your fingers to see what comes next."[98]

When asked at a September 24, 1994, VQT Conference panel discussion in Los Angeles what he thought the audience expected from his show, creator Chris Carter responded, "To have the pants scared off them, and in a smart way."[99] He added that he wanted the story to be the star and the characters to serve the story. He did not want it to be *about* the lead characters. But the show became as much about characters Fox Mulder and Dana Scully as about the story, because fans grew attached to them and were intrigued by their relationship. Carter insisted, "But it's not romantic; it's professional and I think that's the difference."[100]

An *X-Files* fan, Mary Platt of Costa Mesa, California, wrote an essay in VQT's January 1995 newsletter about the quality level of the show; she thanked creator Chris Carter for bringing us "television that is continually surprising, challenging, imaginative and fun." She described the show's hero, Fox Mulder, played by David Duchovny, as "a subtle, subjective protagonist, adrift in a world he wants desperately to understand." She credited Duchovny with playing Mulder "with a nuanced intensity matched only by that of his co-star, Gillian Anderson," whose character, Dana Scully, she referred to as "that rarest of TV species: a female professional who is, without question, the equal of her partner." Mary explained that "together they are avatars of new world explorers on the edge of the millennium, paranormal proceduralists whose investigations take them past ancient superstitions—wolves, vampires, mutant worms and crop circles—to the really scary stuff: just how far governments might go to achieve their occult, arcane ends." She labeled *The X-Files* "eloquent theater for the paranoid." Mary was careful to explain that what made viewers come back week after week was the *human* element; we liked these characters because amid all the paranormal, "they're so real that we care about them and what happens to them. They care about each other, too."

That was the secret. Viewers cared so much about these characters because they cared so much about each other. Perhaps unintended, the characters became the story.

Conclusion

Professor Robert J. Thompson concluded in his *Television's Second Golden Age* that "if you can't find anything good on network TV today, you just aren't looking very hard."[101] Just a few years later, one has to look harder. Of the thirty-five series that premiered in September 1997, only five survived the season—a 14 percent success rate. (The fall 1996 season saw a 45 percent success rate.) VQT endorsed only *Ally McBeal* and *Nothing Sacred,* and the latter was canceled. The 1998–99 season was nearly as dismal. Two network series were endorsed, ABC's *Sports Night* and NBC's *Will & Grace.* (The only other new series to be endorsed that season aired on Lifetime [*Any Day Now*] and HBO [*The Sopranos*]). NBC's *The West Wing* was the 1999–2000 season's only endorsed show. In September 1998, the *Washington Post's* Tom Shales predicted that the "next golden age of television will be put off for at least another year."[102] He accused the networks of "serving up mainly a digitally remastered mishmash of last year's crum-bummy claptrap."[103] He explained: "You can't expect much innovation or experimentation by the networks when their main goal is just to hold on desperately to the viewers they still have. With their share of the total TV audience continuing to erode, the networks don't want to air anything so new and bold it might scare anybody away."[104]

Having said that, even though there is regrettably less quality on network television than in previous years, quality *can* still be found there. If you can't find it, just ask any member of Viewers for Quality Television where to look.

AFTER GRASSROOTS
The Growth and Development of VQT

THAT Viewers for Quality Television graduated from concept to reality is due to Barney Rosenzweig's intercession; that it enjoyed time to grow and develop is because the nation's television journalists felt it was an idea whose time had come. Viewers for Quality Television has from the beginning been a positive force for the good on TV, not a negative drive against what one might perceive as bad. Through VQT, viewers have applauded, encouraged, and constructively criticized the television that they watch. We believe the way to do that is through letter-writing campaigns, encouraging individual, personalized letters. At our 1989 convention, NBC Entertainment president Brandon Tartikoff responded to the letter-writing strategies employed by VQT by saying, "If it looks like it is clearly an individual letter where there is individual thought, it will certainly be distinguished by the people who go through the mail. And that mail is shared with the programmers."

My primary tasks through the years have been to disseminate VQT's information to the television industry and to the viewing public; to let viewers know we are here and that they can participate; to increase awareness and credibility of the organization; and to encourage the industry to consider our information a valuable resource.

It is a fact that very few shows can be saved from poor Nielsen performance by viewers, and almost never once they are canceled. So VQT encourages advocacy while the show is still on the air—better yet, as soon as a quality show presents itself. As NBC's Brandon Tartikoff told the VQT audience the first time the big three entertainment presidents addressed VQT, "It's disheartening for me as a programmer that the time of the greatest outpouring of support, sentiment, and passion generally comes after a show is canceled. I'd love to be aware of that kind of support [sooner]."

VQT's greatest asset has always been its participants, those disenfranchised viewers without Nielsen boxes who want to be counted, to have a say in the television they watch. They are the ones responsible for my fifteen years of persistence in this apparently unwinnable battle to educate the networks on how their audience really feels about their programming—to get them to care about us, their audience—and to educate the public to demand that quality.

VQT never assumed an agenda other than the quality content of programming. As TV critic Steven Cole Smith wrote in 1992, "The good thing about Viewers for Quality Television is that it is just what the name suggests. Most advocacy groups have a more specific agenda: too much/not enough religion, sex, violence, ethnicity. VQT doesn't threaten, boycott, throw firebombs. They just insist that all programs be good—nothing more. Not that this is a small requirement."[1] Because of the support of such TV critics as Cole Smith through the years, VQT had an outlet for its advocacy.

Peter J. Brown identified VQT aptly in *OnSat,* the satellite TV guide, in January 1993. "It is remarkable that VQT members have such visibility in an industry where everything revolves around numbers, big numbers. And yet, since its inception in December 1984, VQT has battled its way right to the top. Every major network executive with any degree of responsibility for programming decisions is very much aware of VQT. This is no inflated claim, it's a fact."[2] Brown went on to clarify:

> Nobody is suggesting that VQT is an all-powerful heavyweight in media circles. The shows that have been endorsed by and fought for by VQT are given credibility by the group's swarming tactics. VQT reinforces and activates other media outlets including this nation's TV critics. VQT serves as a valuable lobbying group which has established itself as a constant and reliable force in the ongoing struggle over what ultimately winds up on your TV screen.[3]

Walt Belcher challenged his readers in the *Tampa Tribune* in January 1993 by writing, "Maybe if more people stopped complaining about how bad TV is and started supporting good programs, TV would get better. If you are serious about supporting quality, try Viewers for Quality Television. They are trying to honor and save good programs."

Television executives, producers, and actors appreciated that we took a stand on behalf of television, not against it. I have always felt that VQT could not be constantly adversarial with the networks; we had to earn their respect if we were to have a seat at their table.

Kim LeMasters, CBS Entertainment president in 1989 when he appeared on a panel discussion with the other presidents during our convention, understood our mission. "What you represent is an intense desire to see television get better; and that is something in a day and age when we're hearing people decry television and say that it's a wasteland, that there is nothing redeeming about it. You are here endorsing shows and talking about shows and really uplifting the entire landscape of network television." He added, "You have a lofty voice and point of view to which we may avail ourselves." Tim Reid told us during the same convention, "You can save [a show] by reacting *when it happens.* Don't wait for it to get there and see how it's going to do—*you are* how it's going to do." Jeff Melvoin, an executive producer of *Northern Exposure* and *Picket Fences*, told a group of VQTers during our September 1995 Conference on Quality Television that "you *care,* and that is extremely important, and you must keep caring, because the networks will only give the audience the lowest common denominator, and you've got to tell them, 'That's not good enough!'"

However, as the years go by, the networks are giving us less and less reason to care as their regard for their audience erodes along with the audience itself. When I suggested to Warren Littlefield, NBC Entertainment chief, that his network's "Must-See-TV" slogan was overused, he snapped, although in good humor, "Well, it's our label and I guess it's for us to decide, not you, Dorothy." (See "What's Wrong with the System?")

What drew viewers to VQT, and what made them stay? Cindy Stabile from Hayward, California, wrote in the June 1994 newsletter: "I joined VQT because I love television. I find that at its best, television is an art form. The thing I like most about VQT is its philosophy. I like the fact that it is about quality television, not politics or money. It is not about censorship or imposing my views or others' views on everyone. I like the fact that the organization does not threaten or coerce the networks, studios, producers, or advertisers."

"It's about empowerment," wrote Robert Yale from Hazleton, Pennsylvania, in the August/September 1994 newsletter.

> Members go to great lengths, and against tremendous odds, in an effort to save a show or in an attempt to invoke a change, realizing that there is strength and hope in the knowledge that they are not alone in their convictions and, thanks to VQT, have an opportunity to be heard, anytime, on any matter, in any fashion, and with a voice and a vote that can ultimately make a difference. It's about appreciating art and

beauty, about laughing or crying or cheering in response to an actor's moving portrayal, or a producer's consummate skill—feelings that most assuredly come from the heart, and often in defiance of the conventional attitudes toward programming generated by networks, advertisers, and other adherents to the ratings game.

"The real goal is to promote viewer awareness of and support for quality," wrote Mark Silverstein from Forest Hills, New York, in the same issue. "That needs to be accomplished both by communication with the industry *and* the viewers. After all, the networks would not need to be convinced to keep low rated quality series on the air if those series could be turned into high rated shows. While I am only one viewer, VQT has served to make me a more informed and discriminating viewer."

The VQT newsletter (named *The Viewer* in 1991) was, from the beginning, the organization's forum through which its members communicated with one another and with the television industry. The first newsletter was one typewritten, photocopied page in February 1985; the 100th issue, consisting of twenty-eight pages, was printed in April 1997.

VQT's newsletter was printed bimonthly until November 1990 when it became monthly. Although I wrote and compiled it, until I had the proper equipment, I relied on volunteers to produce it—first Cheri Jenkins in Houston, Texas, then Randy Schultz and Steve Lenius in Minneapolis, Minnesota. When the newsletter became monthly and I had the necessary computer hardware and software, I began to produce it myself; I was taught WordPerfect in a crash course by volunteer Ron Wagner, learning as I produced my first newsletter.

Throughout 1985 there was no fee to belong to VQT and receive the newsletter; members sent voluntary donations of dollars, envelopes, and stamps. In October 1986 the newsletter was expanded and a $15 subscription fee was established. There was no other way to survive financially.

The set subscription fee was abolished in November 1992 and replaced with a self-determined donation, entitling the contributor to VQT's newsletters, surveys, polls, and ballots. I wanted to encourage greater participation, at whatever level viewers were comfortable.

Not only viewers, but also television executives and journalists valued the grassroots nature of VQT's publication. Bill Allen of MTM told me in 1987 at our first convention that when he received the newsletter, he closed the door of his office to read it because the information in it was "unfiltered." Journalist Steve Bornfeld called it thick and information-packed in his January 31, 1992, column in the *Albany Times Union*. *Dave's World* executive producer

Jonathan Axelrod complimented VQT in an interview for the April 1995 newsletter: "Your viewers and your writings tend to be the most intelligent I've read anywhere about television; and I include *Broadcasting Age* and *Advertising Age* and all the networks when I say this. They don't have nearly the insight that your readership does." Axelrod also said in the same interview that "it's probably the only [viewer] organization in America that the networks really listen to."

It was always gratifying when journalists and television industry executives understood our mission. TV critic Mike Antonucci covered our convention in 1993 and wrote in the *San Jose Mercury News* that *Detroit Free Press* critic Mike Duffy told him, differentiating VQT from special interest groups, that "clearly, she [Swanson] provides a more sane, open-minded viewpoint than Rev. Donald Wildmon," referring to the Southern minister who attempted various boycotts of sponsors of "offensive" shows.[4] Duffy described me to Antonucci as "a one-woman life force."[5] At first I was bothered by that, but came to accept that it may have been an accurate statement. Leslie Moonves, at the time president of Warner Bros. Television, told Antonucci he thought that "Swanson forces the TV business to confront its collective conscience."[6] He added that "VQT is one of the few organizations that gives them [network executives] credit for trying to do the right thing."[7] Antonucci said of Ted Harbert, then president of ABC Entertainment, "Harbert says he can't discern much influence from VQT when ABC makes a programming decision, but he said he cares about the organization because 'I care about anybody who is that passionate about television. What I like about Dorothy's organization is that they've got a love for good storytelling.'"[8]

I was heartened when Kim LeMasters, CBS Entertainment president, told Diane Haithman of the *Los Angeles Times* that "unlike the single viewer, VQT has the advantage of organization and media access. I think there is tremendous publicity to what they do."[9]

By November 1988 I determined that it was time for VQT to supplement, if not challenge, the networks' reliance on the Nielsen ratings as the sole determinant of what is successful on television. I wanted to be able to tap into trends and know not only what viewers were watching, but also their satisfaction level. The first VQT Viewer Survey appeared in the November 1988 newsletter, and asked respondents to note what they watched over a one- or two-week period and rate it qualitatively. Throughout the ensuing years, I would occasionally mail (and ultimately fax) the results of these viewing samples to journalists; occasionally, some would publish them. I was gratified that it seemed to matter what discerning viewers preferred to watch. When it could be of benefit, the networks used the information in print and on the air to draw attention to a show that needed additional promotion. NBC used our Viewer Survey results in advertising *Law & Order* in its first season and *Mad About You* (as best new comedy of the season) on February 20, 1993. ABC used it for *NYPD Blue* (November 16, 1993) and CBS used it for *Under Suspicion*. I never took for granted that this would happen, and always experienced a rush of satisfaction when it did.

There would have been no unique VQT Viewer Survey program without skilled volunteer services. Such information could be accurately and completely processed only by computer. VQT member Steve Lenius created the first program, and Malcolm Austin created the second, still in use in 1999.

Semiannual endorsements were also tallied on the computer (once I had one!), first using a bare-bones program called Survey Master, then switching to one I found on the Internet, called Simply Survey, that seemed to be based on the former. Both were rather rudimentary, but they processed the information I needed. In 2000, new volunteer, Sandy Marshall, created an endorsement reporting program in Excel.

VQT launched its unique Sponsor Program in the spring of 1989, because we felt, as Barney Rosenzweig had often said, that sponsors appreciated positive comments from viewers. ABC Entertainment president Robert Iger reiterated that viewpoint at our 1989 convention when he said, "I think we would all be better served if sponsors heard from our viewers about the quality programs, not only to keep them on the air, but to maintain a fertile breeding ground for more quality." For years, VQT had a sponsor program coordinator who collected the names and addresses of the corporations and the products they owned; then when each sponsor chairperson sent the sponsor coordinator a list of advertisers for a particular show, the list would be compiled and was then ready to mail to viewers upon request. For a number of years, Jane Marie Best of Rochester, New York, supplied us with master lists that she assembled from books at the library. Mark McClelland, of Baltimore, Maryland, prepared the lists of the individual shows to send on request. By 1995, it became obvious to me that information kept in this way quickly became obsolete. We were fortunate to find Donna Schulman, of Forest Hills, New York, who had access to computerized files of this information; we could stay current.

By 1997, however, I had formed the opinion that although it was important to communicate with sponsors of television programs to commend them for sponsoring a particular show, this was no longer a priority, given the frequency with which shows were being moved from time slot to time slot. It was my understanding that sponsors at first purchased time in a specific slot for a specific show, then when that show moved, the sponsor remained behind with the replacement show, and the show that was moved inherited new sponsors. Alternately confusing and enlightening! I felt that if people were to write *one* letter to save a show—and experience proved that they were more likely to write just one—I wanted that one letter to go to the entity that had the power to cancel or extend the show—the network. As of late 1997, VQT still had its sponsor program, but I was not highlighting it as I once had. By 1998 I decided that although advertisers were perhaps most responsible for the problem (of shows being canceled by the networks for not immediately delivering enough viewers or viewers of the "right" demographic breakdown), our letters were meaningless to them. Also, from the responses to viewers from advertisers that were shared with me, it was clear that they had no role in programming decisions.

When campaigning for shows found its way to the Internet, I noticed that sponsor lists were usually included. With one click and little thought, a viewer could send a protest or an E-mail of support. I doubted the effectiveness of this type of communication for this purpose, because it was too anonymous, but felt gratified that VQT's suggestion of writing sponsors had found such a broad audience.

Always looking for a new way to get VQT opinion to the public, I developed a New Season Opinion Poll in 1990, asking VQT participants each fall to name what they considered the best new drama and the best new comedy, along with other questions to keep it interesting—such as which show was their biggest disappointment and which their greatest surprise. Television journalists picked this up as a way to measure the new season for their readers, passing along to them what other viewers thought of the new season. At the beginning of the 1992–93 season, two shows, a quirky drama and a thoughtful comedy, were off to a shaky start—and VQT chose them both as the best of the new shows. *Picket Fences* was best new drama and *Mad About You* best new comedy; this information was widely publicized and hopefully made a difference (a *Picket Fences* producer said it did in the press), as both went on to enjoy many successful seasons. This is what David E. Kelley was referring to when he told Kathy Baker to "make sure that they know that we know they were here for us first."

VQT has twice been the subject of an educational study. Cheryl Harris, a VQT member who was a doctoral student at the University of Massachusetts in 1990, chose VQT as the subject of her dissertation research. She designed a comprehensive survey that was mailed to VQT members asking questions about their experience with television and their thoughts on various topics related to TV. Having received a grant for this project, Cheryl was able to enclose a prestamped envelope with each questionnaire. Cheryl conducted informal group interviews as a follow-up at the 1990 convention. VQT reported some results of Cheryl's study in its October 1991 newsletter, and Cheryl gave a report at the September 1991 convention. A total of 1,117 questionnaires were returned. Geographically, during the year of Cheryl's study, the VQT membership was representative of all fifty states and paralleled the distribution of the U.S. population as a whole. Other indicators suggested that the group represented an unusually upscale and educated demographic. On average, VQT members watched just under four hours of television a day, like the average exposure of the general audience. However, basic and premium cable subscriptions were higher than average, as was the ownership of VCRs and home computers. Using the VCR to time shift programming was also frequent. This indicated to Cheryl that VQT members were comfortable with new technologies and tended to be early adopters of these new advancements. Cheryl also found that interest was highest among VQT members in drama programming, followed by situation comedy, news programs, action-adventure shows, and comedy-variety. According to the *Chicago Sun-Times*'s Lon Grahnke, most mainstream viewers preferred sitcoms and "reality" shows.[10]

Elements ranked most important in evaluating whether a program was of good quality were, in order: imaginative storyline, acting ability of cast, interesting dialogue, believable or real situations, and familiar characters.

Cheryl found that 52 percent of respondents first heard about VQT from a newspaper article. Only 7 percent heard about the organization from another member, and another 3 percent from a friend or relative. This suggested to Cheryl that VQT's public relations with the media was excellent and that visibility through the media channels was good. It also suggested that very few members had been recruited through personal contacts; she suggested that recruitment of new members by current ones would be a very effective method of strengthening the organization.

Further study of the survey results showed that 34 percent of respondents joined VQT to influence television, and 21 percent joined to save a specific show. Sixty-seven percent of VQT respondents had been involved in letter-writing campaigns, while 33 percent had not. Of those involved in letter-writing campaigns, 60 percent wrote to a network executive, 40 percent wrote to a producer, 25 percent wrote to advertisers, and 15 percent wrote to a local newspaper editor or TV critic. Cheryl concluded, from suggestions from the network executives and producers attending the 1991 convention, that the percentage writing to advertisers and TV critics be increased, as both were considered essential elements in any successful letter-writing campaign.

Fifty-seven percent of respondents discussed their favorite program with coworkers; 70 percent discussed the program with other loyal viewers or fans. (This study was completed before the advent of the Internet.) Fourteen percent belonged to a fan club organized around their favorite program or its stars.

Cheryl Harris received her doctorate in communication in 1992 for her 350-page thesis on the findings of her year-long study of Viewers for Quality Television.

Two professors of communication at Santa Clara University, headed by Stephen Lee, researched VQT as a project while attending the 1994 convention. Professor Lee thanked VQT for "extraordinary access" in our November 1994 newsletter, telling us that he found "the rank and file of the organization" to be "open, articulate and passionate about the goals of VQT and their own roles in the organization."Although the plan was to write up their study for two venues, a communication research conference and for submission to an academic journal in communication, it was never completed because of the illness and death of Prof. Lee's associate, Moira McLoughlin.

I conducted my own VQT member survey in the winter of 1994. Only six hundred VQT members (out of about twenty-five hundred at the time) returned their surveys, probably because I was not able to supply return postage. Who were VQT members in 1994? Seventy-eight percent were female. Half fell into the 40–60 age-group. Fifty-five percent were married, 44.3 percent were not. Thirty-seven percent of respondents' household income was in the $30,000–$50,000 range, with 40 percent above that. Seventy-two percent lived in single-family homes, with 80.2 percent owning their own homes. Twenty-eight percent were college graduates, with 26 percent having completed some college. Seventy-five percent subscribed to cable TV, 98 percent received PBS. Thirty-one percent of respondents felt that television was not responsible for the violence in our society, while 16 percent felt that it was. The percentage of those who felt that the networks and producers should curb any violence on television was 46.6, while 3.9 percent felt that the control should be legislated. The percentage of those who had more than one operational TV in their home was 80.4, and 93.6 percent had more than one operational VCR. Only 10 percent of respondents had never written to a network in support of a TV series. The percentage of those who *always* voted in elections was 81.4, while 13.8 percent *usually* did. On average, 3.5 people read each member's newsletter.

From this study, I found that 82.8 percent of VQT members learned about the organization through a newspaper or magazine article, while another 12 percent discovered VQT through word of mouth, suggesting that individual recruitment had increased since Cheryl Harris's study. The percentage of those who favored drama series was 54.7, 28 percent favored comedy series, and only 6 percent liked reality shows. As for laugh tracks on sitcoms, 38.6 percent found them "very annoying," 25.7 percent found them "distracting," while 31.1 percent did not pay much attention. Another 3.7 percent refused to watch a show with a laugh track.

The percentage of respondents who had been with VQT eight years was 4.9; 2.3 percent for seven years; 7.2 percent for six years; 9.8 percent for five years; 14.7 percent for four years; 16.6 percent for three years; 11.2 percent for two years; 18 percent for one year; 15.4 percent for less than one year. These statistics confirmed what I already had surmised: most viewers tire of advocacy and do not stay with VQT for a long time.

By 1994, VQT had an archivist. The State Historical Society of Wisconsin approached me that spring about keeping archives for VQT. It had initiated the Mass Communications History Collections to document the importance of the mass media in twentieth-century American life. It was interested in VQT because of its grassroots history. The Mass Communications History Collections attract scholars from throughout the United States and abroad who find these outstanding sources vital to their work.

For the first and only time, in October 1992, VQT was listed in *Entertainment Weekly*'s "Power 101" naming the most influential people in entertainment, along with two other organizations, GLAAD (Gay and Lesbian Alliance Against Defamation) and Accuracy in Media. The unlikely trio made number 82, and were identified as "television watchdogs."[11] The reason given for the inclusion: "Networks don't always obey them, but they listen." Misunderstanding VQT, the magazine listed as the "X-factor" (disadvantage): "No group has ever mounted a successful national boycott, but that doesn't mean the networks don't fear the possibility." I wrote a letter to the editor, which they published in their November 20, 1992, issue, thanking them for naming VQT and explaining that it was not a watchdog, rather an advocacy group, and that it never boycotted. I clarified that "VQT educates and informs viewers on how to have a voice, while it strives to make the networks and producers of prime-time television accountable for quality, i.e., intelligent, thought-provoking, interesting, illuminating content." I concluded, "We 'watch,' but we don't 'dog.' But thank you for noticing."[12]

My greatest frustration has been the attrition of VQT participants over the years. Sometime in 1991 I conducted a poll asking viewers why they left

VQT. All responses struck a similar chord—disenchantment with network television and impatient that change was taking so long. I published some of the responses in June 1991. Barbara Heinzen of St. Louis, Missouri, wrote that "I am not disappointed with VQT, but with commercial television. I am grateful to VQT for teaching me to look for quality when I watch television, but I have found that true quality on commercial television is a very rare thing indeed, and usually short-lived."

Lorie Freeman of Irvine, California, concurred: "Although I applaud your efforts to secure quality viewing on television, I truly believe you are fighting a losing battle. My belief is very firmly based on this fact: money talks, but it does not listen."

My frustration was based on the belief that if everybody who had ever joined VQT had stayed, not taking into account the thousands more who had written for information but had not joined, we might be forty thousand strong and our advocacy would truly make a difference. It could even be powerful. Every television viewer who stayed with VQT over the years strengthened the organization, as every viewer who left weakened it.

The ones who stayed energized me. Rob Killian of West Jordan, Utah, wrote in the June 1991 newsletter, "I realize that I am not alone. We are finding our voice and learning to speak. It is a thrill to be involved in this process." (Rob dropped out several years later.) John Courtney of Crestview, Florida, wrote in the same issue, "If we don't let [the networks] know there is an audience for quality, then we shouldn't complain about the garbage they give us." (John, too, dropped out.) Viewers are leaving VQT as they leave network television.

Achieving 501(c)3 status in 1989 was crucial to our development. Several producers helped us qualify by writing testimonial letters for our use. Their letters were submitted with our petition for tax-exempt status and have been printed in various VQT newsletters and brochures over the years. Stephen J. Cannell wrote, "I believe the VQT organization to be a positive force in the area of recognition of quality programming and, as such, is probably the only organization in the unique position of being able to educate the public on how to have a voice in television. Such a group is absolutely necessary as a medium for providing this very important public service."

Dr. William Baker of WNET (a PBS station) in New York wrote,

This is a letter of commendation for Viewers for Quality Television, Inc.,
a singular advocacy group for the public good in an arena where the
public good is too often overlooked. As a public television broadcaster,
with a 30-year career in commercial broadcasting, I value the strides

VQT is making toward educating viewers on how to improve the quality of the television they watch. VQT makes a unique contribution to our society and is eminently worthy of our encouragement and support.

The cast of *Designing Women,* Delta Burke, Annie Potts, Dixie Carter, Jean Smart, and Meshach Taylor, all signed a letter dated November 30, 1988, in which they stated,

> As those who toil in the trenches of the television industry, we are most impressed by the work of Viewers for Quality Television. This tireless group has rallied support nationwide and has positively influenced programming in a significant way. We believe it is very important to educate the public as to how to have a strong voice—to have any voice, for that matter—in a medium that is increasingly dominated by corporations and their desire for profit.

Ron Koslow, executive producer of *Beauty and the Beast,* added, "I'd like to register my approval of the work done by VQT. They serve an important role in educating the television viewer *and* the networks—and by doing so, encouraging quality. Their work is worthy of praise and should be supported."

Stephen Cragg, at the time supervising producer of Universal's *Almost Grown,* wrote, "Viewers for Quality Television is a necessary, vital group which gives the public an arena in which they can voice their opinions about the quality of TV programming. It's important that viewers have such a group to represent them."

Producer/writer Patricia Green (*Cagney & Lacey, China Beach, Chicago Hope*) wrote, "Viewers for Quality Television is a vitally necessary group that performs a unique function by facilitating communication between the people who make television programs and the people who watch them."

Harry Thomason and Linda Bloodworth-Thomason strongly and eloquently advocated VQT's mission.

> In our opinion, Viewers for Quality Television is one of the most important cultural institutions in the nation, because it represents the only grass roots movement in television, which is the most influential medium in this country. In this age of corporate takeover of the entertainment business, it is more important than ever for the people— especially discriminating, intelligent people like those who belong to VQT—to have a say in what goes out over the airwaves. And it is increas-

ingly more difficult. We salute the determination of VQT to make its voice heard, and admire its rather incredible feats of organization to rally membership and influence the direction of network television. For those of us who work on the inside, this is an amazing accomplishment. We understand how much tax exemption would aid Viewers for Quality Television in its important work, and we urge you to grant it.

Viewers for Quality Television owes its tax-exempt status to those individuals as well as to David Masterman and Kathleen Harmon.

I had my first, and so far only, encounter with advertisers March 27, 1993. I was invited to address and participate in a Q&A session with the twelve members of the board of directors of industry consultant Jack Myers's Worldwide Marketing Leadership Panel in Washington, D.C. The board of directors of this panel meets annually to discuss topics of interest to major national advertisers. Pat Murphy and I were invited to meet with them, because Myers believed VQT's constructive efforts were important to them. Advertising executives were present from Clorox, Warner-Lambert, Coca-Cola, Nabisco Brands, AT&T, Kmart, and Sony Corporation. We were thrilled, and anticipated the opportunity to begin a dialogue with advertisers. We were going to talk to them as representatives of the audience they wanted to reach. And we were going to try to interest them in helping VQT with funding. It was interesting to meet with individuals who were responsible for placing ads on television programs, and it turned into an informative and enlightening exchange for both sides. And we truly represented "two sides," hardly agreeing on anything. Pat and I left the meeting realizing more than ever that the system had to change if marginally rated quality shows were ever to survive on network television. I learned at this meeting that the fault did not lie solely with the networks, that advertisers definitely do want "the most bang for the buck." *Brooklyn Bridge* had just been canceled because it had "only" eight million viewers. They were not interested in placing an ad on a network show with "only" eight million viewers, no matter how excellent the show was—not when they can reach 35 million with another show. I learned that eight million viewers on commercial television are "valueless" as a market. They did not want to hear that people zap their remote controls from program to program to avoid commercials, or that if viewers are watching a mindless program, they are also mindless during the commercials. They weren't interested in my theory that if viewers are watching a show that requires concentration, that concentration might carry over into the commercial. The jobs of the executives who determine which shows to sponsor are on the line—they are accountable for an uptick in sales as a result of their decision.

The advertisers, not just the networks, totally rely on the Nielsen numbers and what is desirable as an advertising vehicle, and are as much focused on the bottom line as the networks. This meeting confirmed my understanding that advertisers really do consciously steer away from controversial programs, even *good* controversial programs.

I also learned from this group that it was highly unlikely that VQT would ever receive a grant or a donation from a corporation, because our cause is only television. Corporations have two levels for which they dispense funds: charity—and other charities will receive higher priority than VQT—and marketing, in which case they want to know what they will receive in return for their support.

In departing the meeting, I spoke for the 8 million "valueless" viewers and told the advertisers that unless things change, network television may very well cease to be a viable marketplace for their products and that intelligent viewers were abandoning network television. I still believe, more strongly than ever, what I so haughtily told them in parting practically over my shoulder.

Jack Myers, chairman of the Worldwide Marketing Leadership Panel, continued the dialogue by responding to my report of the encounter in our May/June 1993 newsletter. He stated in a letter I published in our January 1994 issue that I "somewhat misrepresented" the position of the panel, and asked that I do not take away from "our meeting together a message of discouragement."[13] He said they had only intended to make "you and your members more aware of the realities that must serve as a foundation for a constructive continuing dialogue between our organizations." Myers applauded VQT's efforts and explained that advertisers "have had a significant impact on the networks' decisions to dramatically alter the amount of violent and controversial programming." He suggested something that was not within VQT's purview, that we encourage research into the causal nature of programming content on advertising effectiveness. He reminded me that "advertisers have a responsibility to be fiscally sound in their investments," and that "shows in which they place their ads must be good financial investments." And as if we didn't already know it, "the reality is that a network has a limited supply of time to sell, and advertisers are in the business of reaching as many people as possible for the lowest possible cost." He told me, and all of VQT, that "your message is being heard loud and clear, but your specific goals of 'saving' programs that are not serving the needs and interests of the larger mass of viewers is unrealistic." Myers offered a "more realistic objective" that his board had urged me to adopt: to communicate directly with the television production and talent community about the high cost of network production that "makes many of your favorite shows economically unsound." He logically argued that "if costs can be reduced so that these same programs can be financially attractive to cable networks, then smaller audiences can be financially acceptable and advertisers will be thrilled to support them." Although that made sense, and still does, it was not within VQT's scope to try to have an effect upon the high cost of network production.

In my answer to Myers's response, in the same issue, I replied to his statement about advertisers wanting the networks to alter the amount of violent and controversial programming by reminding all readers that VQT's position was that "we want advertisers to be *less* influenced by special interest groups that would make viewing choices for us, and take risks with sometimes controversial programming." I contended that some controversial programs are quality programs.

To my surprise, Jack Myers stayed in contact with VQT, and helped me put together a panel discussion, which he led, for our 1994 convention. He also enlisted me for his short-lived, though well-intentioned, National Media Advisory Board in 1996. Myers tried to launch a television ratings system once it became mandated, and had a number of industry individuals on board, including Brandon Tartikoff and myself. But he couldn't get the networks on board, as (1) they believed the battle would be decided in court and (2) they distrusted any advertiser-based system.

More audience opinion on television advertising can be found in "What's Wrong with the System?"

The Future of Viewers for Quality Television

Because of the *Parade* article, I was able to stop teaching in 1989 and devote all my time to the growth of VQT. The board of directors determined that to do this, I would need a salary. That salary has varied over the years, according to the organization's financial stability, but has remained between $20,000 and $25,000 annually. In the early 1990s, at my request, the board voted to compensate me for the fact that VQT could not afford a pension fund, an IRA, or any health benefits for me; the board set my "salary" at $35,000, at least $10,000 of which I would "defer," that is, leave untouched in VQT's bank account. This would guarantee a small security package for me when and if VQT had to close down operation. By winter 2000, the amount of money VQT had in the bank was less than the amount I have deferred. In essence, I am again out of pocket.

Sharon Gless and Barney Rosenzweig greet Dorothy Swanson at 1990 VQT convention. Photographer unknown. Courtesy of VQT.

John Sacret Young, VQT's Pat Murphy, and Dana Delany at the 1990 Quality Awards banquet. Photo by Karen Hurst. Courtesy of VQT.

Sherry Stringfield with VQT member David Masterman at 1996 Quality Awards banquet. Photo by Laurie Strollo. Courtesy of VQT.

Fred Savage with VQT member Marcia Anderson at VQT's 1992 Meet 'n' Greet. Photo by Karen Hurst. VQT file.

Author on set of *Cagney & Lacey,* March 1984. Courtesy of the author.

Linda Ellerbee, Dorothy Swanson, and Pat Murphy at VQT's first convention, September 1987. Photo: VQT file.

David Hyde Pierce with VQT board member Laurie Strollo at Quality Awards banquet. Photo by Rosie Ricciardi. Courtesy of VQT.

Pat Murphy and Dorothy Swanson on set of *Cagney & Lacey,* c. 1986.
Courtesy of the author.

Dorothy Swanson pre-
senting Quality Award
to Julia Louis-Dreyfus at
1992 Quality Awards
banquet. Photo by
Elizabeth Ford.

Linda Bloodworth-
Thomason, Pat Murphy,
and Harry Thomason at
1989 Meet 'n' Greet.
Photo by Tony Ricciardi.
Courtesy of VQT.

Dorothy
Swanson and
John Ritter at
VQT panel
discussion,
1989. Photo by
Ginger Sagau.
Courtesy of VQT.

Dorothy Swanson, Tim
Reid, and Pat Murphy
on set of *Frank's Place*.
Courtesy of VQT.

Dorothy Swanson and Pat Murphy on set of *Designing Women,* January 1986. *Rear:* Pat Murphy, Dixie Carter. *Front:* Dorothy Swanson, Linda Bloodworth-Thomason, Jean Smart, Delta Burke, Annie Potts. Courtesy of Mozark Productions, Harry Thomason.

Network entertainment presidents Peter Roth (Fox), Warren Littlefield (NBC), and Leslie Moonves (CBS) with author at VQT Conference on Quality Television in 1997. Photo by Ellen Gershman. Courtesy of VQT.

VQT members Barbara and Chuck Adams with Kathy Baker and her "Q." Photo by Tony Ricciardi. Courtesy of VQT.

VQT Conference on Quality Television greeters Sharon Johns, Shan Stafford, Laurie Strollo, David Masterman, Rhea Baldino, and John Baldino. Photo by Rosie Ricciardi. Courtesy of VQT.

Gary David Goldberg, Dorothy Swanson, and Marion Ross at Quality Awards banquet. Photo by Karen Hurst. Courtesy of VQT.

Pat Murphy with *The X-Files* creator, Chris Carter, at 1995 VQT panel discussion. Photo by Karen Hurst. Courtesy of VQT.

VQT member Sharon Johns with Scott Wolf (*Party of Five*) at VQT panel discussion in 1995. Photo by Rosie Ricciardi. Courtesy of VQT.

1992 Quality Award winners. Left to right: Scott Bakula, Marg Helgenberger, Michael Jeter, Alice Ghostley, Dana Delany, John Sacret Young, Park Overall, Robert Picardo, Joel Shukovsky, Diane English. Photographer unknown. Courtesy of VQT.

Lauren Holly and Jim Carrey with
VQT member Rosie Ricciardi at
1994 Quality Awards banquet.
Photo by Tony Ricciardi.
Courtesy of VQT.

Joanie and Dennis Franz at
Quality Awards banquet 1996.
Photo by Rosie Ricciardi.
Courtesy of VQT.

VQT's Quality Awards. Photographer unknown. Courtesy of VQT.

GROWING CAMPAIGNS

SINCE 1985 Viewers for Quality Television has spearheaded numerous viewer campaigns to rescue quality shows from the edge of oblivion. The shows highlighted in this chapter all could have, and should have, had longer network lives. They were beautiful, interesting, valuable, and worthwhile sources of quality entertainment. Each was destroyed by a network's reliance on the Nielsen ratings as the only determining factor of successful programming.

I have often said that campaigning for a show after it is canceled is futile. In a story about VQT's letter campaigns for the *New York Times* in 1993, Peter M. Nichols wrote that "a campaign might help prolong the life of a show because the publicity makes it harder for the network to kill it."[1] NBC vice president Sue Binford told Nichols, during the *I'll Fly Away* campaign, "We look at Viewers for Quality Television as a vehicle to help get the word out and stir up the public. But in the end the letters have to translate into on-air performance."[2]

In deciding whether or not to launch a campaign, I was always mindful of something the late John Carmody of the *Washington Post* cautioned me about early on: "You need to be careful about which shows you go to the well for." He meant that I would be risking journalists' disinterest if I announced campaigns too frequently. He was right. Unfortunately, too many zealous and sometimes ambitious viewers "went to the well" for anything and everything, compromising the system VQT had successfully employed. The defining example of this occurred in 1999 when Rob Owen, TV editor for the *Pittsburgh Post-Gazette*, mentioned a campaign for CBS's *The Nanny* in his article about campaigns for TV shows.[3] In quoting my reaction to the news, Owen wrote, "For Swanson, who picks which shows to trumpet carefully, a *Nanny* campaign is unimaginable."[4] I had sounded off, "This is the kind of thing that has ruined campaigning."[5]

An assistant of Tim Reid told me during the *Frank's Place* campaign of 1988 that there is no system in place that allows ordinary viewers to express their opinions. VQT became that system. As its leader, I expressed the views of the disenfranchised viewer, earned respect and attention for VQT and for the shows it fought for, and ultimately saw the overused letter-writing campaign diminish in impact.

In this day of instant communication, Internet campaigns must be addressed. Anita Gates wrote in the *New York Times* in 1995: "Clearly, grass roots aren't what they used to be. In the Internet age, fans can get their message across faster and farther than ever."[6] Indeed, well-organized and media-savvy fans of shows can have executives' E-mail addresses and fax numbers up on a Web site within minutes, and complete sponsor addresses can be compiled and posted. Fans wanting to save their favorite show can gather and become a force almost immediately. In the same time it might have taken to type a letter, put it in an envelope, find a stamp, and mail it, they can send ten or twenty letters with as many keystrokes. Too easy? I think so.

Jack Curry, managing editor of *TV Guide*, told Gates, "I think grassroots campaigns do have impact, but one thing working against them is how they're being run today. The networks don't really know who the cyberspace people are, what they buy."[7] Gates gave perspective to letters by adding that although 50,000 letters may be a big bag of mail, they represent only $1/19$ of a rating point.[8] Yes, but 50,000 letters represent the opinion of 700 million people if you follow the common theory that one letter represents 14,000 people (a rule of thumb I first heard on the *Hour Magazine* show with Sharon Gless and Tyne Daly in 1983). And a letter sent to a specific individual requires more thought than a click of a keyboard.

For a while, before it became commonplace, before producers went onto the Internet to organize their own campaigns, before viewers sprang into action every time a mundane show got canceled, before television journalists became jaded about campaigns because everybody was doing it, letter-writing campaigns for exceptional shows had meaning and impact. These campaigns all had one important, common element—what I call the outrage factor. Without the outrage factor being extremely high and widespread, there simply is no valid campaign.

Frank's Place

Set in New Orleans and starring Tim Reid and his wife Daphne Maxwell Reid, *Frank's Place* was introduced on CBS in September 1987. Created by Hugh Wilson and Tim Reid, it immediately enchanted viewers who preferred some intelligence behind their laughter. Shot on film, there was no distracting laugh track; the show assumed the audience would know when to laugh. Sophisticated, intelligent, and warm, each episode was a flavorful and nuance-filled short story. And it had "only" 10 million viewers. As with too many quality series, *Frank's Place* proved itself too good for network television. CBS shortsightedly canceled it one week before it was to go back into production for the 1988 television season. The previous spring, CBS had lulled concerned viewers and critics by ordering thirteen episodes for use as a midseason replacement. CBS blamed the audience for failing to find the show. But the network moved *Frank's Place* six times in its first season, making it practically impossible for even loyal viewers to find. It ended its run buried on Saturday nights, its final broadcast ranking forty-seventh out of forty-nine shows. The audience had given up searching for it.

Frank's Place could have been saved, based on the amount of passionate mail I received and the involvement of television journalists. But no amount of passion, no amount of mail, could make up for the fact that the show's primary creative force, Hugh Wilson, walked away before the cancellation was even announced, into a deal with Columbia. He was frustrated at the lack of commitment from CBS and left its star, Tim Reid, to handle a shocked media and outraged fans. *Frank's Place* without Hugh Wilson was unrealistic. I knew that, but we fought anyway, because, overwhelmed by wishful thinking, we thought the show could be saved.

Frank's Place suffered from musical-chair time slots from the start. It premiered on Monday, September 14, 1987, at 8 P.M., where it aired until November 30, when it was moved to 8:30. On February 8 it moved to 9:30 Mondays. It moved March 15 to 9:30 Tuesdays. It was taken off the air after the March 29 broadcast, and returned July 16 to 8:30 Saturdays. At some point it aired on a Wednesday night. Its final CBS showing was October 1. The total ratings were not all that terrible. In its Monday night outings, *Frank's Place* averaged a 19 share with a 12.7 rating, higher than *Murphy Brown* would earn in its ninth year when it was surprisingly renewed for a tenth season. Predictably, on Saturday nights *Frank's Place* garnered only a 10 share and 5.6 rating. *Frank's Place* did better than its successors on both Monday and Wednesday night, but finished a poor second in its Monday night time, ending 1987 with a rank of forty-fifth with an average audience of perhaps 20 million. Twenty million viewers is a bona fide hit today.

VQT backed the show immediately. I wrote a letter of praise to CBS Entertainment president Kim LeMasters, and he released my letter to the media. VQT and a network joined forces to promote what both recognized as a quality show. It was a sign of progress.

When the fall lineup was announced that May, *Frank's Place* was not on the schedule. But CBS promised to deliver the show midseason and ordered thirteen episodes, thereby effectively halting any campaign. Although no production date was given, Daphne Maxwell Reid believed the network and gave VQT a statement for our June/July 1988 newsletter that made us somewhat complacent: "CBS is going to wait to see where their best slot will be for *Frank's Place* because they believe in the preservation of the show. Tim and I are very satisfied with this decision." If I had it to do over again, I would have started the campaign the moment CBS announced it was not on the schedule. By waiting, we lost time, momentum, and the executive producer.

But *Frank's Place* nonetheless had the support of inflamed television journalists and irate viewers, usually an unbeatable combination. Viewers hadn't seen anything like it before—each episode was its own carefully told short story. It could be poignant drama or it could be slapstick comedy, but what held all the stories together was the quality of writing and acting.

Inspired and angry, talented VQT member Wesley A. Wright from Kensington, Maryland, sent VQT original cartoons, which were published in our December 1988/January 1989 newsletter.

CBS announced that *Frank's Place* would not be on the fall schedule after all—one week before it was scheduled to go back into production. A CBS representative told John Carmody, "The audience just hasn't come to the show."[9] LeMasters told Carmody, "Unfortunately the viewing audience simply failed to respond to the show."[10] I pleaded for *Frank's Place* to television journalists on October 5, 1988, in an effort to mobilize frustrated viewers. I began my letter, "After nine Emmy nominations, critical acclaim, and promises and assurances from CBS about how much it was valued and would be protected, *Frank's Place* has been canceled, one week [before] the start of production." I lamented that the networks couldn't seem to find a time slot for quality any-more, and stated that VQT could not let *Frank's Place* go without voicing an outcry. I reminded journalists that *"Frank's Place* had class and heart and soul and moments of brilliance." In an October 19 letter to journalists, I quoted from letters I had received, largely from the Washington, D.C., area (thanks to the *Washington Post's* Tom Shales) and Orlando, Florida (Greg Dawson). I believed that the more journalists that became involved, the more viewers I could rally. That strategy worked; more journalists came on board, and more viewers wrote me, and more letters went to CBS. One quote summed up the frustration so perfectly that I used it in every television interview, including *The Oprah Winfrey Show,* a morning and an afternoon talk show in Washing-ton, and another talk show in Pittsburgh. I was heard all over the dial all over the country saying, "It is irresponsible of a network to move a show around as much as *Frank's Place* was moved, and then to blame the audience for the show's failure." Passionate, articulate, angry letters poured in to VQT's post office box. I didn't hear from every one of *Frank's Place's* 20 million viewers, but if every letter represents 14,000 people, as has been suggested, I heard from 9.8 million of them.

From Baltimore came *"Frank's Place* is the type of quality that should be an anchor for a network to point to with pride." A viewer in Connecticut wrote, "Cutting this show is an injustice to television audiences everywhere and points to the hypocrisy of those networks claiming a focus on quality pro-gramming. I would think that alternatives such as an innovative advertising campaign would be thought of and attempted as viable alternatives to can-cellation." From Georgia, I read, "I can't help being peeved about the network president's conclusion that 'the viewing audience failed to respond to the show.' I watched *Frank's Place* religiously, whenever I could, until I just couldn't find it anymore. If someone like me, who *wants* to watch it, can't find the show, how does CBS expect those who might just casually watch it to find it?" A viewer in West Virginia had a broader view: "If television is ever to be a force in strengthening rather than assaulting a rapidly deteriorating American cul-ture, the quality of network television programming must be improved."

Viewers refused to accept the blame; they held the network accountable. From Syracuse, New York, I received "The people at CBS were responsible for the problem of low ratings by their frenetic manipulations of the time slots. A show of this nature needed time to build an audience, and was never given the opportunity." Across the board, viewers could not fathom CBS's strategy. But they weren't supposed to understand it and they weren't supposed to question it. They were expected to follow the show no matter where CBS put it. Television journalists agreed with the audience. Greg Dawson of the *Orlando Sentinel* was particularly irate when he wrote, "If CBS insists on burying *Frank's Place*, it may as well jump into the grave, too, and let us say last rites for the Promise of Network Television."[11] Truly, CBS developed what many referred to as the curse of *Frank's Place*. Every show that CBS put into its time slot failed to achieve the numbers of this canceled gem.

DeWayne Wickham wrote that *Frank's Place* was a "cultural achievement that is unmatched in American television history. In the short span of one television season, it did more to correct decades of media caricatures of blacks than any other program on TV."[12] He seemed to have only disdain for CBS's programmer Kim LeMasters when he wrote, "Nobody is about to accuse LeMasters of going too far with *Frank's Place*. More likely, his name will find its way onto a list of those who broke and ran when more courageous people would have stood their ground, at least for one more season."[13]

TV critic Alec Harvey wrote in a November column that I had reported that "the *Frank's Place* campaign is gaining momentum, with more than 30,000 letters in support of the show received by CBS."[14]

VQT's campaign received much positive press, and resulted in numerous requests for broadcast interviews. Besides the ones already mentioned, J. C. Hayward, channel 9 anchor in Washington, came to my home and was seen on camera sitting on my living room floor going through a box of mail, reading the letters aloud randomly.

At the suggestion of Tim Reid, the NAACP contacted me about rallying the support of its members behind the show. I tried in vain to persuade the representative who called not to go forward with the planned postcard campaign, rather to urge every person to write that all-important individual letter. I did not and do not believe that postcards mean anything.

Tim Reid was honored with VQT's Quality Award for Best Actor in a Quality Comedy in September 1988. He told us, "I think there is a place for *Frank's Place,* and that's what television *should be* all about. It should be a place where you can tune in and find all kinds of comedy, not just the same kind of mass appeal shows. The tragedy of it is that unless viewers come together and make yourselves known, you will be given one kind of show—one kind of entertainment format—which is very wrong."

Susan Tick, vice president of media relations for CBS, told a VQT audience in September 1993 that "Kim LeMasters has said on several occasions that the cancellation was the biggest mistake he ever made." Hearing those words just made the loss all the greater. I don't think LeMasters knew what he had in *Frank's Place*. He certainly didn't know what to do with it. Responding to the issue at VQT's 1989 convention panel discussion, LeMasters admitted, *"Frank's Place* was a show that I absolutely adored. It was beautifully executed and performed; [but] it got bettered [in every time slot]. We probably over-moved it, maybe destroyed the audience." His admission was no consolation.

Viewers have not forgotten *Frank's Place* to this day. Ellen Gray of the *Philadelphia Daily News* lamented the loss of *Frank's Place* as recently as December 1996 by fantasizing that *Frank's Place* was on the "TV Critics Channel." She dreamed, *"Frank's Place* is in its 10th season. The bar-based sitcom, which still doesn't have a laugh track, has outlived *Cheers,* and everyone knows its name, if not what it means to miss New Orleans. Frank Parrish married mortician Hannah Griffin six seasons ago."[15]

Twenty million viewers were dismissed by CBS along with *Frank's Place*.

A Year in the Life

From *St. Elsewhere* creators Joshua Brand and John Falsey, *A Year in the Life* chronicled three generations of the Gardner family on NBC. Richard Kiley was a widowed patriarch; other cast members included Wendy Phillips (*Homefront, Promised Land*) and Adam Arkin (*Northern Exposure, Chicago Hope*). It premiered as a miniseries in 1987 and enjoyed a 27 share for that debut on NBC.

VQT members embraced it for its character-driven story. The only flaw was its somewhat slow pace. From VQT's December 1987 newsletter, Mary Anne Montgomery from Bloomington, Indiana, wrote, "The characters seem real, with real feelings, cares, flaws and foibles. I care about them and look forward to being with them each week." Mark Cooper from Norcross, Georgia, added, "Each episode assumes that the viewers are intelligent. Viewers must pick up on the subtleties of action and dialogue to understand the characters. A viewer must participate. It is a slice of life rarely captured on film."

By spring there seemed little doubt that cancellation was imminent, because of unacceptable ratings. The "quality" network, NBC, and Brandon Tartikoff, its Entertainment president, could not excuse the show. This time VQT sprang into action before NBC announced its schedule. I wrote Brandon Tartikoff and reminded him of the risks NBC had taken with *Hill Street Blues, St. Elsewhere,* and *Cheers* when they did poorly in the ratings their first season. I likened cancellation of *A Year in the Life* to a "book burning," telling him, "We read a chapter each week, and we're not finished with this novel yet." I wanted to alert fans of the show to the very real probability that this show would be canceled if they didn't act *now*. Again TV journalists notified their readers of our campaign—they loved *A Year in the Life,* too.

Cocreator John Falsey felt that *Life* would have had a better chance if NBC had promoted it better early in the season.[16] He also attributed the problem to good reviews, saying to Gary Mullinax, "I think we were all lulled into a degree of false security. The reviews were so terrific that NBC and the studio didn't bother to put money into promotion."[17]

As expected, *A Year in the Life* was not on the schedule for the following fall. Journalists told their readers how to get in touch with VQT. Campaign wheels were in gear. Letters arrived by the box, and I relied on volunteer staff to open and sort them. I read and replied to each letter, trying to mobilize the enthusiasm that existed for this show. But *A Year in the Life* was a quiet, subdued, low-key show; so, I learned, were its fans. I perceived their letters as less irate than those received in previous campaigns. This group was far from resigned to the loss of the show, but they seemed to not possess the passion that *Frank's Place* or *Our World* viewers had demonstrated. I was urging these viewers to write regularly and passionately to the network, columnists, and sponsors. But most, as far as I could tell, wrote only the one requisite letter. Still, I knew that at least five thousand letters had been sent through VQT to NBC. That meant there were at least triple that, for not all viewers knocked on VQT's door first.

Journalists pressured Tartikoff into putting a number on the pieces of VQT-inspired mail he had received on behalf of the show, and he went before *Entertainment Tonight* cameras on July 12 to respond and to state that he wasn't swayed by a letter-writing campaign. He was also forced to respond to the campaign and the cancellation at that summer's TV critics' meeting. I told critic Joe Stein that this wasn't the summer for viewers' opinions to matter. "The public wants to be heard, but NBC doesn't want to listen. But we're making our voices heard anyway."[18] I reacted to Tartikoff's response to viewers by saying, "NBC dismissed a quality audience; they dismissed a quality program."[19] Tartikoff and I seemed at odds with each other that summer. He told the TV critics that VQT was unable to produce the "groundswell" it had hoped for in support of *Days and Nights of Molly Dodd,* another acclaimed show that NBC dropped.[20] I was able to respond to Stein that "we never got *Molly Dodd* off the ground because Lifetime (the cable channel) picked it up. Tartikoff was saying we failed even before we began. VQT was going to do something, but we didn't have to. People just want to watch *Molly Dodd*—they don't care what button they have to push."[21]

Wall Street Journal critic Martha Bayles wrote about the campaign on July 11. She was one of the journalists I had targeted to receive copies of letters viewers wrote to NBC. "As a critic cited by VQT for having written favorably about *A Year in the Life*, I personally have received a tall stack of letters, most of them copies of letters sent to NBC."[22] Questioning whether VQT's coordination of the campaign didn't hurt as much as it helped, Bayles thought that "too many of the letters seemed coached," and felt that advising people to mention specific episodes that had moved them or characters they related to made the letters seem "less than genuine."[23] I was undeterred in my belief that it is important to demonstrate a familiarity with the show in a letter. Bayles did allow as how "[*Year*] was the best family program on TV," and that "its cancellation reveals the hypocrisy of the TV industry, which has spent several seasons sanctimoniously extolling the importance of TV in helping families cope with everyday problems."[24]

Kay Gardella of the *New York Daily News* also reported on the volume of letters to NBC. "I don't know what the desk of NBC Entertainment President Brandon Tartikoff looks like, but mine is buried by letters directed to him—all pleading for the return of *A Year in the Life*."[25] She declared our campaign worthy of support and quoted from a few of the letters, including one from VQT member Richard Brown of Silver Spring, Maryland. Gardella said in no uncertain terms that "NBC should listen to the voice of the people—and not the ratings—when it comes to a show of this calibre."[26]

Tartikoff told Monica Collins of *USA Today* on July 27, 1988, "I have not read every letter, but I have been keeping tabs on how many we get. I labored far harder than Ms. Swanson to make *A Year in the Life* as competitive and compelling as it possibly could be."

Brandon Tartikoff and I would finally meet—at VQT's 1989 convention in September. I had written him before the 1988 convention and asked if he would appear before the group. He called just as our events began and said he had just found my letter; he asked if I had a spot for him. Regretting that I did not (we had a full roster of guests), I asked him to commit for the following year to a panel discussion with all the network entertainment presidents. He said he would gladly do that. Thanks to Tartikoff's generosity and interest, I had the hook I needed to convene all the network entertainment presidents for the 1989 convention even before the 1988 one got under way. Carole Smith, still Barney Rosenzweig's assistant and helping us with convention details, admonished me for saying no to Brandon Tartikoff. She insisted I should have eliminated someone else to make room for him. "This is why you'll always be a two-bit organization," she told me, hurting me deeply. But I felt I had done the right thing. It would have been rude to jettison an invited guest at the last minute to make room for a "bigger" name.

Tartikoff would call me in 1996 for assistance in saving his New World Television family show *Second Noah*. He wondered if he could enlist me for a campaign. I told him that while *Second Noah* was a lovely family show, Viewers for Quality Television had not found it interesting or compelling enough to warrant endorsement, and that I had no mandate to campaign for it. It was a pleasant conversation, and it was not easy to decline his request.

Wiseguy

This show was one of VQT's victories. Producer Stephen J. Cannell believed that the organization was instrumental in keeping *Wiseguy* on the air, and said so as guest speaker at our 1989 Quality Awards banquet. Fragile as most quality shows are, *Wiseguy* required ongoing viewer advocacy.

Premiering in fall 1987, it was canceled in May 1990. CBS brought it back in midseason 1991, minus Ken Wahl. As a result of my naïveté and Wahl's seductive charm, I became embroiled in a controversy that pitted Wahl against Cannell. (See "Misunderstandings, Misconceptions, and Manipulations".)

Wiseguy introduced former CBS publicist Terri Corigliano (Terri Soreco then) to VQT and brought VQT to Terri. From the start of our relationship, Terri personalized the network for me and gave it a soul. We would fantasize about the Terri and Dorothy network. As she would say seven years later to critic Rob Owen, "Dorothy always seems to be there for the shows that haunt me."[27] *Wiseguy* was one of those.

Wiseguy was presented in "arcs" of anywhere from three to six or seven weeks long. The first, introducing Ken Wahl as Vinnie Terranova and featuring doomed actor Ray Sharkey as mobster Sonny Steelgrave, exploded onto the screen and into peoples' consciousness and hearts. The two actors played off each other with provocative intensity and the characters they played endeared themselves to the audience. One of the final scenes in the Steelgrave arc showed Terranova and Steelgrave sitting on the floor, exhausted from confrontation, listening to a song Steelgrave had programmed the jukebox to play, "Knights in White Satin." The camera work between the actors and the powerful eye contact between them was riveting and mesmerizing to watch. These two adversaries had come to mutually respect each other, and viewers knew they had never seen anything quite like it.

VQT members easily articulated why the show was special. "The show has an almost palpable texture: rich, dark, ominous. The stories make one empathize with Vinnie, and that's a very uncomfortable place to be," wrote Elizabeth Ravan of Nashua, New Hampshire, for the October/November 1988 newsletter. "This is a show that establishes a lot of context over several episodes." Michael Kirby wrote for the October/November 1988 newsletter, "Unlike most TV entertainment, *Wiseguy* is not a diversion; it is not an escape. Rather, it is a weekly one-hour foray into those deep, dark, hidden parts of ourselves. It is a program that visually and verbally articulates the ongoing dilemma of our body/soul duality. *Wiseguy* is a show about people trying to achieve goodness, perhaps even spiritual purity, in the face of man's inhumanity to man. Not only will I remember the Sonny Steelgrave epic tomorrow, I'll remember it for the rest of my life." Michael Smolinski, of Grand Rapids, Michigan, expressed in the April/May 1989 newsletter that "the dialogue is rich and raw. Every episode involves intelligent people (good and bad) who can allude to philosophy, psychology and democracy in their speech and mannerisms without losing credibility or appearing haughty or overly-intellectual. The action is plentiful and rough. Every week, the producers, cast and writers walk the tightrope between brains and brawn and successfully combine the two for an always intriguing premise." Linda Crothers of Tucson, Arizona, embraced its "dark, brooding, mean streets vision," and liked that it "is willing to show the reality of violence. It often probes the frail, less-than-perfect psyche of its heroes and reveals the human/redeemable side of characters that in lesser shows would be simply stereotypical villains. The writing is always sharp and quick with one foot in the gutter and the other soaring with the poets and philosophers."

Elizabeth Ford of Long Branch, New Jersey, observed in the August/September 1989 newsletter that "a recurring theme in *Wiseguy* is whether the ends ever, always or never justify the means, and the answer to that question is never the same twice."

How important was Wahl as Vinnie Terranova to the series? Cindy Thompson was so inspired by Wahl's performance that she wrote an essay for our September/October 1989 newsletter.

"I discounted the importance of Ken Wahl to the effectiveness of the series until his absence from the Jerry Lewis arc just shut it down. It was still an interesting story, but because we were no longer watching the characters through Vinnie's eyes, they lost their importance and went back to being strangers." She continued,

Is Ken Wahl a great actor, or is this just a happy marriage of actor and role? I do know that he has presented us with a multi-dimensional character of flesh and blood, more fully realized than any character I have ever seen. Vinnie is a man doing the job of an American hero—I use that phrase in its most derogatory sense—whose personal life has had everything to do with the public man he has become. He has frightening weaknesses disguised as virtues that could finally destroy him and a core of inborn strengths that could be his salvation. He is as real, as complete, as the man who sits across from us on the bus. It is sad that we have to leave this man, who has earned our regard.

Wahl had left the show over a feud with Cannell. It does not matter who was right, who quit, who got fired, who wanted to change the show or why. Without Vinnie Terranova, *Wiseguy* was simply not compelling. The half-hearted attempt by viewers to resurrect *Wiseguy* without Wahl just fizzled out.

Beauty and the Beast

Created, produced, and written for Witt-Thomas Productions by Ron Koslow, *Beauty and the Beast* premiered on CBS in September 1987. Based on the fairy tale, it told the story of Vincent, the beast (played by Ron Perlman), who lived below the city in an other-world of tunnels, and Catherine Chandler, the beauty (played by Linda Hamilton), who was nursed back to health by Vincent after she was attacked by hoodlums. TV critics were charmed. John J. O'Connor of the *New York Times* called it "a lesson in going beyond surface appearances."[28] O'Connor added that the "most startling aspect" of the show "is its old-fashioned, shamelessly lyrical romanticism."[29] Viewers agreed, and in fact found it to be as O'Connor described it, "the season's most unusual and compelling love affair."[30] In his review of September 25, 1987, O'Connor called it "the most fascinating show of the new season [that] manages to touch on some unsettling contemporary realities."[31]

In his *TV Guide* review in December 1987, Don Merrill described the two worlds of *Beauty and the Beast:* "Above ground, New York is a place of fear where man's inhumanity to man is evident in all aspects of life. Below ground, in mile upon mile of tunnels and caverns, there exist people who live simply but serenely."[32] Merrill wrote of the deep bond between Vincent and Catherine and how "the love story continues through each week's episode, and it is the sensitive, convincing treatment of the romance by the writers and the actors that is the heart of *Beauty and the Beast*."[33]

The *Philadelphia Daily News* spoke to the way women were flocking to it. "This fantasy romance seems to have done something to inspire the female population to great admiration. They're turned on in a very new way."[34]

Dismissing the show at first, I was persuaded by my friend Pam Calligan to watch it one evening while I was visiting her in Michigan. Her attention was focused on the TV set when she said to me, "It's not what you think. Listen—he reads poetry to her." I then realized how literate the show was, and soon, so did most VQT members.

Creator Ron Koslow believed that the lure of *Beauty and the Beast* was grounded in the emotional dimension of the show, that people responded to the depth of feeling portrayed.[35] He said the show "maximized the capability to convey moments of great depth of feeling. The reason people respond strongly to this show is because it is a basic myth; it resonates very deep in our collective unconscious." Indeed, *Beauty and the Beast* stirred television fandom not only to its maximum, but also to the outer bounds of the realm that separates reality and fantasy. Its hard-core fans *believed* it. Although the show enjoyed fervent support from mainstream viewers who enjoyed a literate and interesting story, its loyal followers gave new meaning to the term "fervent." They created fanzines, some of which were the most professional-looking and articulate of any I had seen. In 1989 I counted thirty-one different fan clubs. They organized themselves into one entity with a central clearinghouse of information that would be to their advantage when it came time to campaign for the show. One thing drove them: passion.

"The concept of taking a fable and modernizing it is not a new one, but the way in which the producers and writers have molded the fabled story line of unrequited love is unique. The idea of people from two different worlds interacting and creating a new reality is beautifully played out," wrote Kathy Brogan for VQT's October/November 1988 newsletter. "The writing is sensitive, evocative, literate and thought-provoking. The use of literary allusion, as well as quotes from great authors, is refreshing. The characters are multidimensional, with behaviors and reactions that are compelling, ennobling and true to life." Betsy Sprouse of Alexandria, Virginia, commented for the February/March 1989 newsletter, "It is a show that touches the heart, the soul, the brain and our dreams. The relationship between Vincent and Catherine is totally believable, and makes you feel that anything is possible."

This one was my favorite: "People like me who adore this show have at least one foot firmly planted on the ground, *honest!* It's just that the other one is stuck in this steam grate," admitted Margaret Zumas of Bethlehem, Pennsylvania, in the April/May 1989 newsletter.

The show also attracted men, such as Stanley Hocevar of Euclid, Ohio, who wrote in the June/July 1989 issue: "It is the realization of a world that once only existed in the mind of its creator." Ditto Michael Leary of Morehead City, North Carolina, in the August/September 1989 issue: "This show, although a fantasy tale, provides important reinforcement of the values and feelings that are representative of the very best that humankind has to offer."

The ratings were never great but the show earned a full second season. Its fandom continued to grow and mobilize. VQT endorsed it and awarded Ron Perlman the Quality Award twice, in 1988 and 1989. Perlman told the VQT audience during our 1989 Quality Awards banquet that "I'm here because Viewers for Quality Television is a miracle for us."

By spring 1989 the well-organized fans got wind of CBS's reluctance to renew the show (it had finished fifty-third out of seventy-three programs)[36] and mobilized. Aligned with Viewers for Quality Television, the combination of dedication and wills was strong. VQT dispensed information to all who inquired and channeled the passion. Still before the onset of Internet communication, the fans commenced a telegram campaign that caused CBS to cancel, then pick up the show within a two-day period. Only thirty-six hours elapsed between the time CBS announced that *Beauty* was not on the fall schedule and the hasty announcement that it would be back midseason. It was a true grassroots response—letters from here, telegrams from there, phone calls from somewhere else. Again, a low-rated but critically acclaimed show was saved because viewers spoke and the network listened.

Ron Koslow wrote to the heads of his fan groups and to VQT on May 24, 1989, thanking them for their support. "The power and depth of your feelings raised a voice that the network simply, and finally, could not deny."[37] They would produce at least twelve new episodes for the 1989-90 season that would begin airing "as soon as a suitable time slot opens."[38] Endearing himself to his fans, Koslow wrote, "Please know that there is power in dreams. You've proved that. We consider ourselves truly blessed to have so many sharing that dream with us."[39]

David Poltrack, vice president of research and planning for CBS, addressed the fan phenomenon on WRGB-TV in Schenectady, New York, on May 23, 1989.

Beauty and the Beast is a show that has created a phenomenon nationally. It will definitely be back on the air; we have been listening to all those people who have been writing, calling and sending us telegrams. The response of *Beauty and the Beast* fans certainly helped us make the decision to keep it in production and to bring it back next year. There's no question about it, we do pay attention to this. This is probably the biggest public response for a program that we've had since *Cagney & Lacey.*

Ah, but there were conditions for the show's return and circumstances that required that changes be made. By May 1989, journalists were reporting that indeed CBS insisted on retooling (that meant reworking) the show. The *Philadelphia Daily News* reported on June 2, 1989, that fans were distressed that "the series may return in a form that brings down the romance and pumps up the violence and adventure."[40] Linda Hamilton was pregnant and reportedly wanted to work less so she could spend more time with her baby. Paul Witt told critic Tom Feran in June 1989 that the number of episodes in which Hamilton would appear had not been determined but "dismissed reports that she will disappear for good."[41] Critic Jerry Krupnick spoke to Koslow in December and delivered the following interesting perspective on the Hamilton angle: "'Linda came to us at the start of last season,' Koslow said, 'and told us she wanted to start up her family and have a child. When that happened, we knew she would not be coming back. Certainly, despite her contract, we had no intention of interfering with those plans.'"[42] But rumors had surfaced that Hamilton's departure was due as much to creative differences with Koslow as her desire to spend more time with her child. Witt insisted to Feran that "hard-core fans will be able to recognize [the show]."[43] Taking him at his word, I wrote television journalists that VQT wanted to make sure that *Beauty and the Beast* "does indeed air at the earliest date possible."[44] *Frank's Place* was too fresh in our memory; we would not be calmed by a network's promises again.

Critics wanted *Beast* back, too. David Freedman wrote about the show "where man and woman come together without fear of shame or embarrassment, where honesty is its own justification, where grace counts for more than guile, where courage is measured by kindness. It is a place that exists in all of us. *Beauty and the Beast* teaches. If only we'd take the time to find it."[45]

As the third season approached that winter, the fandom split into two factions. One side was concerned that without Hamilton the show would lose its premise and its soul. The other side was the Vincent-at-any-cost group.

I interviewed Ron Koslow for the VQT newsletter where he responded to my question about what the "retooling" meant. He was pleased to be able to assure us "because there are so many rumors going around now that it would not make any sense to respond to them or to attempt to address what any of this means. All I can tell you is there are going to be some surprises."[46] Then he said something that turned out to not be the case: "None of us are going to be doing anything that is going to violate the spirit of the show."[47] In September, during a VQT panel discussion, he vowed he would not add anything new, but did reiterate his pledge to keep the spirit of the show intact. One *Beauty* aficionado stood and assured him, "We trust you implicitly."

Then in December *TV Guide* leaked some unattractive and fairly gruesome particulars of the two-hour movie that would begin *Beauty*'s return: that "Catherine would be kidnaped, tortured and die at the end."[48] CBS trumpeted the return in advance promos, "It's not a fairy tale anymore."[49] It certainly wasn't. Fans who considered themselves purists (most VQT members fell into this group) were appalled and offended at the insensitive and truly brutal way that Hamilton was written out of the show. It seemed almost sadistic. Fans noticed other changes, too, that compromised the quality. The return episode contained inconsistencies and was illogical. For example, why would Catherine threaten the health of her unborn child to protect a mysterious notebook? It went against a mother's basic instincts. Fairy tales do not have to make sense, but now the show was not a fairy tale and did not have that excuse. Not only was the beauty gone, but the show was no longer beautiful. Enough viewers shared this feeling that the show had lost much of its "cult" audience. The males the network had hoped to attract by making it an action-adventure show did not come. Critics trounced it. Ratings plunged—worse in the third season than the *repeat* episodes of the first two seasons. I announced the network's cancellation of the show in the March/April 1990 newsletter. Not even all twelve episodes would air. I also announced something that I knew would be unpopular. "It is almost impossible to save a cancelled show once; it *is* impossible to save it twice. At this point, the future of *Beauty and the Beast* is in the hands of Witt-Thomas. There are business and legal decisions that viewers cannot impact upon." Still, hard-core loyalists tried to campaign, but something was missing. I explained in the newsletter: "This time around, *Beauty and the Beast* lacks the support of the press. An important campaign element is missing."

While the hard-core fans were scathingly critical of my refusal to campaign again, many VQT members eloquently expressed their disappointment with the third season in the newsletter.

"I honestly tried to find the same qualities in the show when it returned. Sadly, I could not. I feel betrayed. The writers and producers caused their own downfall. The original series had joy, tenderness, feeling. I cannot in good faith support an effort to extend the run on another network," wrote Ronee Siegel of New York City for the March/April 1990 newsletter. Diane Bellino of Waterbury, Connecticut, wrote in the same issue, "CBS ruined something special for many of us. With Catherine dead, it is no longer the show we all took to our hearts. CBS removed hope from Vincent and replaced him with a bitter creature, for whom hope arises only when it is time to quote something." Maria Nott from Barberton, Ohio, wrote frankly in the same issue, "I'd prefer to forget that this season ever happened. I want to remember the love and the inspiration that *Beauty and the Beast* was in seasons past."

Rosemarie Salvatore of Bloomfield, New Jersey, declared, "All of the hope, the magic, the spirit that made it special was gone. I'm not a writer, and even I could think of a dozen ways in which the [departure] could have been handled better."

"I can't believe the writers could think that fans could accept such a painful and unsatisfying end to a romance that we were made to believe was unalterable. I would rather have seen the series end last season in a more uplifting and positive manner than to have witnessed the selling of its soul, at least in part, in a vain attempt to raise its ratings," declared Mary Carver of Spartanburg, South Carolina. Cindy Henderson of Bluefield, West Virginia asked in the same issue, "Did Witt-Thomas really think, really believe, that what they offered us would be acceptable?"

Perhaps the most scathing and unforgiving remark came from Mary Hester of Tryon, North Carolina:

> Of all the senseless and completely destructive changes that CBS forced upon *Beauty and the Beast* as the price of renewing it, the most difficult to understand, and the most abominable, was the deliberate destruction of the beautiful, romantic, inspiring love story, and the cruel and needless death of Catherine. Every effort should have been made to keep Linda Hamilton in the role. That failing, another actress should have been found to play the part of Catherine.

Ultimately, all fifty-six episodes, including three that never aired, were sold to cable's Family Channel for one year of airing. No new episodes were produced. The Family Channel acknowledged that the letters from *Beauty and the Beast* fans contributed to their interest in the show.

What viewers did for *Beauty and the Beast* cannot be discounted—the show came back and had another chance, if only for nine episodes. Viewers had a voice, and made a difference.

Quantum Leap

Quantum Leap was another show that earned and enjoyed a large and actively involved fan base, many of whom joined VQT to champion the program.

Starring Scott Bakula as time traveler/scientist Dr. Sam Beckett and created and executive produced by Don Bellisario, its appeal reached beyond the allure of Bakula, whose sensitive portrayal of Beckett captured the hearts and minds of millions of fans. The premise was that Beckett's time machine experiment went wrong and he was sent on a never-ending journey. Each week he leaped into someone else's body to help right a wrong. Bakula portrayed somebody new each week besides already being Sam Beckett: among the roles he played were a retarded man afflicted with Down's syndrome; a pregnant teenager; a woman enduring sexual harassment in the 1960s; and a black man in the South in the mid-1950s. *Quantum Leap* was, for a time, part of the reason Wednesday nights were "quality" nights on network TV. The other reasons were *China Beach* and *Wiseguy.*

Viewers appreciated that "every leap gave Sam, and by proxy, the viewer, the chance to see life from a different perspective, which is the first step toward tolerance and understanding."[50]

Fan Cynthia Shannon of St. Petersburg, Florida, for VQT's November 1990 newsletter wrote:

> It is not limited by genre, time period or tone. It has explored many elements of the human condition, from mainstreaming of mentally handicapped persons to women's liberation and sexual harassment to the plight of Native Americans to the heart-wrenching plight of the wife of an MIA. But it doesn't always limit itself to social issues. It also spotlights personal dilemmas and relationships. The show does all this while still entertaining the audience with humor and poignancy.

VQT's Cindy Thompson from Pittsburgh, Pennsylvania, believed that

> Scott Bakula's apparently absolute belief in the value of what he is doing contributes to the growing credibility of this fantasy that is taking on allegorical overtones. He is developing Sam Beckett into a person with whom we are comfortable having the power to change history. With his gentle ways and latter-day hippie love for mankind, we believe without question that he does indeed care for the people into whose lives he intrudes.

Fans united to share their enthusiasm, many of them through VQT. Several newsletters developed. One, "The Quantum Quarterly," was still going strong years after the show left the air.

In 1991 NBC decided to move *Leap* from its successful Wednesday night at 10:00 slot (have we heard this before?) where it had finished the season with an acceptable 10.6 rating and 19 share of the audience. When Bellisario learned the show would air on Fridays the next season, he conducted "a text-book campaign," enlisting the help of the already- organized fans and VQT.[51] It wasn't necessary to enlist us; we were already convinced. NBC was inundated with letters. As feared by Bellisario, the show slipped to an 8.3 rating and 15 share in the move to Friday (its average as of November 11, 1990). It lost approximately 3 million viewers.

NBC finally returned the show to Wednesdays as a result of the mail. An on-air ad by NBC showed an executive at his desk holding several letters in his hand. He says, "How dare they tell me what to do." He is then deluged from above with a shower of letters, and he shouts, "Okay, I moved it to a weeknight! You got what you wanted, now stop writing me!"

VQT members Elizabeth Wilson and Karen Hurst were among the three hundred fans honored by Bellisario at Universal Studios on February 25, 1991, with a special screening to express his appreciation. Bellisario was there, as was his wife and coexecutive producer, Deborah Pratt, and stars Scott Bakula and Dean Stockwell. That September, Bellisario was guest speaker at VQT's Quality Awards banquet.

NBC gave an early renewal notice to the series for the 1991–92 season. I announced in our May 1991 newsletter that an NBC prime-time marketing sheet directed to advertisers touted the resurgence of *Leap*'s ratings. NBC told their advertisers that Viewers for Quality Television endorsed *Leap,* and that it also headed our monthly roster of quality programs for March 1991. NBC had turned to VQT as an alternative source of viewer feedback for promotional purposes to help increase awareness for their quality shows. In my mind this is how it was supposed to work.

Of course, it couldn't last. In spring 1993 it was revealed that for *Leap* to be renewed again, NBC wanted to retool the format. *Quantum Leap* aficionado and VQT member Heidi Sanchez recalls that fans were told at the time that to keep the show on the air, Bellisario would have to make creative compromises.

At the second annual *Quantum Leap* convention in February 1993, Bellisario told "leapers" that NBC wanted to take the show in a "different direction."[52] It was a condition of being picked up. Bellisario told his fans that the network always wants him to make changes "because they always feel the show has peaked or interest is lost in it." He said they wanted to change it to make it better.[53] "Next year they want me to come up with something such as leaping him into the future permanently and sending somebody along with him [such as] a teenager." This got as far as a scripted but not filmed alternate ending to the series's last episode, but Bellisario told fans he would "rather see the show leave network TV than to let NBC ruin the show's premise."[54] Already, the theme song had been changed to a faster-paced number that most *Leap* fans hated. The production schedule had been cut from eight to seven days. There were leaps into, or around, real-life people such as Elvis Presley, Marilyn Monroe, and Dr. Ruth Westheimer. Previously, leaps involved only unknown people. Sanchez feels that this was a major change and that it was harmful, not helpful, to the show. The suggested new premise sounded like a perfectly logical thing for a network to do—and the sure end of the integrity of the show.

Fans wanted the show back as it was. They collected the money and placed an ad in *Variety;* they ran a coupon in *USA Today* that was to be mailed to NBC; and they held a rally outside NBC headquarters in Burbank. So many faxes were sent to NBC at one time they had to shut down their fax machines. More than a hundred calla lilies (a significant *Leap* flower) were sent to Warren Littlefield asking for the show's renewal. He thanked the fans, but in the end the show was canceled. Twenty-two weeks into the 1992–93 season, *Quantum* had an 8.6 rating, a 14 share, and ranked eightieth.

In paying tribute to *Quantum Leap* in our August 1993 newsletter, Genia Shipman from Studio City, California (now a television writer), remembered the following scene because it demonstrated what was best about *Leap:* the small, personal moments.

> The quintessential *Leap* for me will always be a moment from "The Leap Home, Part I." Sam, as himself at 16, sits on the porch swing with his sister Katie, playing the guitar and talking about the future from whence he came. She asks about the Beatles—are they still together in the future, what are they doing now? Then she asks about John Lennon. Sam tells her that "John is going to write my favorite song." He begins to play "Imagine" and Katie listens, skeptical at first. But as she listens, enraptured, she realizes that she's never heard that song before. Maybe Sam's telling the truth—maybe [her brother] Tom *is* going to die in Vietnam. As she lets out an agonized "no!" and falls into her mother's arms, sobbing, Al [the hologram who advises Sam] tells Sam he's not changing anything, he's only making things worse. In agony himself, Sam tearfully tells his family he made the whole time-travel story up.

In September 1994, *Leap* creator Don Bellisario told a VQT audience that Brandon Tartikoff had both saved and killed the show. "He was a double-edged sword for me. Brandon loved the show and because he loved it, he kept it on the air initially when it probably would have been taken off. But at the same time, he tried to have it perform in time slots that he felt he had to put it into that I totally disagreed with." Bellisario added, "Sometimes they support you and sometimes they don't at the same time."[55]

Jamie Greco of Washington, Pennsylvania, remembered *Quantum Leap* in VQT's July 1993 newsletter. "Sometimes a series is so [well done] that you look forward to its weekly arrival into your home. The characters, as illogical as it seems, feel like friends. The network exiles these friends forever when they cancel a show. When this happens, you don't just feel disappointed, you grieve. This is how I feel about *Quantum Leap*. Quality television is diminished with its loss."

A total of 12.5 million viewers were dismissed by NBC along with *Quantum Leap*.

China Beach

The campaign for the survival of *China Beach* began before it ever aired. Believing it was a show VQT would like, a Warner Bros. publicist sent me the pilot. I was immediately taken with it, and it was only a matter of time before the rest of VQT embraced the show. That first season, beginning in late March 1988, *China Beach* aired six episodes on ABC. It ranked between sixtieth and seventieth place for the next two seasons, while often winning its Wednesday time slot as part of a successful Wednesday lineup that also included *Wiseguy* on CBS and *Quantum Leap* on NBC.[56] ABC moved *Beach* to Monday in spring 1990 and VQT went into campaign mode.

TV critics came to the defense of the show. Marvin Kitman was one. He wrote on April 16, 1990,

> Tonight is the start of the Tet Offensive against *China Beach*, a sneak attack by the network aimed at its own program. Just when they were seeing the light at the end of the tunnel, *China Beach* has finally turned the corner—and run into a dead end. ABC wants to get out of *China Beach,* and a poor rating in a new time period is the perfect way to grease the skids. It will just prove to them how hopeless it is trying to get the public to watch quality TV.[57]

He added, "This has got to stop. There has to be a better way to deal with quality TV drama. The system is suicidal and destructive. It's time to end the killing fields for quality TV."[58]

VQT kept up the pressure all spring. Countless television journalists responded to my reasoned pleas and urged their readers to write to us for information on how to save *China Beach*. Viewers poured out their hearts to me in their letters of support for *Beach;* I printed some of them in our May/June 1990 newsletter.

"When a Golden Globe and Emmy-winning show becomes a pawn in the ratings game, it makes me wonder about the intelligence of the network programmers. I find [*China Beach*] to be thought-provoking, heart-wrenching and humorous, all without insulting my intelligence," wrote Mary Mitchell of Lansing, Michigan. Brett Griffin of Glendora, New Jersey, felt that "Dana Delany is one of a select few actors I would refer to as pure. By pure, I mean she seems to possess a natural ability to control, channel and express the spectrum of emotions needed to manipulate the viewer into actually experiencing what she is feeling." Janne Swearengen from Jackson, Mississippi, asked, "If it's cancelled, where will we go for quality?" "No one has ever called me or sent me a survey to see what I watch. Well, I watch *China Beach* and would like the privilege to continue to do so!" declared H. A. Bickert of Lansing, Michigan.

> Granted, the dark side of life and its experiences are exposed more frequently than in most current programming. Very often our reaction results in somber thought and reflection. We get a mature look at an event that still carries a lot of baggage for those of us who lived, fought, saw others die, and ultimately survived the experience. We hope that common sense and a realization that quality still counts for something will penetrate ABC's collective decision regarding the future of *China Beach*.

Thomas and Barbara Allen of Fredericksburg, Virginia, contributed those words to the cause of *China Beach*.

Beth Lawrence of East Lansing, Michigan, wrote, "We have allowed a whole generation to grow up knowing nothing about Vietnam. Please do not remove this extraordinarily well-written, insightful, humane program."

"*China Beach* is an accurate depiction of the pain and pathos experienced by the millions who served in Vietnam, and the millions more family members and loved ones who lived in anguish back in 'the world.' For that reason, it makes for both important and compelling television," wrote David Narsavage of Washington, D.C.

VQT member Peter Staley of Fairfield, Connecticut, sent this definitive statement to Robert Iger as a thank you for renewing *China Beach*. I printed it in our September/October 1990 newsletter.

> This weekly trip through the conscience of the most influential generation of this century keeps gnawing at me. Friends who fought in Vietnam say that their sleeping hours are filled with the scrambled visions of a place they will never forget. For these men and women for whom sleep is never restful, whose memories are all too clear after 20 years, the Vietnam War needs to be better understood by the rest of us. We need to join up, sign on and feel it the best we can. For me, *China Beach* is one of the most important ways I can accomplish this act of bonding. For an hour each week, *China Beach* lets me peer into the world of what might have been for me. And through that harsh, captivating, often-painful vision, I see fact and fiction brought to life. The gift that *China Beach* has given me is the chance to feel the horror of that war, and to relive that point on my own continuum, through the show's excellent ensemble. Will the world be better served if *China Beach* stays on the air? That's hardly the question. I do feel that there is a place for what the show has to say and the way that it says it. I know that this show never fails to reach me. It says something important about a particular part of the human spirit. I feel that *China Beach* still has some unfinished business to take care of.

Under enormous pressure, ABC renewed the show. Robert Iger reportedly told affiliate stations that Viewers for Quality Television had made it impossible for him to cancel the show. But he banished it to Saturdays, a little-watched night, against two NBC sitcom hits, *The Golden Girls* and *Empty Nest*. Predictably, ratings plunged. As of November 11, 1990, it was holding a 7.1 rating and 13 share. Wednesdays at 10:00 P.M. it had averaged an 11.5 rating and 21 share. Six million viewers were lost in the move.

John Sacret Young wrote me in June 1990 thanking me for VQT's efforts in helping get the show renewed. This brilliant, sensitive, talented man would call occasionally to talk about the show *and* about VQT. He believed in the potential of the organization and valued our Quality Awards.

Journalists applauded the renewal of the show. Rick DuBrow of the *Los*

Angeles Times wrote on May 22, 1990, "*China Beach* reportedly was a close call, but ABC has been under pressure to renew the series by Viewers for Quality Television, among other admirers."[59]

Jerry Krupnick gave VQT its due when he wrote, "At least the renewed *China Beach* vindicates all those Viewers for Quality Television efforts in that show's behalf. Certainly, their insistent campaign, aided by strong support from the critics, made some kind of impression on the network bigwigs."[60]

That December, *China Beach* was put on indefinite hiatus with seven episodes unaired, among them a two-hour finale set at the Vietnam War Memorial. John Sacret Young knew it was over, so he was able to wrap up the series with a special episode. The final episodes were burned off by ABC that summer. Ironically, because they aired during that time frame, the show and its cast were eligible for Emmy nominations the following season. Dana Delany took her second Emmy for a show that hadn't aired in more than a year, reminding the world and ABC of the glory that was *China Beach.*

The show had won a Golden Globe for best drama, two Emmys for Delany, a Humanitas and a Peabody Award, as well as seven Quality Awards from Viewers for Quality Television.

When asked by Pat Murphy at a Viewers for Quality Television conference panel discussion why he had moved *China Beach* from Wednesday to Saturday, Iger responded, "I don't know. My mom liked it too." When I asked him if there were a show on his network in the last five years that he now wished he had on his schedule, he answered, "*China Beach.* I think had we kept *China Beach* in that time period [Wednesday nights], it would have outperformed the shows that succeeded it."[61] However, defending his decision to cancel it, he added that the show's life in that time period long-term would have been short-lived. "I think we would have seen continued erosion of ratings in that show."[62] I thought that was a lame excuse.

Viewers were not resigned to the end of *China Beach.* They felt that ABC had mismanaged the show. They were angry. They were resentful. VQT's newsletter was a forum for them.

"*China Beach* is very real, and played close to the bone. For the network to abandon *China Beach* is to admit that they have lost all humanity and decency, and will allow ratings and money to always rule their actions. With that kind of indictment, who are they to unleash this money-grabbing garbage into our homes via the TV? And who are we to let them," wrote Robert Leigh of Hawaii. C. J. Bonfig of Havertown, Pennsylvania, lamented in our August/September 1991 newsletter that "it was a program that consistently touched the heart, tweaked the brain, chided the conscience, and still managed to see some humor in it all. The vision that this show possessed was unequaled and will surely be missed."

Journalists were not resigned, either. Robert Goldberg lamented the loss in December 1990 in the *Wall Street Journal*. "Never before on television has there been a show so unflinchingly somber, so unrelentingly devoted to death and pain as *China Beach*."[63] Goldberg wrote, "As a show, *China Beach* was never afraid to slap its viewers across the face: 'Some guy's telling you about his hometown one second, the next second you're scraping him off your sunglasses.' Yet perhaps because the program focused primarily on the women of war, it was a strangely appealing blend of hard and soft, of cold metal and warm shoulders." Goldberg ended the article, "This, then, is something of a eulogy for a sad and lovely show that was finally so dark that few could bear to watch it."[64]

At our 1991 Quality Awards banquet, John Sacret Young told a combined VQT and industry audience, "*China Beach* was about two wars, one in Vietnam and the other to keep the show on the air. And we lost both. In a certain way, the last year, when we knew we were doomed, we tried to take even more chances. There were so many stories to tell about Vietnam and they were so important. We couldn't tell all the stories, but we feel very lucky and proud that we told some. Our thanks to you."

Dana Delany, who had flown from Boston to Los Angeles the previous night just to attend our banquet, said, "I don't know why the show came into my life when it did, but it obviously had an enormous effect on me and has become a part of my subconscious. It will always be there. And you will always be there. I had to be here tonight. I just couldn't miss it, because this is really the end of *China Beach*, this is our last gathering. I feel like you are all responsible for the show staying on as long as it did."

China Beach was lost to viewers and to network television in what I called at the time "the May Massacre."[65] Also lost that spring 1991 were *Equal Justice, Shannon's Deal, Midnight Caller, WIOU, Guns of Paradise* (*Paradise* until CBS changed the title), *thirtysomething, Twin Peaks,* and *Gabriel's Fire.* In referring to VQT's June 1991 newsletter as "an edifying outlet for grassroots debate on TV's best," Matt Roush told his readers that "this [newsletter] issue was more a howl of pain."[66] Roush quoted a member from Florida who had written, "If we don't let them know there is an audience for quality, then we shouldn't complain at the garbage they give us."[67]

China Beach remains a sad reminder in the hearts of millions of viewers that all too often quality shows are prematurely canceled.

Ten million viewers were dismissed by ABC along with *China Beach*.

I'll Fly Away

Premiering in fall 1991 and telling the story of the Bedford and Harper families during the turbulent civil rights movement, *I'll Fly Away* was a fragile commodity from the beginning—so fragile that Warner Bros. publicist David Stapf screened it in advance for VQT members at our 1991 convention. The word "breathtaking" was gleaned from a VQT member's written comment after the screening. NBC used that, with my permission, to demonstrate immediately that discriminating viewers liked the show. The official endorsement followed. *I'll Fly Away* was named VQT's Best New Drama for the 1991–92 season, and topped our Viewer Survey for quality many times. Before it perished, VQT gave it four Quality Awards.

TV critics shouted its merits. Jonathan Storm called *I'll Fly Away* "network television's most engrossing series—a subtle, challenging and ultimately uplifting weekly dramatic event."[68]

Critic Susan Stewart offered that "it is not always easy to take. It offers few answers. It creeps along toward uncertain conclusions. Its premise means that many of its stories are about race," and that "politically, *Away* usually is more complicated than correct. Watching, you are simultaneously bored and transfixed."[69] Stewart explained *I'll Fly Away*'s slow pace in describing the unforgettable scene where Lilly tries to register to vote. "The scene unfolds in real time, not TV time."[70] Executive producer David Chase illuminated the moments with young Jon Aaron Bennett, who played the youngest Bedford child. "John Morgan gets more than the usual number of emotional beats. That's because, when you're six, it's your job to learn things."[71]

VQT members found it remarkable, too. "It's about ordinary moments played out against extraordinary times," wrote Nina Pan from Hastings-on-Hudson, New York, in VQT's February 1993 newsletter. "A child's innocent blunder, adolescent awkwardness, park bench gossip, family quarrels and intimate moments are as finely nuanced as the more explosive race riots, trials and demonstrations." Michael Smolinski from Grand Rapids, Michigan, said in the November/December 1991 issue, "Quiet, intelligent and subtle, the show steeps in our subconscious and builds realistically. Timely, important and extremely relevant." In the same issue, Mary Anne Montgomery of Bloomington, Indiana, wrote, "I treasure this multifaceted series [that is] so full of potential. I hope its network will protect and nurture it." Sharon Johns from Belmont, North Carolina, added, "[It's] one of those rare shows where you have to watch the faces as closely as you listen to the words." Patty Latham of Warren, Ohio, appreciated that "every character has an internal life and a personal dignity."

But by November 25, 1992, in its second season, only seven million viewers tuned in every week.[72] By December 1992, it ranked ninety-ninth,[73] the lowest-rated series on network television that season.[74]

Worried about the ratings and NBC's intentions, I issued a press release announcing VQT's first "Tune in to Quality" hour in February 1992. NBC had moved *I'll Fly Away* from Tuesday nights where competition was high to Friday nights where expectations (and viewers) would be lower. It would follow *Matlock* at 9 P.M. I wanted to draw attention to the new time slot. Many journalists ran the item, including *Electronic Media* on February 24.

The 1991–92 season saw VQT doing its heaviest campaigning yet. That May, *I'll Fly Away* was renewed along with *Brooklyn Bridge, Homefront, Reasonable Doubts, The Trials of Rosie O'Neill, Civil Wars, Life Goes On,* and *The Young Indiana Jones Chronicles.* As Jerry Krupnick said, "That would be seven out of eight for VQT, an incredible victory for those of us who still believe good television has a future."[75]

NBC Entertainment president Warren Littlefield seemed sincerely committed to *I'll Fly Away.* I published a June 9, 1992, letter from him in July's newsletter: "Thanks to you and VQT, we are able to present *Reasonable Doubts* and *I'll Fly Away* on NBC's fall schedule. I appreciate all you've done to give these wonderful shows the attention and viewers they deserve."

By November 1992, early in the show's second season, it was reported that NBC was ready to pull the plug. The network did not appear to be inclined to order episodes beyond the original thirteen, indicating an imminent cancellation. I prepared a major campaign, and on December 4, faxed an alert to journalists and Lorimar Television. That afternoon Warren Littlefield ordered three additional episodes, *after* having announced that production would stop. In one of the most savvy moves toward viewers ever by a network president, Littlefield called me the evening of December 4 to tell me personally that he had just ordered three more episodes. With four still unaired, it was assured that the show would run through the end of January. Besides episodes on December 11 and 18, there would be five hours of *uninterrupted,* well-publicized episodes every Friday in January. Littlefield confided to me that NBC had spent upwards of $50 million promoting the show. I asked him what the show had to do; he responded that "there has to be some growth." I didn't realize how much until Steve Hall reported on January 7, 1993, that Littlefield said that *I'll Fly Away* must increase its share (percent of audience) from a 12 to a 16.[76] I questioned to Hall how *any* show could jump from a 12 to a 16 share.[77]

I'll Fly Away also suffered from "undesirable" demographics. Its audience was not "broad" enough, meaning they did not represent enough age-groups. It attracted women over fifty-five and black viewers. It had to demonstrate not only an increase in ratings, but also a broader demographic range. The producers were told to shift some emphasis to teenagers in an attempt to lure younger viewers. So we saw a lot of young Bedford and his friends on motor-cycles. We criticized this, preferring the earlier focus on the Bedford and Harper families, not the Slocums. But the important thing was that *I'll Fly Away* was still on network television.

I'll Fly Away did not get the 16 share that January as deemed necessary by NBC; it averaged an 11 rating/13 share. David Chase, executive producer, said to Steve Hall on January 7, "I'm beginning to think America gets the TV it deserves. We've got an audience that doesn't read, that doesn't care about quality, that doesn't do a lot of things. You can't really blame the networks for programming junk, if those are the only shows people will watch."[78]

NBC's scheduling of the program must be considered when assessing why the show suffered a huge drop in ratings its second season. *I'll Fly Away* began the 1992–93 season on Fridays at 10 P.M. opposite *20/20*, where it had been slowly building an audience despite inappropriate and hindering lead-in shows (that were all canceled). For the November sweeps period, it was moved to 8 P.M. Fridays—with no advance notice—and after the print deadlines of all the TV listings magazines, including *TV Guide*. NBC's programming vice president, Preston Beckman, justified the action to TV critic Jonathan Storm. "We felt we had an obligation to our affiliates to provide them during the sweeps period with as strong a lead-in to the local news as we could."[79] I decried the action to Storm, telling him it left viewers baffled. A source at Lorimar told Storm the studio believed NBC had "panicked."[80] Beckman acknowledged that "the switch might have hurt ratings."[81] After sweeps ended, NBC returned the show to 10 P.M. But the damage had been done.

On February 8, 1993, TV critic Mike Duffy reported that NBC had received more than twenty thousand letters about *I'll Fly Away*. He claimed that it easily broke the record for the network's single-season fan mail.[82]

By this time, PBS was expressing interest in the show should NBC pass on it in May. Tom Shales reported in the *Washington Post* that the producers were interested, but skeptical of a financial agreement.[83] Shales added, "Dorothy Swanson thinks some public-minded company might be willing to underwrite such a project."[84]

The press blamed NBC for the failure of *I'll Fly Away*. But Warren Littlefield's courtesy in keeping me informed and explaining the situation, either directly or through his media-relations staff, made me more sympathetic to the network's efforts. Advertiser demand for the biggest bang for their buck helped kill *I'll Fly Away.*

New York Post TV critic David Bianculli wrote that "it's ironic, but if NBC cancels *I'll Fly Away,* a show that aims to teach by examining history, it'll be because the network failed to learn anything from its own history."[85] Its plight was announced even beyond the TV sections of newspapers. Dennis Byrne, a member of the *Chicago Sun-Times* editorial board, went to bat for the show on February 4, 1993. "It's more than just a show about living through the emerging civil rights movement. It's about growing up, loyalty, friendship, integrity, caring—without the usual dose of TV cynicism. It's important to write about it here, and not on the TV preview pages, because it is one of the few shows that makes people of us all, and thereby brings us all closer together."[86] He noted that the show had received a Peabody Award, two Humanitas Awards, many Emmy nominations, and "the award of excellence from Viewers for Quality Television."[87] He noted also that *Sun-Times* readers had picked it as TV's finest drama by wide margins. Byrne proclaimed that "this show is being axed because of the incompetence of the network," citing the many times *I'll Fly Away* had been moved and taken off the air, disrupting viewing habits. Byrne scolded the network for having the "brass to run an ad campaign warning viewers that if we didn't tune in, *I'll Fly Away* would be cancelled—as if it were our fault. Congratulations, you later told us, you did it, enough of you tuned in to keep it alive. To be killed, I guess, another day."[88]

Not every television journalist was sensitive to the cause of *I'll Fly Away*—or to VQT, for that matter. Michael McWilliams of the *Detroit News* described Viewers for Quality Television as "a national network of busybodies," and noted that the cancellation of both *Brooklyn Bridge* and *I'll Fly Away* "would be a merciful end to mediocrity. Neither show is very good."[89] I wondered why Mr. McWilliams was a TV critic if he did not recognize and appreciate good television.

By spring 1993, TV critics were declaring *I'll Fly Away* gone. A third coproduction partner would be necessary before it could proceed to PBS, and was being sought with no success.

I'll Fly Away did go out in a blaze of glory on PBS. On October 11, 1993, the two-hour *I'll Fly Away: Then and Now* wrapped up the show's plotlines. At the end, quotes were run showing what the show had meant to people. Most were from journalists, but one—from a VQT newsletter, by Michael Smolinski—was credited to Viewers for Quality Television. It felt wonderful to be linked in this indelible way to such a historical and noble television event.

Then, for thirty-seven weeks, PBS ran repeats of all episodes of the series for viewers to enjoy for the last time. It was a public service. This was one discarded quality show that did not "fade into oblivion."[90] Sam Waterston told *TV Guide*, "I think the noise that they [the viewers] made was heard by PBS and had a lot to do with its decision to pick up the show."[91]

Waterston also praised viewers in the *Los Angeles Times* that June. He told Rick DuBrow, "[The return] is a big vindication of viewer participation. Obviously the bottom line is money in all this. But the fact is that viewers who cared about it cared enough to take time out of their lives to fight for that. I think it's all because of the viewers. People should feel encouraged to participate more actively in what they care about on TV. I think the networks hear that, even when it doesn't work out."[92]

It was a bad spring for quality television. Pat Murphy, myself, and other VQT members were quoted about the losses in the *Los Angeles Times*. The article explored what it feels like when viewers lose characters to whom they have become attached.[93] Pat Murphy said,

> The networks should not dismiss the powerful connection between viewer and characters. When a viewer loves a show, attention stays focused, even when the commercial comes on. We pay attention because we've invested some emotion and some time. But when the connection gets broken, many people don't come back. Those cancellations are heartbreaks. Viewers aren't as willing to invest or get attached. [Networks] want us to be loyal to their shows and their products, but then after they hook us, they show no loyalty back.[94]

VQT member Rob Killian of West Jordan, Utah, paid final tribute to *I'll Fly Away* in our August 1993 newsletter. "It was a poignant look at ourselves—our beauty as a nation and as a people—and our hideousness—the ugliness of our hatred, our pride, our self-indulgence. Yet it offered a glimpse of hope and belief in a better tomorrow."

Nine million viewers were dismissed by NBC along with *I'll Fly Away*.

Homefront

Homefront lived on ABC from fall 1991 to spring 1993. Its primary strength and appeal was its nostalgia; ABC never capitalized on the show's charm. The network never realized what it had.

TV critics disagreed on what *Homefront* was—a quality drama or a "high-principled soap opera."[95] "Trash and class have never mingled so well," wrote Mike Duffy.[96] But it was more than that.

At first glance, *Homefront* could be mistaken for a prime-time soap opera. The storyline continued from week to week, but that is all it had in common with a soap opera. It was really a continuing story of generations in a small Ohio town in the post-war 1940s. It possessed a strong sense of history. It delved into relationships in families and among friends. The evolution of vital political issues was woven into the characters' daily lives. The real tragedy is, of all the series VQT fought for, of all the shows the networks canceled, *Homefront,* had it not been mishandled and then so carelessly discarded by ABC, could still be an interesting, informative, viable show today. The subject—the lives of soldiers and their families post–World War II—could have continued to evolve into the 1950s and 1960s, and be relevant in the 1990s and beyond. The subject matter was inexhaustible.

In his book *GenX TV,* Rob Owen declared that "*Homefront* was not a failure. It exemplified all the good things about television. Most of the time TV is a passive, sedentary experience that doesn't engage the viewer. *Homefront* introduced audiences to memorable, realistic characters and offered mini-history lessons, with each episode serving as a new chapter in a great novel. Despite its period setting, if the show had been handled more carefully by ABC management, *Homefront* could have been a Gen X hit in spite of itself."[97]

The twenty-four episodes that aired the first season did fairly well Wednesday nights at 10:00. *Homefront* was renewed in May as part of VQT's victory package. But only eighteen episodes were ordered, not enough to cover a full season, necessitating numerous reruns and preemptions—what John Engstrom called "always killers of viewer loyalty."[98]

Homefront was the choice of *TV Guide* readers in its 1992 Save Our Shows campaign, demonstrating its wide appeal.

Trish Elliott from Oakland, California, wrote of *Homefront* in VQT's January 1992 newsletter, "*Homefront* depicts our country during a specific time in history and brings that time and those events into its stories in a way that provides a living, breathing history lesson every Tuesday night." John Salada from Grosse Pointe Woods, Michigan, wrote in November 1992, "The fine threads that contribute to making a tapestry have been delicately interwoven to create a compelling drama." Kathleen Bergeron from Mojave, California, felt that "its characters feel like my parents' memories given life."

In December 1992 *Homefront* was placed on hiatus by ABC just before it would have enjoyed a run of seven consecutive first-run episodes in January, as ABC had promised producers Bernard Lechowick and Lynn Latham.

Latham provided statistics proving the show had experienced a steady climb in ratings during the four times it was allowed consecutive airings in the same time slot earlier in the season. It reached sixteenth place once, but it had (expectedly) slipped during reruns, preemptions, and time slot shifts. By the time it was placed on hiatus, it ranked 94th out of 109 shows.[99] Still, it reached seven million homes, "and that's a lot of viewers who may be outraged at the treatment of the show."[100] The show had not aired consecutively since October 1 and 8, disruptive if not disastrous for a continuing series. As Matt Roush argued in *USA Today* on December 7, "As a serialized ensemble piece, *Homefront* requires two critical elements: visibility and continuity. ABC gave it neither. Renewing it only to place it opposite *Cheers*, which shares much of the same young female viewership that carried *Homefront* through a shaky first year, ABC added insult to injury by pre-empting the show almost as often as it aired."[101]

I faxed a press alert, and again, thanks to journalists who believed in *Homefront*'s cause, began hearing from viewers. It seemed obvious to me that ABC would recognize the potential hit it had with the series. Punishing it for being on opposite *Cheers* seemed illogical. Having lost the viewers it so painstakingly built up, *Homefront* had to start over building an audience when it returned in the spring.

"Dear Abby" joined the crusade and ABC heard from her readers in droves. Bob Iger told the *Cincinnati Enquirer* that the network received twenty thousand letters in two weeks, and that viewer mail often helps him reaffirm his instincts.[102] Producer Lynn Marie Latham told critic John Kiesewetter, "Letters certainly tipped the scale in our favor."[103]

Homefront finally did return on Tuesday nights at 10:00 on March 9 with nine new episodes. The expectation was a 21 share, but it pulled "only" a 19. VQT kept fighting, because we felt that with this show we had a solid argument.

Despite an average 18 share and a loyal audience, *Homefront* was canceled. The campaign had been ongoing for two seasons. Heartfelt letters poured into ABC; television journalists wrote about it. We finally gave up, but not before encouraging viewers to write thank-you letters to Latham and Lechowick for all the pleasure they had given viewers.

Mimi Kennedy, who played Ruth Sloan with her usual flourish, felt that the erratic scheduling and constant preemptions sabotaged their efforts.[104] She told me in an interview that "we lost any vestiges of habitual viewing that we'd managed to hold onto despite three schedule shifts."[105] She theorized that *Homefront*'s treatment had been determined by financial decisions by ABC and that the recently changed syndication rules, where a network can reap the syndication money for a show if they own it, was not a golden goose for ABC, as *Homefront* was not under the new rule.[106] She questioned why the network would turn someone else's moneymaker into a hit when they could do the same for one of their own.

> The frustrating thing is that *Homefront* should be a growing hit. Maybe the networks got sick of seeing independent producers become rich, while the network got publicity and ratings and watched it all fade away when the show did. I still think the value of the nation uniting to watch particular TV shows with fervor, and discussing them over the phone afterwards or at the office the next day, is an important part of our national glue. Stories are important to a culture, and mass audiences aren't that easy to come by. It's sad to see the networks—one of our last meeting places where we can all get the same story on the same night—give up on a show with potential mass appeal, particularly one that addresses our history.

National glue. Whenever Mimi talks to me, writes to me, or E-mails me, I have a pen in my hand to catch this wordsmith's gems.

The *Homefront* campaign was an opportunity to speak out to the three networks about their self-destructive programming practices. John Engstrom of the *Seattle Post-Intelligencer* wrote in December that "Viewers for Quality Television denounced ABC's decision to pull *Homefront* from the schedule. VQT said the show hadn't been allowed to air enough original episodes this season. The group also complained that networks 'place their best programs in the worst time slots, depriving them of success.'"[107]

What were viewers feeling and saying? "I found the newsreel coverage in the polio episode fascinating as it recalled what that time was like," wrote VQT's Trish Elliott of Oakland, California, in the February 1993 newsletter. "Imagine what viewing it was like for those not yet born at the time. *Homefront* found a way to link the generations together that was important."

In my poll of TV critics that summer, I asked what they felt was the most unjust cancellation of the previous season. *Homefront* was the most mentioned, with Nancy Sweid of the *Nashville Banner* insisting, "It could have been a ratings contender." Joel Brown of the *Daily Southtown* in Chicago said, "Has strongest argument for having been screwed by schedule and pre-emptions." Tim Sosbe of the *Ft. Wayne Journal-Gazette* agreed, saying, "The numbers were okay and the show could have had broader appeal had the network handled it better." Lon Grahnke of the *Chicago Sun-Times* was more blunt: "ABC killed

Homefront through mishandling." Matt Roush of *USA Today* agreed, saying, "ABC blew it." In this poll I asked them to send a message to programmers. Almost to a person, TV critics echoed VQT members. Matt Roush told programmers to "attach less importance to the value of mass household ratings numbers in making programming decisions, or you will bland yourselves out of existence." Joel Brown echoed VQT: "Stop screwing with the schedule! Leave good shows in one place so viewers can find them." Greg Dawson of the *Orlando Sentinel* suggested they "aim higher." John Voorhees of the *Seattle Times* urged networks to "stop testing everything and let creators do their thing." John Kiesewetter told the networks, through VQT's newsletter, to "remember *Cheers* in 1982; let a well-written show alone; believe in it; don't bounce it all over the schedule, and you'll be happy in 18 months."

Homefront was also the most-mentioned unjust cancellation cited by VQT members in a similar poll.

VQT member Eleanor Closs of Rhinebeck, New York, said good-bye to *Homefront* in VQT's July 1993 newsletter. "I said goodbye to *Homefront* with great regret as they hurriedly tucked in all the loose ends. For those of us who lived through those post-war years, it was a memorably accurate trip down memory lane—the clothes, hair-dos, language, the mores, the unrecognized prejudices. Does anybody today realize the need to learn from the past?"

It was my privilege to award *Homefront* the Founder's Award for unheralded excellence the following September. When it was announced in the trades, the Lechowicks sent *me* flowers. I was astounded! I couldn't wait to meet them. They attended the Quality Awards banquet that year with Mimi Kennedy and Wendy Phillips who stood together clasping hands with tears in their eyes while the Lechowicks accepted the award. They all stay in touch with me to this day. It's gratifying when the people for whom you advocate not only appreciate it, but also return the regard.

Two years later at VQT's September 1994 Conference on Quality Television, cocreator Lynn Marie Latham expressed mixed feelings about ABC's treatment of the show. She told an audience of VQT members,

> We actually were very successful on Wednesday nights; we had a 20 share. We were growing. Our demographics were good, but they gave the time slot to *Civil Wars*. I wasn't angry with the network, but I knew if we were left alone, we would continue to build. So when [ABC] put a show in [that slot] that had already shown it had not been able to [deliver a 20 share], it broke my heart. But they said, "Oh, don't worry, you're against *Cheers*. All we want you to do is go in and double the

female demos in that spot." So we went in and we more than doubled the female demos. We did exactly what they wanted and got yanked off. *Matlock* was put in, which brought down the demos. But they had a higher overall share, so they could win sweeps. It was a heartbreak. But I was grateful to the network for even putting it on the air.[108]

In sharing the story of *Homefront*'s origin, Latham explained that she went to the network to sell a story about 1945, calling the show by that name. She envisioned changing the title in January every year, from *1945* to *1946* to *1947* and so on. She had not expected anyone to buy it. She went into the network meetings with stacks of books with little tags marking pages to show pictures from a given period. She showed the network executives the pictures and said, "Remember these pictures from this period?" And explained to them that where we are today really came to be after what happened when the men returned home. She told us it was like a history class. "I didn't expect to sell it. When we did, I was thrilled."[109]

Ted Harbert was challenged about his cancellation of *Homefront* at VQT's 1993 convention, on a panel discussion with other producers and executives. He said that although he took *Homefront* off the air when it was holding an 18 share, first on Tuesdays, then on Wednesdays, he assumed that the viewers who loved the show would follow it to Thursday. "[That] didn't really happen," he admitted. He explained further. "We kept it on for two years. I think that's patience." And he stated the "problem" as if that would justify the action:

> The 18 share is okay. It's right on that fence. The world's not going to come to an end with an 18 share. Where the world comes to an end is that you can't repeat that show. That is a serial drama that in repeat turns into an 11 share. All networks lose money off of a first-run program. The only place you have to make any money is off the repeat. And there's pretty good money there. So when you pay $900,000 a week for *Homefront,* that works great if you get an 18 share, and a 15 or 16 share in the repeat is fine. If it goes down to an 11, there's no way to even keep that on the summer schedule and that's what really kills it.

I followed through by asking, "So you expect more out of a serial show. It must do better because it will do worse in repeats? Is that what you're saying?" He affirmed that "our only chance at profit is in the repeat business. I'm stuck in a system that really only works with past successful programs." I guess when ABC presented *Homefront* they didn't know it was a serial? How enlightening. How discouraging. How ridiculous! We continued to learn.

I miss *Homefront* to this day. I was a World War II child whose father finally came home to stay when I was six. I remember my mother singing two great songs of that time, "The White Cliffs of Dover" and "Now Is the Hour." I remember the era that *Homefront* had depicted so vividly and brilliantly.

Eleven million viewers were dismissed by ABC along with *Homefront*.

Brooklyn Bridge

Brooklyn Bridge, Gary David Goldberg's affectionate, nostalgic look at his own multigenerational family in 1950s Brooklyn, premiered on CBS in fall 1991, and immediately scored on VQT's quality meter. The show's difficult time could be anticipated.

Marvin Kitman predicted its cancellation the day *Brooklyn Bridge* premiered on September 18, 1991.[110] "It was on the endangered species list at CBS as soon as the first couple of weeks of disappointing ratings came in."[111]

VQT members were articulate about the show they named Best New Comedy of the season. "Gary David Goldberg has crafted a series of remarkable sensitivity, nostalgia, and humor that possesses its own unique quality," wrote Sue Chapman of Johnson City, Tennessee, for VQT's October 1991 newsletter. "It is not necessary to have experienced the era to enjoy the program. Goldberg has given us one from the heart." Harry Noles of Los Angeles wrote in the November/December 1991 issue, "Like *Frank's Place*, it is a sitcom that isn't really a sitcom. Gary David Goldberg's memories of growing up in Brooklyn make us wish for a world like this today, where baseball and family are the most important things."

"I don't relate specifically to the events and slice-of-life incidents that have been depicted thus far," admitted Jane Marie Best of Rochester, New York, in the January 1992 newsletter, "but I can definitely recall the feelings they evoke. Regardless of our individual childhood experiences, the feelings stirred by this show are universal."

Because of its disappointing ratings, *Brooklyn Bridge* was iffy for renewal that spring. Its rating for the week of April 15, 1992, was a 9.0, ranking eightieth.

VQT's advocacy for the program was well known. In February 1992 I published a portion of a letter from Goldberg: "I want to offer very sincere and heartfelt thanks to you and your organization for all the recognition and support and positive energy you've sent our way. For a new show starting out, your group is a nurturing source. One we very much appreciate. And, one we turn to on those dark, low-ratings-ridden nights."

CBS tested *Brooklyn Bridge* on Mondays at 8:30 P.M. for two weeks in April 1992. Two weeks is not much of a tryout, and I've never thought that moving a show around to find an audience while the audience is trying to find the show is an effective strategy.

The viewers who loved it were passionate about it. I was told by a publicist that the amount of mail CBS was receiving for *Brooklyn Bridge* was second only in volume to that for *Northern Exposure*.

By spring 1992, CBS representatives were unofficially telling me the show "has a pulse" because viewers had not discovered it yet. It's not like they had sampled it and left; they had never been there. But now license fees became a problem. (A license fee is what the network pays a studio to produce a series.) CBS and Paramount could not agree on what it should cost to produce the show in a second season. CBS wanted to order thirteen episodes; Paramount did not want to do less than the full twenty-two. The studio wanted the network to demonstrate a commitment, or Paramount could not justify the investment. Twenty-two episodes were agreed upon, and *Brooklyn Bridge* was renewed. Jeff Sagansky had told John Kiesewetter the previous summer that he took his mail very seriously.[112]

When VQT members voted it Best Quality Comedy in 1992, Cheri Annau of Elgin, Illinois, gave her reason in the August/September 1992 newsletter. "How many shows can spend a half hour talking about the trade of a baseball player or what goes through the mind of a kid at the free throw line at a basketball game and make it interesting?"

"It doesn't rely on one-liners for laughs," added Frances Boyd of Terre Haute, Indiana. Ruthanna Amy of Bay View, Michigan, voted for it "because it is nostalgic and doesn't pretend to be anything else. It shows changes in the generations and pictures them so well." Susan Ivey in Palatka, Florida, liked that "it demands your attention; the reward is total enjoyment and involvement in the lives of these characters."

I called for VQT's second "Tune In to Quality" on November 7, 1992, on behalf of *Brooklyn Bridge*. Journalists latched onto my entreaty as an excuse to write about the show, among them Jerry Krupnick in Newark, Greg Dawson in Orlando, and Michele Greppi in New York.

Again I printed part of a letter from Goldberg: "I can't tell you how much all of us here at *Brooklyn Bridge* appreciate your efforts on our behalf. We have always tried to write 'up' to our audience, to respect our audience, and to challenge our audience. To have our best instincts validated by you and your group is at the same time gratifying, satisfying and humbling. We are in your debt."

CBS halted production in November 1992 with seven completed episodes yet to air. They called it "hiatus," but with production halted on what was a twenty-two-episode commitment, *Brooklyn Bridge* was clearly not destined for the CBS schedule. On November 14, the last time it aired before hiatus, 9.7 million viewers tuned in to the show, according to A. C. Nielsen, meaning that 39.5 million chose to watch something else.[113] It was ranked 93rd out of 106 shows.[114] The ax fell so swiftly that we—and journalists— were caught by surprise. I immediately began a VQT campaign to demand that CBS air the remaining seven episodes in a time slot where it would have a fair chance to draw viewers. I admitted to Peter Johnson of *USA Today* that all we wanted was for the seven remaining episodes to be aired in a consistent time slot. "Any weeknight, any time, as long as it stays in that slot for seven weeks in a row."[115] I promised that if the show did not increase its numbers under those circumstances, the network would not hear any further complaint from me. I wanted a hundred thousand fans to write in. Johnson asked, "Could it be that these nostalgia shows just don't work on network TV?"[116] I responded that I blamed the network, not the era.[117] Greg Dawson also wondered if the musical time slots were "the show's only, or even main, problem."[118] He posed what he admitted was an uncomfortable question: "Could it simply be that not enough Americans want to watch this program?"[119]

TV critics' responses to our campaign were overwhelming. As of December 2 I had responded to six thousand viewers. I needed TV critics to spread the word to rally these viewers, and they did: Tom Shales of the *Washington Post*; Peter Johnson and Jefferson Graham of *USA Today*; Rick DuBrow of the *Los Angeles Times*; Michele Greppi of the *New York Post*; Duane Dudek of the *Milwaukee Sentinel*; Mike Antonucci of the *San Jose Mercury News*; John Kiesewetter of the *Cincinnati Inquirer*; Alec Harvey of the *Birmingham News*; Bob Wisehart of the *Sacramento Bee*; Nancy Sweid of the *Nashville Banner*; *The Hollywood Reporter*; Steve Bornfeld of the *Albany Times Union*; Ruth Butler of the *Grand Rapids Press*; and Dusty Saunders of the *Rocky Mountain News*.

Journalists were outraged. Ruth Butler declared on November 29, "That one beacon of quality, of family fun and sentiment, has been cancelled."[120] Butler reminded her readers that CBS had placed the show on Saturday, the least-watched night of the week.[121]

But Sagansky defended his treatment of *Brooklyn Bridge*. He told Tom Shales in November that no matter how popular a lead-in the program had in its many time periods, it never held onto viewers in sufficient millions.[122] Shales termed the cancellation of *Brooklyn Bridge* "another sign that the commercial networks have surrendered their status as innovators and groundbreakers."[123] He accused all the networks of "programming the safest

mediocrities they can find" in their desperation to keep audiences from erod-
ing further.[124] In a final blast, Shales stated, "The networks forget why they
are networks and then sit around wondering, 'Where'd everybody go?'"[125]

Rick DuBrow was one of the TV critics to whom I suggested viewers vent
about *Brooklyn Bridge.* He reported the content of some of those letters in his
December 6, 1992, column.

> What is even more significant than the write-in campaign itself is the
> content and thrust of the letters, which are telling the networks that
> they are driving away many intelligent, selective, financially comfort-
> able viewers by failing to show them any respect. They are telling the
> networks that they are committing suicide by failing to at least give
> worthwhile borderline shows the time and opportunity to prove them-
> selves. And they are also telling the networks that they are painting
> themselves into a creative corner by catering more and more to the
> semi-literate audience, dragging TV's theory of lowest common
> denominator programming even lower. Many sophisticated viewers
> have come to the point where they simply don't give a damn whether
> the networks go under.[126]

Gary David Goldberg told Tom Shales on November 24, 1992, "It isn't
that every show has to be *Brooklyn Bridge* or *I'll Fly Away,* but some shows
should be. How can there be no room, no room for these shows? That's what
I think is really sad."[127]

Goldberg told Frances Katz of the *Boston Herald* that based on his mail,
"people feel they've really lost something. There's a sense of loss, outrage and
betrayal."[128]

Marvin Kitman proclaimed that *Brooklyn Bridge* "was the one show that
evoked a place-specific, time-specific nostalgia. There was reverence for a simpler time when people weren't afraid of each other. Admittedly, everybody's
memories of the '50s weren't the same as Goldberg's. To some, it seemed like
manipulated reality, the mellowness of a Brooklyn kid gone to seed in L.A."[129]
Kitman also revealed that Jeff Sagansky, the entertainment president who canceled the series, received a bonus for finishing first—as he had the year
before.[130] "There is nothing in his contract about being the poster boy of
VQT."[131] Kitman blamed viewers in the end. "Ultimately, the reason for the
failure of *Brooklyn Bridge* is TV viewers."[132]

Steve Bornfeld recalled some episodes that mixed gentle comedy with
pathos: Joel Grey as Cousin Jacob newly arrived from Europe after surviving

the Holocaust; Sophie's rebellious daughter announcing she's getting a divorce; Alan and his Irish girlfriend, Katie Monahan, introducing their families in a restaurant, set against the music from "West Side Story." Bornfeld called the episode "a beautiful snapshot in time of two families."[133] Taking back an earlier pronouncement that people were getting too worked up over television shows, Bornfeld now declared, "Some shows are worth the trouble."[134] He referred to me as "the indomitable Dorothy Swanson."[135] (I wouldn't say I felt indominatable, but I was not ready to concede defeat.) Quoting from my letter to TV critics, he told his readers that *Brooklyn Bridge* had "aired just three times in its regular time period [before] the baseball hiatus, then one more time before the decision was made."[136]

James Endrst of the *Hartford Courant* wrote on December 17, 1992, "Who's killing primetime television's quality shows, the networks or the viewers? The networks say it's the viewers—bombarded with options, remote control at the ready and impatient for entertainment. Viewers, especially those deeply attached to well-crafted programs that fall into the ratings margins, say it's the networks that are impatient, catering to the whims of the lowest common denominator."

I heard from Goldberg again in January; he wanted me to know that he had met with Sagansky and learned that he "was overwhelmed by and incredibly impressed with the quantity and quality of the letters he has received on *Brooklyn Bridge*." While Sagansky had been expecting a "firestorm" of criticism, he told Goldberg he had been unprepared for the "depth and feeling and emotion and concern expressed in the letters. He seemed genuinely impressed with what he had seen."[137] At this meeting, Sagansky promised Goldberg that the show would return to the air in a "good" time slot, either Saturday night after *Dr. Quinn, Medicine Woman* or Friday night after *Golden Girls* (now on CBS)—that it would air seven times uninterrupted and that "we would be a legitimate candidate for renewal next fall based on how well we did in our April try-out."[138] Goldberg credited me and "all the members of VQT" for securing a second chance for the show. "The campaign was wildly successful, resulting in an avalanche of emotional, well-written, articulate letters that clearly hit home and had an enormous impact on the people at CBS."[139] He thanked us again and ended, "I can't impress upon you enough how much it means to know you're out there and you care."[140]

Steve Bornfeld gave a "spit-soaked" salute to CBS in March for fulfilling only half of its promise: bringing back *Brooklyn Bridge* but minus network support. He reported that CBS had received about twenty-six thousand letters.[141] Bornfeld felt that while CBS would indeed air the seven episodes, the pledge to give it the support it deserved had been broken. "With its fate—a shot at renewal for next season—hanging in the balance, the former 8 P.M. Saturday show will return to Saturdays on April 10 at 9:30 P.M. PPPPHHHHTTTHHHH!"[142] Bornfeld was speaking my language.

Brooklyn Bridge returned to the CBS schedule on Saturday, April 10 at 9:30 P.M., instead of the hoped-for slot following *Dr. Quinn, Medicine Woman.* Goldberg told me that Sagansky finally told him that the reason the show was placed at 9:30 after a new, untried series instead of after *Dr. Quinn* was that "the falloff from *Dr. Quinn* to *Brooklyn Bridge* would be too great."[143] How could Sagansky know this? Goldberg felt this showed that CBS had no confidence in the show, and that that had been the problem all along. "They don't understand the show and what the potential might be."[144] *Brooklyn Bridge* was now lost to us, and there was absolutely nothing more that could be done about it. Twenty-six thousand letters had gone to CBS. Goldberg was bitter and spoke to every journalist who would listen.

After airing just three of the remaining seven episodes, CBS rescinded the promise altogether and pulled the show. It had won a Golden Globe, a Humanitas Prize, four Quality Awards, and was nominated for eight Emmys.

A CBS spokesperson told Katherine Phillips of the *Richmond-Times Dispatch,* "*Brooklyn Bridge* has been the focus of the 'most well thought-out and targeted letter-writing campaign I've ever seen.'"[145]

Its star, Marion Ross, told VQT members about the quality of the letters the show had received.[146] Goldberg gave each cast member a two-inch stack of them, bound in a book. Ross surmised from the letters that people were searching for quality on network television, and when they found it they treasured it. She admonished the networks, through our newsletter: "You cannot keep pandering. There's a tremendous appetite for junk, always has been; but there is also an appetite for quality, and we must not lower our standards."[147]

Matt Roush said on June 1, "[Dorothy Swanson] feels networks are too impatient and should lower their expectations for more challenging shows in today's climate of expanding choices."[148]

In remembering *Brooklyn Bridge* in VQT's July 1993 newsletter, Kathleen Bergeron of Mojave, California, wrote,

> I am not from a large, extended family and I am not Jewish. It is difficult for me to say, therefore, why it was that this sitcom, which detailed the daily trials and tribulations of a family that was all of the above, should have edged its way into my heart and taken up residence there permanently. *Brooklyn Bridge* always made me feel that family is

not something that is bound by those parameters. Family is rather a state of mind, a safe haven to look back upon and base one's life upon. This show was warm and had a way of making me laugh with tears in my eyes. In particular I remember the episode where the Jewish family and the Catholic family attempted to peacefully break bread together. Though the results were hilarious, it also brought home to me the reality that as different cultures and religions may seem on the outside, on the inside, they share far more values than they usually realize. Bless Gary David Goldberg for, even briefly, sharing the warmth and the caring he was lucky enough to grow up with, with all of us.[149]

Eight million viewers were dismissed by CBS with the cancellation of *Brooklyn Bridge*.

NYPD Blue

I was interviewed by *E!* at the end of our 1993 convention about the quality of *NYPD Blue* before its premiere. The stir about the show was already at fever pitch.

The Rev. Donald Wildmon's American Family Association (AFA) tried to sabotage the show through advertiser boycotts before it even aired in September 1993. Wildmon protested its "violence, brief nudity and use of coarse language."[150] Besides threatened boycotts of sponsors, the AFA dissuaded affiliates from carrying the show through fear tactics. The approach was marginally successful—fifty-seven affiliates refused to air the adult series its first season. That fell to nineteen the second season. A hit is a hit is a hit.

VQT rallied behind the show's gritty, adult quality immediately, giving it number 1 qualitative status in that season's first Viewer Survey. For the first time, ABC used these results in on-air and print ads. By November VQT had named *NYPD Blue* the season's "best new drama."

That spring, in anticipation of the summer buying season, Wildmon stepped up his media assault on *NYPD Blue* with full-page ads boycotting its sponsors. Even though it was by now in the top twenty and had been renewed for the 1994–95 season, I was offended by the expensive negative campaign and decided to publicly counter it. I faxed a press release to that effect to the nation's TV journalists, encouraging viewers of *NYPD Blue* to send letters of support to each of the show's advertisers. There was a valid concern that the program was not winning much support from mainstream advertisers. I wanted advertisers to know that there *was* a segment of the population that appreciated controversial programming.

This counterattack was widely publicized, as *NYPD Blue* was the current darling of journalists. Joe Mandese of *Ad Age* quoted me in April 1994: "We don't usually get involved in any kind of anti-boycott situations, but we felt viewers who are seeing all this advertising from the AFA should know that there is an alternative to this and that is to write a positive letter to the sponsors."[151] Mandese reported that Wildmon was "concentrating the group's entire $3 million annual media budget on targeting *NYPD*'s advertisers during the network up-front buying period this summer."[152] VQT's *entire* budget was less than $100,000 and had *no amount* set aside for advertising. Still, I wanted to rally viewers who felt strongly about what the AFA was doing, activities that to me amounted to creative censorship. The *Los Angeles Times* reported that I wanted to "stir up those complacent viewers who through their silence are allowing the Wildmons of this country to have their power."[153]

As a result of all the press, viewers from around the country wrote VQT to request the *NYPD Blue* sponsor list. Based on their letters, I trusted that they would be positive. From VQT's May 1993 newsletter:

> I accept [the violence in the program] as a real and unfortunate depiction of life in America. But I believe the series shows the senselessness of violent acts. I am neither titillated or offended by the language or nudity expressed, and I am sure this holds true for most level-headed, mature adults. Television needs more *NYPD Blue*–type programming, not less.
>
> My wife and I are regular church-going Christians and have never seen anything on any episode that offends us in any way.
>
> Without the publicity that was generated by [Donald Wildmon's] campaign, I would never have known of this terrific show. His type of condemnation is by far the finest commendation of this show's excellence, one that could not have been purchased at any price.

VQT members were likewise on the offensive. Lansing Bailey of Austin, Texas, wrote in January 1994, "What little violence there is is always in the context of the story, never gratuitous. The brief nudity is always tasteful. It doesn't particularly further the plot, but is a pleasant change from the gritty, stunning realism of the show." Nora Mandel of Forest Hills, New York, added in the same issue, "It actually assumes that viewers are adults. It deals with shades of gray and moral ambiguity; that's what makes for quality TV."

Viewers even sent me copies of their letters to sponsors, some of which I printed in the June 1994 issue: "At no time has this show offended us, although the way we live is nothing like the show's portrayal of that life. We believe *NYPD Blue* accurately depicts the criminal life in New York City, and should not be criticized for it."

> Please do not be influenced by the bigots criticizing the wonderful writing, good production, and superb acting. We believe many of the people writing in to object are prodded by the bigots and perhaps even financed by them. Many people like us, but without such prodding and financing, will not take the time or buy the stamps to do what we are doing, but there are undoubtedly thousands out there. Let us represent them in your thinking. We hope you continue sponsoring *NYPD Blue* without change.

In the same issue, we printed a reply from the Consumer Affairs Department of Warner-Lambert sent by a viewer. It was obvious that the company was being very careful.

> We thank you for your letter of support for *NYPD Blue*. Viewers and organizations bring an important voice to the issue of program content and your assessment of this programming is valued. Warner-Lambert believes that a diversity of types of entertainment and issues can be programmed on television. Our policy is basically to make evaluations on an episode by episode basis. We look to see that episodes of programs or movies are not excessive or too graphic. We recognize, however, that programming decisions are subjective and open to honest difference of opinion. Thanks for sharing your thoughts with us.

At some point during this campaign, a publicist for the show suggested that we should direct letters *not* to the sponsors who *were* advertising on *NYPD* but to the major network advertisers who were not. This seemed beyond what viewers would normally do, so I declined to take on that cause.

As Jefferson Graham said in *USA Today*, once "*NYPD Blue* began to click with viewers, Wildmon's newspaper ads decrying [the show] all but disappeared."[154]

NYPD Blue settled into success, brought about partly by curiosity aroused by so much negative campaigning and fear. Viewers discovered, as I had said on *E!*, that the only thing about *NYPD Blue* worth shouting about was the quality.

Homicide: Life on the Street

Homicide: Life on the Street, executive produced by *St. Elsewhere*'s Tom Fontana, triumphed over irregular scheduling by NBC. It premiered after the Super Bowl in 1993, and nine episodes were aired. But only four new episodes were made for the 1993–94 season.[155] Journalists and viewers confronted NBC and argued for its reinstatement. Curt Block, an NBC spokesperson, responded to David Zurawik of the *Baltimore Sun,* "*Homicide* is still under midseason consideration. That does not mean it's a midseason replacement. It means they still have to make a call on it."[156]

Whenever possible, usually through our poll results, I attempted to draw attention to this little-watched show. *Picket Fences* was on opposite it on CBS; I couldn't favor one show over the other. But steadily and consistently, VQT's admiration for *Homicide* just enhanced the critical acclaim.

Only when the four midseason episodes performed in the ratings in *L.A. Law*'s old time slot on Thursday night did NBC finally order a full season's worth of episodes for 1994–95.[157] Viewers for Quality Television, along with television journalists, trumpeted *Homicide* for its quality, and viewers finally discovered the show.

EZ Streets

EZ Streets was easily the most morally ambiguous quality drama ever offered on network television. CBS is to be commended for even attempting to interest an audience in such an intricate program. It was uncompromisingly, relentlessly bleak; deep, moody, haunting, tangled, risky, masterful, brilliant, complex, subtle, deeply disturbing,[158] and like a mini art film. And according to Sue Chapman, who echoed too many viewers, "needlessly complicated."[159]

There was hardly time for advocacy. CBS yanked it from the air after its first two outings in the same week in October 1996, on the same day VQT named it best new drama of the season.

Jeff Feindt of Dayton, New Jersey, admitted that there was "nothing easy about it. It's not only challenging, but rewarding. The plotting is multi-layered, but it's the characters that suck you in."[160] Monica Zullo of New York City found that "although this series demands a lot from its viewers, it rewards us with a level of complexity and intensity rarely encountered on TV."[161]

TV critic Marvin Kitman called it "a daring show" that explores "the gray area in life, the place between good and evil where heroes do questionable, or even bad, things and villains do good things. There are no smoking guns and neatly wrapped-up stories; instead, there are moral questions left unanswered. It leaves you with something to think about."[162] He declared it "the TV equivalent of lyric poetry."[163]

When asked about the complexity of the show at VQT's 1996 conference, creator Paul Haggis told us he wanted the audience to be able to understand it, but to also reach for it.[164] He said that although he didn't want to alienate viewers, he'd rather fail making people think and talk about it. He admitted that he "had a really good chance of failing at it. I wanted to do something that just terrified me, that I didn't know if I could succeed at. I always like to do something that I think I can fail at."

CBS made good on its promise to return *EZ Streets* to the air, but stopped short of a total "relaunch" by deciding not to rebroadcast the two-hour pilot. Fans correctly feared that new viewers would be unable to familiarize themselves with the complicated storyline without benefit of the pilot. Television journalists, themselves fans of the show, cooperated with CBS to interest new viewers by urging them to watch the show. Through CBS's Terri Corigliano, who had found another show to haunt her, VQT members held viewing parties in various cities across the country. Terri sent tapes of the pilot and first episode to the viewing party hosts so people could be brought up to date. *Entertainment Tonight* covered one of them, hosted by Nora Mandel in Forest Hills, New York. On March 3, *ET*'s Bob Goen stated that *EZ Street*'s return to the CBS schedule was mainly due to a campaign launched by VQT. Our Web site logo was prominently displayed. The publicity was everything CBS, journalists, and fans wanted.

Despite the exposure, millions turned away from the show with each new episode, and the audience decline escalated. On March 26 *EZ Streets* had an audience of 8.2 million with a 6.1 rating and an 11 share in its first half hour. During the second half hour, viewers dropped off to 7.5 million with a 5.6 rating. A similar, more devastating decline occurred the following week. The hour averaged an 8 share with a 4.6 rating and 5.8 million viewers.

After airing nine of the ten episodes that Universal had filmed, CBS pulled the plug for good on April 4, 1997, leaving viewers unfulfilled, unsatisfied, and angry. *EZ Streets* had plummeted to an 8 share by the April 2 episode. CBS would replace the final episode of one of television's greatest series with a *Walker, Texas Ranger* rerun, which earned an even worse rating.

This is where I parted company with CBS, having praised the network publicly in our April newsletter for bringing the show back. I understood the cancellation—no one really expected a renewal—but I shared the anger of the nearly six million who were still committed to this show. One more week, one more episode; what would it have cost? And did it matter when weighed against the goodwill of 6 million people? But as Terri Corigliano had told me, there is the plaintive wail of the viewer, and then there is the business of television. Would the two ever reconcile? Now I truly doubted it.

I was one of those 5.9 million viewers who reached every time I saw it. Reached to understand it, reached to remain with it, reached to overcome its darkness.

Five and one-half million viewers were dismissed by CBS along with the brilliant *EZ Streets*.

The Practice

David E. Kelley's much-awaited 1997 midseason offering, *The Practice*, did not disappoint. Starring Dylan McDermott as a dedicated and struggling defense attorney, with a strong supporting cast of likable characters, the show immediately garnered critical acclaim, drew passionate viewers, and disappointed network executives because it failed to maintain the numbers of the hit whose time slot it was borrowing (*NYPD Blue*). Still, the show had good numbers. *NYPD Blue* ranked number 12 while *The Practice* hovered around number 40, allowing NBC's *Dateline* to take over first place in that time slot. Yet *The Practice* gained, not lost, audience. On April 1, 1997, it could boast 11.9 million viewers with an 8.9 rating and a 16 share, ranking number 34. Television journalists lamented ABC's lack of commitment to the show. Alan Bash of *USA Today* wrote on April 8 that ABC was giving *The Practice* a "last chance to woo audiences. Where it will land next, or when, is anybody's guess."[165] ABC Entertainment president Jamie Tarses admitted to Bash that ABC couldn't find room for the remaining seven episodes before the season ended in late May, but "the shows might run during the summer."[166] Couldn't find room? How many quality shows did ABC have? By VQT's count, there were four, and three were going to be canceled!

Critic Marvin Kitman took on ABC over *The Practice* in his April 7 column, questioning, "Now that they have hooked us on what is the best of the midseason replacement shows so far, what are they going to do with it? After the thrill of victory in finding a good show, will we now have to go through the agony and despair of wondering where it went?"[167] He howled along with viewers into the wilderness, "I'm getting tired of how the networks handle new programs these days. They expect everybody to keep up with all their hot news flashes about scheduling changes usually buried in TV notes columns. They need to put electronic ankle bracelets on shows so we can keep track of them."[168] Kitman called it "the best socially class-conscious law show since *Shannon's Deal* (short-sightedly cancelled by NBC in 1990)."[169] He even suggested that *The Practice* had another problem besides ratings: people were angry at it for replacing *NYPD Blue*.[170]

Livid, and acting on behalf of the VQT members who had endorsed it and the hundreds of viewers who had written me about the show, I placed an ad in *Daily Variety* on April 25, 1997, "Open Letter to Jamie Tarses." I had not spent VQT funds to advocate just one specific show in the twelve years of VQT's existence. But I thought, if not now, when? I was incredulous that a new show, in just six episodes, was expected to measure up to the performance of the hit it had replaced. A quality show by a proven quality master would be thrown away because the network had no place to put it? Then why was it ordered in the first place? Why was it shown at all? Why were these original characters allowed to shine and endear themselves to the audience? This was now *more* than the plaintive wail of the viewer conflicting with the business of television. It was *good business* for television to retain interesting shows! This struck me as a *terrible* business decision. It was time to take a stand against the mass destruction of creative genius on network television. The president of David E. Kelley Productions, Jeffrey Kramer, and the "quality master" himself were stunned and appreciative. Kramer told me in a phone call that because the support had been unsolicited, it was especially meaningful.

Simultaneously with my open letter, fans of the show launched an Internet campaign that resulted in thousands of ABC Web site hits on behalf of the show. There is no way of gauging how much influence viewers might have had on ABC's decision to renew *The Practice* for the 1997–98 season. But it was given a Sunday night at 10:00 time slot, the one that had killed *Relativity* the previous season. ABC gave the show time to build an audience there, and it won the Emmy for Outstanding Dramatic Series in September 1998. It also won the Quality Award from Viewers for Quality Television that year and the next, and David Kelley with his wife, Michelle Pfeiffer, and cast members Dylan McDermott, Steve Harris, and Kelli Williams attended the 1998 Quality Awards banquet.

Conclusion

One discouraging conclusion can be reached as a result of VQT's myriad campaigns, only a few of which were mentioned in this chapter. Networks and advertisers care only about the bottom line: how much money they can make. Even if a show is making money, if another show comes along that might

Viewers for Quality Television, Inc.

P.O. Box 195, Fairfax Station, VA 22039 • 703/425-0075

Open Letter to Jamie Tarses
President, ABC Entertainment

April 23, 1997

Dear Ms. Tarses,

Viewers for Quality Television, which appreciates and advocates compelling, challenging television, implores you to keep *The Practice* on your schedule.

I have read that *The Practice* disappointed you because it did not measure up to the performance of the hit whose time slot it had borrowed. No new show should carry the burden of those expectations. Still, *The Practice* managed to place 33rd in the 18-49 demographics—with an audience that was angry because it displaced *NYPD Blue!*

11.9 million viewers told you on April 4 that they want to see this refreshing, absorbing program continue. With audience erosion a concern, I ask you not to discard a quality show by a proven quality master (David E. Kelley). Viewers are incredulous that ABC cannot find room for the remaining seven episodes before this season ends.

For 13 years I have been balancing the plaintive wail of the viewer (my job) and the business of television (your job). Viewers' pleas for *The Practice* are loud and clear and eloquent. The business of television must be re-evaluated if audience erosion is to be curbed. *The Practice* is a good place to start.

Sincerely,

Dorothy Swanson, President and Founder
Viewers for Quality Television, Inc.

make more, the first show is canceled. Audience is regarded as product and easily discarded. Add them up:

Frank's Place:	20 million viewers
Brooklyn Bridge:	8 million viewers
I'll Fly Away:	9 million viewers
Homefront:	11 million viewers
Quantum Leap:	12.5 million viewers
China Beach:	10 million viewers
EZ Streets:	5.8 million viewers

I count 76.3 million viewers with just those shows alone. If only half of this audience did not return to network television after each show was thrown away, that's still a loss of 38 million "products." It is time for network executives and advertisers to look in the mirror and at their own practices when asking "Where have all the viewers gone?" They have been dismissed with a cavalier lack of regard. The networks canceled them.

UNCONVENTIONAL IDEAS

IF you have ever planned a wedding or a large party for very important guests, you have some idea of the logistics involved and stress associated with producing VQT's annual convention. For weddings, there are established protocol, guidebooks, and consultants available. Our convention was uncharted territory, and proved to be a crash course in planning and public relations.

Why did we undertake something of such magnitude year after year? VQT's annual convention (renamed Conference on Quality Television in 1995) presented the unique opportunity to bring face-to-face the people who made television shows and the people who watched them. At these annual gatherings most of our contact with television producers, executives, and actors occurred.

A year after our first convention in McLean, Virginia, in 1987, we decided to hold it in Los Angeles. Thanks to the influx of members from the *Parade* magazine article, we could now afford an L.A. event. We booked the Beverly Garland Hotel in North Hollywood. It had everything we needed—an intimate, beautiful setting, a state-of-the-art theater, and a brand-new ballroom—or so we thought. The ballroom was still under construction! Nobody had told us it would not be ready as promised. Once on site, we gazed in horror at a shell of a room that was sawdust and cement, knowing we had a formal banquet to host in a few days.

Assurances were given that the room would be ready. Beverly Garland herself supervised the sweeping and painting, and even pitched in. The carpet was not installed in time, so Garland decorated the room to look like a Western sound stage.

To prepare for the various speakers and the awards banquet, Pat Murphy and I met in my suite with a small staff of inexperienced but enthusiastic volunteers. We were convinced, along with our convention co-coordinators, that we had everything covered down to the last detail. So when we unveiled our plan to the staff—that the teenage son of one of our convention planners would meet celebrity cars and direct the guests inside (after all, he was young and energetic)—Nancy Lutzow (who happened to be Joan Baez's assistant) interrupted and quietly suggested that this procedure was not going to work.

So with Nancy's help, a more detailed and complete course of action was invented, one day before the convention was to start. We appointed designated greeters and escorts. We had handlers in place to move people. Nancy's ideas have been fine-tuned over the years, but her expertise helped us prepare for the experience of a lifetime.

That first Quality Awards banquet was pure terror. I found myself hostess of an event that was totally outside my experience. Guests for the night were Quality Award winners Sharon Gless, Barney Rosenzweig, Linda Bloodworth-Thomason and Harry Thomason, Ron Perlman, Tim Reid, Daphne Maxwell Reid, Stephen Cannell, Ray Sharkey, Larry Drake, Susan Ruttan, and Julia Duffy.

When I found myself at the microphone on the platform that was our stage and looked out at the ballroom full of industry guests and VQT members, I froze. There was no TelePrompTer (nor has there ever been). My speech was slow and deliberate, my mouth dry. Pat called for water. Sharon Gless told me later that her manager, Monique James, had whispered to her, "Dorothy is paralyzed." And I was. Over the years, with experience, it gradually became easier. The panic, though still present, became less severe. We keep water at the lectern now. Not until 1998 did I overcome my drymouth. Still, every year I wonder, Why am I doing this? and, Should I ever do it again? The answer is simple: the convention is our only opportunity to bring in the funds (through our auction) necessary to survive one more year. And once we started the Quality Award, we needed to continue it.

Paul Reiser told the assembled group at our 1994 Quality Awards banquet: "I wish I knew as a kid that if you were at home watching a show and you liked it, you could call them to a hotel and they would show up. I had no idea that you could do that. It's just a phenomenal interaction here. 'We like your show, come on down, we'll give you a 'Q', have roast beef, go home.'"

Well, sort of. Paul's humorous perception that it was that simple was understandable. Who would think that if you hold a viewers' convention, industry executives and actors will attend? Common sense dictates that such a gathering is not feasible. But it worked for VQT, from the very first convention in Virginia 1987. In that first year, Linda Ellerbee and Ray Gandolf came from New York, Harry Thomason and Bill Allen came from Los Angeles, and television journalist Matt Roush of *USA Today* was a guest speaker who stayed the whole weekend. *Entertainment Tonight* came to feature it. Over the next ten years, numerous producers, network executives, and actors came because they were appreciative of our support and interest.

But you don't just call them up, offer them roast beef and a "Q" and they come. The process is arduous and complicated and involves many layers of representatives, mainly publicists, some cooperative and some not. In fact, with only a few notable exceptions, personal publicists became the bane of my existence.

If stars, producers, or executives are to attend our events, their first choice, of course, is to come to receive an award. They *might* participate in a panel discussion. To come just to meet VQT members and mingle informally is not a popular choice; they must be offered an event worth their time or one that will benefit them in some way. This is understandable.

Why did they come to us? What motivated them?

I'm sure some of the reasons had to do with politeness, regard, and even self-promotion. The *Los Angeles Daily News*'s Diana Lundin asked some of our guests at our 1990 Meet 'n' Greet why they were there. Sharon Gless told her: "These are old friends. Dorothy Swanson has done a great deal for us and for other shows. It has tremendous impact. She has been a very loyal friend to us and we look forward to it [the convention]."[1]

Barney Rosenzweig told Lundin he was the founding father of VQT. "They sometimes give me credit, they sometimes don't, but I am a proponent of people being involved."[2] He added, "I'm interested in their opinion. I think they can be a force."[3]

Delta Burke told Lundin she was there because "I think these people are great. They kept [*Designing Women*] on the air, they have integrity, and they're wonderfully supportive. And if people support you, you want to be there for them."[4]

Ed Bark of the *Dallas Morning News* also solicited some basis for attendance when he covered the 1989 convention. Linda Bloodworth-Thomason told him at the Meet 'n' Greet that "we always come, but actually, what's so hard about coming and hearing yourself complimented all night? These are hard-nosed, critical people who know every line you've written and have studied every show you've done."[5]

Dixie Carter added, "Viewers for Quality Television saved *Designing Women*, so I'm here to thank them for that. I give them complete credit for the fact that our show is still on the air."[6]

Paradise creator David Jacobs, who also created *Dallas* and *Knots Landing* and was an executive producer of *Homefront,* also attended the 1989 Meet 'n' Greet. He brought cast members from *Paradise.* Jacobs told Bark why he was there. "VQT was accurate in both its praise and criticism of *Paradise*. An organization that defines itself as dedicated to the improvement of this medium deserves the same recognition from me as I get from them. It's good manners."[7]

In 1995, during a New Series panel discussion, Patricia Wettig told us why she had come. "It's fascinating for me to be here, because in all the work I've done in television, this is the very first one that I've done with viewers. It's always critics or press or network; it's never the people that are actually watching the television show."[8]

Frasier executive producer Peter Casey had occasion to explain his reason for attending the 1996 Quality Awards banquet to VQT member Gerry Ashley. Just as the conference that year was getting under way, Kelsey Grammer crashed his car and subsequently entered the Betty Ford Clinic. Kim Conant, the Paramount publicist for *Frasier,* was on the phone with me daily as their plans changed and then changed again. The producers were in turmoil over whether to come; they did not want to speak to the press at this sensitive time. I assured Kim that together we would be able to keep journalists and entertainment newsmagazines away from Peter Casey, John Mahoney, and the group of producers who planned to attend. With Conant's able assistance, we did indeed keep everybody associated with *Frasier* protected from *Entertainment Tonight, Extra,* and *E!,* all of whom wanted to interview Casey. I did not score any points with those newsmagazines, but I kept my promise to Conant. She had told me that the only reason they came was their regard for VQT.

No one knows why Sherry Stringfield attended that same Quality Awards banquet in 1996. Just a few weeks later she announced she was leaving *ER* and Los Angeles. She arrived alone, was gracious and friendly, and stayed for a while afterward signing autographs, posing for pictures, and talking to people. She told her VQT escort, David Masterman, that she hated L.A. and the whole celebrity trip. Perhaps it was her private good-bye to Hollywood.

In 1989, at our second Los Angeles convention, all three network entertainment presidents—Robert Iger (ABC), Kim LeMasters (CBS), and Brandon Tartikoff (NBC)—agreed to meet with us for a panel discussion, the first time network executives would hold a dialogue with viewers. What did I think I was doing? Now that I had them, I had to prepare intelligent questions. I asked David Masterman to comoderate the panel. He is an attorney and used to public speaking. I was a teacher, unused to addressing more than thirty people over the age of twelve.

We formulated our questions and were ready. They all arrived early at the Beverly Garland Hotel. A problem with the sound system delayed the start of the discussion. One of the presidents suggested we begin without microphones. Tension mounted. Finally we were under way. David and I look nervous and stiff in the photos. I don't think either of us displayed a spontaneous moment.

Ed Bark, covering the three-day event for the *Dallas Morning News*, found our questions "deferential."[9] I suppose they were. We were afraid to offend. Yet, I feel I made a valid, if somewhat naïve point, when I asked about the feasibility of setting aside a ratings-free, quality hour of prime-time programming where extraordinary shows could thrive and be protected. LeMasters responded that such a move would be a "blue sky" approach to an aggressive broadcast market. Tartikoff said that the problem with the concept was that it suggested that the network was not trying to present a quality hour anywhere else. I still think it's a good idea.

Iger made a valuable suggestion: "All interests would be better served if viewers indicated their support for various quality programs by writing to advertisers who are pressured by the attempts at coercion by certain special interest groups that are trying to superimpose their own realms of power as a particular hamper on creativity." As I reacquaint myself with this bit of advice ten years later, I realize how crucial it is for viewers to encourage advertisers to commit to quality shows, no matter how "controversial" they might be.

The presidents diplomatically said encouraging things to the press afterward. LeMasters told Ed Bark he found the meeting "collaborative."[10] Tartikoff told him, "I think they were sophisticated questions from a non-industry audience," and stated, perhaps criticized, that it was a more "gentle" session than he might have anticipated.[11] I admitted to Bark that I was disappointed in myself.

My performance, as well as David Masterman's, improved in 1991 when they returned—Iger for ABC, Warren Littlefield for NBC, Jeff Sagansky for CBS, and Peter Chernin for Fox. Still, *Variety's* Brian Lowry found the questions "conciliatory rather than confrontational."[12] But we grilled Iger about *China Beach* (see "Growing Campaigns"), Littlefield about *Shannon's Deal* ("I just didn't know where else I could put it on where it would succeed"), and Sagansky about *Rosie O'Neill* ("Last week it got a 17 share; we're really pleased with the performance so far").

Three of the four network entertainment presidents returned for a panel discussion in 1997 to discuss network erosion. I wanted to confront them with all the reasons why I felt viewers were watching increasingly less of their programming. Four out of four had been my goal, but Jamie Tarses, at the time the beleaguered ABC entertainment president, bowed out the day before to attend a meeting in New York. Present were Peter Roth of Fox, Warren Littlefield of NBC, and Leslie Moonves of CBS. Audience erosion was now a big concern. Network executives were blaming everyone and everything but themselves for viewer defection. In fact, two of the three (Littlefield and Moonves) were in denial that there even was a problem. Warren Littlefield declared that "what's truly amazing is that in the last thirty years the number of channel choices in the average home has increased eightfold, and yet we've retained more than 50 percent of the audience that we had thirty years ago. That's a pretty remarkable retention story, not erosion story." Only Peter Roth seemed to recognize the problem and even take some responsibility for it. He stated during the discussion, "No more erosion can take place, Dorothy. Not a share point more. I've been watching this for seventeen years; I've watched the cumulative share total point go down from 90 to where we are right now. We have got to change the way we do business." Reflecting the opinions of his counterparts, Moonves even challenged critics' contention that quality was declining: "I think right now that pound for pound, show for show, there is more great television than there has been in any other decade since television has been in existence . . . so I wouldn't say that the quality is declining."

Although nothing was resolved during this panel discussion, the third time VQT hosted the network presidents, this time I confronted and challenged.

From 1988 to 1995, I enlisted a guest speaker for our Quality Awards banquet. Over the years, we had the pleasure of hearing Barney Rosenzweig, Stephen Cannell, Gary David Goldberg, Don Bellisario, Steven Bochco, Barbara Corday, Leslie Moonves, Dean Valentine, and John Romano.

My favorite statement is from Stephen Cannell in 1989. He spoke directly to VQT and summed us up: "The thing that makes this group so wonderful is that you talk to us; you tell us what you think. You don't boycott us, you don't threaten our sponsors, you don't attack us. You simply look at the product that we put on the air and you make a decision as to what you think is valuable. And then you call us all together and you tell us. For me, VQT has really been a chance to re-establish my acquaintance with the audience."

Another favorite statement is from Steven Bochco in 1990. He also directed his message to VQT members:

I think there's an underlying message in your letters that those of us who write and produce TV shows should pay attention to, and that is that television gives focus to people's outrage and sense of powerlessness. You can switch the channel with the flick of a finger and make a statement, which overnight translates into ratings, that in turn determines what shows live and what shows die. Or, as you become more and more frustrated and less passive, you begin to do the unthinkable—you stop watching network TV altogether. On the one hand, this has a good effect of causing networks to be more adventurous in their programming, but on the other hand, has the bad effect of making them skittish about committing to less traditional fare when the audience is so quick on the trigger. So where does this leave all of you, the viewers? Are you faced with more quality shows than ever before? The sad fact is, no, you're not. The talent pool, relatively speaking, is finite. So as that pool of talent spreads over a wider TV landscape, it actually gets thinner. And so the catch-22 is that while there's more to choose from, there may actually be less that's worthy of watching. And the few shows that can be defined as quality programming are often prematurely rejected by an audience not willing to sit still long enough to get used to something different when there's so much out there to choose from. Audiences are under no obligation to watch something just because it's different or because it's perceived as quality. TV isn't medicine—you've got to like it or you're not going to swallow it.

He seemed to be addressing the networks when he said, "What's the point of taking risks if you're not prepared to give it the time that it needs? *Hill Street Blues* didn't become a hit until its second season and after it won eight Emmys." Bochco ended: "You as a group are already doing more than your share. I can only urge you to keep up your good work, and I promise you I'll do my darnedest to keep up mine."

Our first fund-raising auction was at the 1988 convention. Thanks to the generosity of Carole Smith, who was auctioneer for our first four conventions (after which Pat Murphy assumed this task with her usual charm and good humor), we auctioned many keepsakes from *Cagney & Lacey,* which had just ended its network run. Among the numerous items she gave us were some of Chris Cagney's clothing (blazers, jackets, coats, and hats), as well as her wallet, business cards, and identification. These items alone brought thousands of dollars into VQT's coffers. A Day on the Set of *Beauty and the Beast* brought a $4,400 donation; the next year it went for $2,200, both amazing amounts. The auction that first year probably brought in about $20,000, which allowed us to expand our work. By 1998, the total was down to less than $10,000, a disastrous figure for VQT's fiscal stability.

The success of our auctions is vital to our organizational financial sur-vival. VQT's yearly conference is how we make money to stay in business. For the auctions to be successful, we need generous donations of memorabilia and collectors' items from the shows we support. Sounds reasonable and log-ical—but it isn't to the TV industry to whom we appeal. Except for Carole Smith, with both *Cagney & Lacey* and *Rosie O'Neill,* asking for auction items was a formidable task. Many charities seek donations from the television industry. VQT is now just one of them. Unless the producer is a big supporter of VQT, my carefully constructed letter of request gets passed down to the designated charity handler, and is treated matter-of-factly like all the others. As the years go by, less and less of value is set aside for VQT. Some producers and studio and network publicists have us in mind throughout the year and set aside memorabilia for us. Publicists Diann Shaw of Carsey-Werner and Neil Schubert of Universal are always generous and plan ahead for us. Paul Gen-dreau, when he was publicist for Fox, always came through. One year he donated Fox Mulder's wallet and ID from *The X-Files.* (David Duchovny was given a replacement.) Bernard Lechowick and Lynn Marie Latham were always generous, donating memorabilia from *Homefront* years after it was can-celed, making the items even more valuable. Mimi Kennedy let us auction her Warner Bros. *Homefront* parking pass, and years later donated her own (not yet worn) *Dharma & Greg* T-shirt and an autographed script from the show. Dana Delany gave us the U.S. Army shirt off her back as well as Colleen McMurphy's flight jacket. She also had special McMurphy dog tags made up, identical to the one she wore. Peter MacNicol sent a *Chicago Hope* hospital pillowcase autographed by the cast after his VQT escort, Kim Hehe, answered his rare question at a Quality Awards banquet, "What can we do for you?" *Everybody Loves Raymond* producer Philip Rosenthal, remembering our advo-cacy for his struggling quality show in 1997, always gave a rare gift—the use of somebody's name in a script. He also donated, in 1998 alone, a day with *Everybody Loves Raymond,* T-shirts, baseball caps, and autographed cast pho-tos. Others who were particularly generous included Tom Fontana and Henry Bromell from *Homicide;* Harriet Margulies, a production assistant on *Quantum Leap;* Mark Tinker, executive producer of *NYPD Blue;* and Jennifer Freeland, a publicist for Steven Bochco Productions.

Some just didn't understand or didn't care. Others had short memories. John Wells, a producer on *China Beach,* had attended at least one Quality Awards banquet with executive producer John Sacret Young. He can be seen in photographs on the stage along with other *China Beach* producers as John Sacret Young accepts the "Q." Wells took many of the *China Beach* producers and writers with him to his smash hit, *ER*. The first year I requested memorabilia, I was sent the pilot script autographed by Michael Crichton. The second year I received an identical script along with a letter from a staff person that the policy of *ER* was to contribute to a given charity only every other year, but that they would break that rule in our case this one time. I was to expect nothing the next year. Undaunted and bold, I wrote directly to John Wells expressing my dismay, reminding him of our history. The staff person who had written the first curt letter called to say they would send something else—a hospital scrub top autographed by George Clooney. The letter accompanying the scrub top expressed the hope that this would help us meet our financial goals. I am grateful to John Wells for participating in a 1995 panel discussion with Mark Tinker (*NYPD Blue*) and other distinguished producers. But I never got the impression from Wells that he understood or cared how much he could have helped VQT by donating additional items, things he might have considered junk. I've seen the things lying around in producers' offices—not that we have any right to any of it—but it is the one way producers of the shows we advocate can help us stay alive. Too many do not, and this ultimately will spell the end of VQT's financial viability.

The most popular item has always been a Day on the Set, which amounted to a day-long chaperoned visit by a VQT member and sometimes a guest. *Northern Exposure* granted this for several years before it became enormously popular. *The X-Files* allowed visits its first two years. Other shows that generously gave us Days on the Set or walk-ons include *Beauty and the Beast, Designing Women, China Beach, The Trials of Rosie O'Neill, Picket Fences, Murphy Brown, Dr. Quinn, Medicine Woman, Tour of Duty, Sisters, Star Trek: TNG, Homicide, Law & Order, The Practice, Ally McBeal,* and *Everybody Loves Raymond*.

I don't remember where the idea came from to auction seats at the Quality Award winners' tables, but it was brilliant. In 1989, ten seats at Ron Perlman's table totaled $2,400. Only Scott Bakula would top that several years later. The award winners who allowed us to seat them at a table of VQT members greatly contributed to our auction. Nowhere else do viewers get to dine with television stars; and nowhere else are stars and producers asked to do so.

In 1998 Steve Harris, VQT's Best Supporting Actor in a Quality Drama (*The Practice*), learned from a VQT member at his table that his character, Eugene Young, was a role model. Lisa Sharp teaches middle school in the Watts district of Los Angeles, and told him. Upon accepting his Quality Award, Steve shared this with the assembled guests in the ballroom. He told the audience he was going to visit Lisa's school and meet these kids. (And he did.) Once in a while, somewhere, it is important that the Steve Harrises meet the Lisa Sharps.

This policy of seating viewers with award winners was tested in 1994 when both Paul Reiser (Best Actor in a Quality Comedy) and Helen Hunt (Best Actress in a Quality Comedy) attended to accept "Q"'s for their roles in *Mad About You*. Although I had explained earlier in letters and over the phone to their personal publicists how the evening would proceed, both actors expected to sit together. And it was a reasonable expectation. I had to explain to them why they were not at the same table. They were side-by-side at adjacent tables, however, and when it came time for the awards to be presented, both Paul and Helen positioned their chairs next to each other. That year I decided to seat winners from the same show together so they would feel more comfortable.

Those of us who have attended have some amazing memories of our conferences.

At one of the Quality Awards banquets, VQT members sitting at thirteen-year-old Fred Savage's table reported later that when served his dinner, a half chicken on the bone with the wing standing straight up, he asked his mother, "What am I supposed to do with this?" His mother cut his meat for him. Other VQTers at the table said they were tempted to ask her to do the same for them.

Candice Bergen never came to an awards banquet, although she won three years in a row. However, she wrote several letters of thanks that we read at the banquet. If they cannot attend, we always appreciate it when the winners respond or send their thanks by videotape.

Regina Taylor did neither the two years she stood us up. Taylor won the "Q" award for best actress in *I'll Fly Away*. Both years she accepted the invitation to be there. Each time we auctioned seats at her table. The first year, she said she was bringing one guest. The table was set and the meals had been counted. Without explanation, she was a no-show. The following year Taylor was committed for two extra guests. The table was set again, the meal count submitted. The VQT members at her table sat uneasily as the banquet began without her. It soon became apparent that she was again a no-show. This time we had paid for three meals that never got served. We couldn't believe it. Barbara Hall, the *I'll Fly Away* producer who was there for the second year to accept the Quality Award for best drama, told me she was appalled that Taylor had done this again.

Beth Sullivan, who had created *Rosie O'Neill* by writing the first episode and others that first season, had been working night and day to bring *Dr. Quinn, Medicine Woman* to the air in 1992. She took time to drive the distance from the Paramount Ranch where the show filmed to our convention hotel in North Hollywood so she could introduce the show to us. Beth stood at the lectern in the Beverly Garland theater, nearly dead on her feet, and told VQT members how and why she conceived the show, what it meant to her, and where she wanted to take it. We could feel her exhaustion and passion as she spoke. She wanted to stay while the two-hour pilot was shown, but Pat Murphy and Beth's coproducer, Tim Johnson, persuaded her to leave and get some rest. We promised to report VQT reaction to her later.

The year we held our convention at the Universal Hilton and Towers, 1991, Ken Wahl appeared on a panel discussion with Jill Eikenberry, Neil Patrick Harris, David Clennon, and Robert Picardo. Two of our volunteers, Mark McClelland and Ken Nielsen, were standing outside holding signs to direct our guests to a VIP parking area. Nielsen stood in a driveway near the street, McClelland in the parking lot. Suddenly, Mark heard the unmistakable roar of a Harley Davidson and turned to see Wahl speeding toward him apparently unconcerned about where he was supposed to park. Mark told us later he decided that Wahl could park wherever he wanted. Obviously, mine are not the only stories.

Pat and I experienced a moment of terror (within the terror of the actual awards banquet, of course) during the 1994 Quality Awards banquet. Before we present each award, we show a clip of the performance on a large screen TV. We have been very fortunate that this has always gone smoothly. Until this time. I had just read praises of Helen Hunt's performance when I noticed volunteer Don Chapman step out from behind the curtained audiovisual setup and motion to Pat. She went to him, then returned to the microphone. I stepped back to let her handle whatever disaster had occurred. With incredible poise and humor, Pat explained to Helen, eyes locked on hers, that our machine had just eaten her tape, so we had none to show. Pat improvised what the scene would have been, prompting VQT members in the audience to recite the lines from the lost scene with her. A gracious Helen Hunt accepted her award.

Ray Walston belongs in a category all by himself. Never have we encountered anyone more difficult. He was more ornery than Judge Bone, for whose portrayal he won VQT's Best Recurring Player award in 1993.

After I notified all the award winners, a publicist for *Picket Fences* asked me to call Walston because he had some concerns. Walston told me he wanted to attend, but that he had some physical problems that included an intense sensitivity to flashbulbs. He asked that there be no flash photos taken of him. I assured him that I would notify all VQT members not to take pictures of him. He asked if any photographers would be outside. I explained that if there were, I did not have the authority to ban them, but that he could be brought inside immediately.

Mark McClelland and Ken Nielsen, this time manning an elevator down a long corridor from the entrance to the Hollyood Roosevelt Hotel, say they heard his booming voice complaining all the way down the hall. Apparently, there had been photographers outside with flashbulbs. I knew there were problems when I spotted him wearing dark glasses. His VQT escort, Jeanne Levy, was a big fan of his, and was nervous. She lost her bearings and inadvertently took Walston the long way along the mezzanine to the ballroom. She overheard him say to his daughter, who had accompanied him that evening, "I will not go anywhere else with that woman; she's so stupid." He apologized later when Jeanne told him how much she had always admired him and that his words had hurt.

The most chaotic and hectic moment of each conference for me comes as I try to line up the award winners in specific order so they can be brought into the ballroom and introduced as they enter. While I was doing this, Jeanne Levy approached Pat and me with word that Walston wanted to see "Mrs. Thompson." That would be me. He came charging at us, livid because I had promised him "no flashbulbs." Pat and I could not deal with him at that moment. He would either line up with the others or he would not (I believe he did not). Finally, somehow, he was seated at his table with his daughter and some very anxious VQT members who had bid to sit with him. Walston grew even more upset because there were flashbulbs inside the ballroom. I had completely misunderstood—I did not know that his requirement was that there be *no* flashbulbs on the *premises*. Had I known, I would have advised him not to come.

During my opening remarks to the 250 people present, with Pat on the stage with me, Jeanne Levy approached and stood beside the stage waiting for us to finish so she could talk to us. I thought, What now? "Mr. Walston is cold," Levy whispered, and asked us to go to him. He stood and showed us that he was sitting in a draft. The Blossom Room of the Hollywood Roosevelt has an elusive cold spot. Legend has it that it is some kind of ghostly celebrity "presence." You guessed it—Walston was in it. He wanted us to either physically pick up his table and move it to another part of the room or put him at another table. Both were impossible to do, and we tried to explain as he literally walked us both around the room telling us where it was drafty and where it was acceptable. All this while the 249 other people were dining. Walston seemed oblivious to the fact that there was anybody else in the room to consider besides him.

Pat offered to get Walston his "Q" immediately so he could leave, saying she understood if he could not stay. But he angrily said he would not leave now. He wanted to go first, though. I explained that the guest speaker goes first, then Jerry Seinfeld, who could only stay a short time. Then it could be Walston's turn.

Of course, the show must go on, and, trooper that he is, Walston accepted his award with one of the most heartfelt and beautiful—and long—acceptance speeches ever. On our videotape he can barely be seen, though, as we had to instruct those taping the event to turn off the spotlight. The audience applauded enthusiastically after his terrific speech, oblivious to all the commotion and stress he had caused. Walston took his award, walked directly past Pat and me, and left.

Jerry Seinfeld was our "drive-by" award that year. At the height of his show's success, and we believe as a result of some good words from Richard Lewis on VQT's behalf, Seinfeld came to get his "Q" in 1993. He had a prior commitment, so it was necessary for me to pinpoint almost to the minute when he could accept his award. Once he arrived, the murmur "Jerry is here" spread throughout the ballroom to the stage. There he was, sitting where he was supposed to be, at his table full of eager VQTers. They had been told when bidding for those seats that they might have him for an hour or for five minutes, or he might not even sit down at all. They were thrilled with their fifteen minutes with Seinfeld. And we appreciated him making the effort to stop by in the middle of other commitments.

John Ritter was a panelist along with Tim and Daphne Maxwell Reid in 1989. Tim and Daphne were running late because of unexpected traffic. Ritter arrived early and went right to the dais and tapped his microphone to see if it was on. My alert staff hit the "on" switch. I joined him at the table as he began a private entertainment session for his audience. He wanted to share with us a business proposition he had just received in the mail. For the next twenty minutes, he did a hilarious off-the-cuff monologue about an infomercial solicitation called "Encore," a male impotence product. He read us their letter and explained how someone as manly as himself would never need this product. He had the audience weak from laughing as he carried on about "Encore." When the Reids arrived, they were brought into the room to waves of audience laughter. As soon as they sat down, Ritter brought them up to speed. This was a totally spontaneous moment from a gifted and funny actor; those present will never forget this unscripted and unexpected show.

Scott Bakula demonstrated his support for VQT by attending four Quality Award banquets out of five awards won, in 1990, 1991, 1992, and 1993. His presence attracted many *Quantum Leap* fans, who were also great supporters of VQT and its goals, although most of them dropped out of VQT once *Leap* was off the air. Seats auctioned at his table brought thousands of dollars to VQT each year that he attended. These seats tended to sell for about $1,000 each. This may sound extravagant. But imagine it. You have this favorite TV show and favorite TV star and the organization to which you belong gives the star an award—and the star shows up. You have an opportunity to spend an evening dining and talking with your favorite actor. You know he is amiable and in other ways a magnificent dinner guest. So, instead of a vacation that might last a week, you decide to spend that money for one evening's entertainment. You have paid for a once-in-a-lifetime memory.

But in 1992 at the Beverly Garland Hotel, one avid *Leap*/Bakula fan went too far. I started receiving phone messages from her about the same time that diligent *Leap* fans began to warn me about her. I had already determined, from her messages and her tone, that her agenda was Scott and that her devotion was excessive. She wanted to attend the banquet to take photos of him. That kind of message was always a red flag to me. Through the *Leap* network of fans, I learned that this woman was a Bakula stalker, and that she intended to intrude upon the event. We had a description of her and a fan provided a photo. I informed my immediate volunteer staff as well as our convention liaison at the hotel. I was preoccupied with other guests, but learned afterward what a good job these people did.

Once the stalker was spotted, she was invited to sit on a bench outside the ballroom and was immediately surrounded by VQT staff headed by David Masterman. They prevented her from following Scott into the ballroom. We also had hired additional hotel security. One guard stayed with the fan and the other stood just inside the ballroom door near Bakula's table. Scott was completely unaware of the turmoil. That was the goal.

Although the incident was serious and potentially dangerous—and certainly treated so—it was still funny to envision our VQT volunteers following this woman around the bushes and alerting one another with walkie-talkies. Nothing in their pursuit of quality television had ever prepared our volunteers for this type of adventure.

Bakula, usually accompanied by publicist Jay Schwartz, was always the last to leave the banquet, making sure that every VQT member who wanted to meet him and have their photo taken with him had that opportunity. One year I had to ask him to leave because the hotel staff needed to close the room. He always took the time to demonstrate his appreciation of his fans.

Richard Lewis has been an enthusiastic supporter of VQT since the organization campaigned for *Anything But Love*. He understood that his presence at our conference, along with that of other industry people, was important to its success. Because of scheduling conflicts, the only event he could attend was our Sunday farewell brunch. Richard arrived just as everyone was finishing their meal. He had been up most of the night at a comedy club and had not had much sleep.

We thought he might go to the podium, say a few words, and leave. Not Richard. He said he wanted to meet and thank every single person there. So he went to each table, to each person, and said something individually to them. He made jokes, he gestured as only Richard can, and he drank all the orange juice at every table—all twenty of them. He was a hilarious wave of comedic energy. When he got to the last person at the last table, he turned to the group, gave a big wave, and fell to the floor in a mock faint. He gave his all, and continues to stay in touch with Pat and me. He is one of the real ones.

In 1996 both Christine Baranski (*Cybill*) and Stanley Tucci (*Murder One*) canceled out of the Quality Awards banquet the day before, making that year the least attended of Q award winners in our history. We were particularly appreciative that year of the ones who made the effort: Warren Littlefield of NBC, Sherry Stringfield of *ER*, Barbara Bosson (accompanied by Steven Bochco) of *Murder One*, Bonnie Hunt from *Bonnie*, Amy Aquino from *Picket Fences*, Dennis Franz from *NYPD Blue*, Tom Fontana and Henry Bromell representing *Homicide*, and Peter Casey representing *Frasier*. Tucci's publicist later claimed his Q; Baranski's claimed hers several years later. But neither ever said thank you to VQT.

Bonnie Hunt brought her entire cast from her canceled *The Bonnie Hunt Show* to the Quality Awards banquet in 1996. I awarded Bonnie the Founder's Award for her sweet, funny, short-lived show. VQT can only pay for the meals for the award winner and one guest; the winner must buy tickets for any additional guests so VQT's costs can be kept down. Bonnie never questioned this, and purchased twelve additional tickets. She wanted her cast to share the only award either of her brilliant TV series ever received.

John Cullum made a special trip from Washington state where *Northern Exposure* filmed to receive his "Q" in 1992. I never had to deal with a publicist or send additional information. He committed to the event on his own and attended with his customary charm and graciousness.

Kathy Baker called me after hearing she won her first "Q" for *Picket Fences*. Afterward she wrote me a lovely thank-you note, and wanted me to be sure to thank VQT member Mark McClelland for taking such "good care" of her. She also called the next year after the nominations were announced. Baker attended both years. Her genuine warmth and gentle personality made her one of our favorite guests.

Noah Wyle became a nonfavorite in 1997 when neither he nor his personal publicist, Eddie Michaels, ever responded about his Best Supporting Actor Quality Award (in *ER*). My phone calls were not returned, my faxes ignored, even a request for a photo and bio for my Quality Awards banquet booklet went unanswered. (I used the sparse studio bio and a studio publicity still.)

Gloria Reuben, two-time Quality Award winner for her role as Jeanie Boulet in *ER,* was a real puzzler. Attending the Quality Awards banquet in 1998 (along with two *ER* producers—the show won Best Quality Drama that year), she dismissed us the following year without so much as a response. Even with repeated inquiries, Gloria's personal publicist, Robin Baum of Huvane, Baum, Halls Public Relations, never gave us an answer. She would have been in good company had she attended in 1998—David E. Kelley, Michelle Pfeiffer, Dennis Franz, Dylan McDermott, Steve Harris, and other cast members from *The Practice;* Calista Flockhart and fellow cast members from *Ally McBeal;* Fox Broadcasting executives; and Doris Roberts from *Everybody Loves Raymond.*

The Noah Wyles, the Regina Taylors, and the Gloria Reubens discourage me. I feel that we cannot continue to give Quality Awards if they won't come to accept them. I would say that this lack of response and lack of regard by a few diminishes the award in the eyes of future winners—but for a comment from Neely Swanson, business manager for David E. Kelley Productions. She attended in 1998 as a guest of her boss and was impressed at who *was* there. She told me, "Do you realize that David doesn't go to *anything?*" She suggested that those who do not come (Gillian Anderson, Gloria Reuben, and John Larroquette that year) don't "get it" and do not deserve a second thought.

John Sacret Young's belief in and contribution to VQT is the most visible and lasting. He called me one day in 1991 after the winners of our Quality Award had been announced and *China Beach* had won for the second time. He said that this award was "right up there" with the Humanitas and Peabody Awards. And he told me that it should be more than a printed plaque; it should be a real "Q." He asked my permission to commission an artist to create it—and to pay for the creation. I was flabbergasted. Nobody in the industry had ever cared this much. After looking over several of the artist's drawings, John and I agreed on a design: a simple gold Q with Plexiglas in its center on a green marble base. We talked of giving it several different names, but I stayed with "Q." This has been our secret. Only Dana Delany knew. It is time now to credit John Sacret Young with the creation of VQT's "Q" Award. It came about as a result of his admiration for and belief in Viewers for Quality Television.

There are more highlights to share.

In 1991 a large group of VQT members attended a taping of the Thomasons' CBS series *Evening Shade*. The taping kicked off our conference that year. The Thomasons had other special guests that night besides VQT: Bill Clinton (then governor or Arkansas) and Hillary Clinton. Linda was excited and very focused on them. This event occurred just before Clinton announced his presidential candidacy. Pat met both Bill and Hillary, but I did not take the opportunity.

Among our most interesting events are the New Series panel discussions, which began in 1995. Here we learned the arduous and often frustrating process that is involved in bringing a show to the airwaves. Numerous producers told us tales of network intrusion in the creative process. Only the powerful producers, such as Steven Bochco and David E. Kelley, can stave off network interference in their creative vision. Mark Tinker, who ran *NYPD Blue* for Bochco, told a VQT audience during a 1995 panel discussion that Bochco has a special relationship with the networks. He can say, "This is what I'm going to do," and do it. He said that since he'd worked for Bochco, he didn't think they had ever lost a battle that was a reasonable issue, and that he got the ABC executives to agree to a list of words. "It's like the seven dirty words you can't say on radio. He agreed to ten words that you can say on TV. Success will bring a remarkable amount of freedom."[13]

John Wells (*ER*) had problems with NBC at first, but once the show became a hit, the disagreements ended. "Almost all the people I've had to deal with at the network are really good people and quite literate and intelligent. They're just in an unfortunate job," he said.[14]

A favorite remark about network executives came from James Widdoes (*Dave's World, Brother's Keeper*). He said, of the networks' tendency to intrude upon creative vision, "These are temporary people making permanent decisions."[15] Stephen Collins added to that during an actors' panel in 1997 when he explained that "there are a lot of people in television who have to prove that they have a reason to hold the job they have. So if a network development person, who is the liaison between the producers and the network, comes in, he or she wants to show everybody that there is a reason why they got this job. So they want to fix things that aren't broken. Or just fix things for the sake of fixing them."

Why don't the networks leave the creative people alone? I asked a panel of producers at the 1995 panel discussion. Mark Tinker replied, "They're paying the money. They're buying the car. So they say they want this option or that option. So it's their prerogative, but at a certain point you have to say, 'Hey, you hired me to build the car, [so] let me build the car, and I'll put it in your garage.'"

Deborah Joy Levine, guest on our New Series panel in 1995, had created, and for a while executive produced, ABC's *Lois & Clark: The New Adventures of Superman.* She told me a fascinating story to point up just how ludicrous some network suggestions can be. When presenting *Lois & Clark* to ABC executives, she was asked about the character of Superman, "Can he carry a gun?" It reminded me of the much-told story of an NBC executive asking the creator of *Reasonable Doubts* if the Marlee Matlin character would be deaf all season.

When creating *Lois & Clark,* Levine was told she could take the story in any direction she wanted.[16] So she did. However, she had nothing but aggravation from the network because "I wanted [Lois Lane] to be the lead and to be strong; I didn't care that he was a superhero—to the point that I was off the show."[17] Levine said the criticism from the network centered on the fact that "for 50 years people have been buying Superman comic books, so why is Lois Lane bossing him around?" Levine lamented to us that "[the networks] have other priorities that are important to them that clash with what the executive producer or the creative people want to do."[18]

Brett Butler told us at a 1994 panel discussion that the network wanted her character to smile more. "I said, 'Why? I'm mad in the scene.' They said, 'But you have this great smile, it's like a light that goes on.' I said, 'If I don't stop smiling, it's like a light that never goes off.'"

Panels with producers and actors were always interesting and informative. Jeff Melvoin (who took over *Northern Exposure* and *Picket Fences* late into their network lives and was blamed by many critics for the loss of quality of both) said something that few of us comprehended at the panel discussion of producers in September 1995. Until I saw it in print after it had been transcribed, I thought I had misunderstood. It revealed how he perceived his audience. "[The networks] think that the audience tells you what they should be watching. They don't understand that it's our job to tell the audience what they should be watching." Had I grasped the full meaning of the statement at the time, I would have challenged it. Now I realize that Melvoin meant that those who make TV shows are smarter than those for whom the TV shows are made—exactly the misconception Linda Ellerbee is talking about in her foreword to this book.

At the same panel, Amy Lippman (*Party of Five*) said what we all knew, that people watch dramas because they can relate to them. She praised VQT for its role in the survival of her show. "Being called a quality show by your organization from the start is largely responsible for us being on the air."

Lippman explained to us that the idea for the series was not that of herself and writing partner Christopher Keyser. Fox went to them and asked if they would be interested in doing a show about a teenage family. They thought about it and came back with a very different show from the one Fox had originally thought they wanted, which Lippman assumed was "kids on their own, parties, drinking. What they got back was a script that dealt with the difficulty of losing a parent."[19]

Chris Keyser then told us how *Party of Five* had a different problem than *ER* or *NYPD Blue,* because "we're a story about a family. Dramatic things happen all the time to cops and doctors. You can believe that every single day it's life or death. It's hard to believe that with a family. When you start to make that happen, you get melodrama."[20] Which is what eventually happened to *Party of Five.*

At our 1994 conference, producers Beth Sullivan (*Dr. Quinn, Medicine Woman*), David Lee (*Frasier*), Tom Fontana (*St. Elsewhere, Homicide*), Lynn Marie Latham (*Homefront*), and Chris Carter (*The X-Files*) appeared on a panel together. Fontana explained the difficulty of trying to produce quality week after week. "I think that every once in a while you get a really great episode. But I pray every week that I get ten seconds out of an hour that I'm proud of." David Lee agreed. "The rule of thumb is if you're doing 24 episodes of a half-hour comedy a year, you hope to have two or three that [work]. But the reality is, you're probably going to have 15 that are just satisfactory to good, and you're going to have some stinkers in there. What I strive to do is keep the level of stinking from falling below a certain level."

We were told interesting stories about casting. The networks have final cast approval. David Lee and the other creators of *Frasier* wanted Peri Gilpin for the role of Helen in *Wings.* Brandon Tartikoff, then NBC Entertainment chief, said to save her for a supporting role on another series; he wanted Crystal Bernard. The producers and Tartikoff fought over it. NBC won. Lee admitted to us that Bernard was perfect in *Wings* and Gilpin was later cast as Roz in *Frasier.* We know how successful both casting decisions were.[21]

Lynn Marie Latham told us that both sides [the network and the producer] have, according to her husband, Bernard Lechowick, "vomit privileges. You can vomit on their selection and they can vomit on yours. But until you reach an agreement or you have that leverage, you just have to keep slugging it out. The one thing I've always found is they can be wrong, but *I* can be wrong too. I never know until we start shooting if we've got the right people in the right roles."[22]

Chris Carter related how Gillian Anderson was not the choice of Fox for the role of Dana Scully on *The X-Files.* Carter had to fight for her. He said that everyone at Fox was convinced that Anderson wouldn't look good in a bathing suit. "I kept trying to emphasize the fact that she wasn't going to *be* in a bathing suit."

I asked Carter if, when he conceived of *The X-Files,* he thought that the story would be the star or the characters would be the star. He answered, "I always wanted the story to be the star; I wanted the characters to serve the story. I didn't want it to be about the leads in the show. I didn't want it to be about their life."

Dean Cain (*Lois & Clark*) and Brett Butler (*Grace Under Fire*) appeared together on a panel of actors in 1994 that also included Sharon Lawrence and James McDaniel of *NYPD Blue.* We learned the day of the panel that Lawrence and McDaniel would be late because of an ABC photo shoot, so Cain and Butler began without them, carrying on a hilarious, unrehearsed comedy routine. Cain went along with Butler as she led him down her path to laughs. She was even able to make him blush a few times. For one hour, we had a spontaneous, unplanned panel that got away from me. I ignored most of my prepared questions and went with the flow. I found Cain to be very engaging, and VQTers in the audience told me later that they had never seen me gaze at a panelist quite like that. But for all the comedy, both actors made some serious points. One of Butler's gems was "Characters that people can trust are very good, not only for the ones portraying them, but for the people who watch, because in essence the audience allows you to reflect their own magnificence."

Lawrence and McDaniel arrived in time for the last half hour of the discussion. Butler had been with us for most of the day, having graciously committed to both our tenth anniversary luncheon *and* the panel.

In 1992 we had the pleasure of presenting, on one lively panel, Michael Jeter and Elizabeth Ashley (*Evening Shade*), Grant Shaud (*Murphy Brown*), Marlee Matlin (*Reasonable Doubts*), Wendy Phillips (*Homefront*), Alley Mills (*The Wonder Years*), and Amy Aquino (*Brooklyn Bridge*). Ashley arrived late, swooping dramatically into the Beverly Garland theater, apologizing profusely and loudly every step toward the stage. She tended to speak very fast for great lengths of time with a great deal of energy. At one point she told us something that I think fully explains why some characters click with an audience and others do not. "The camera does not photograph, strangely enough, what you say and do. It photographs what you feel and think."

Michael Jeter elaborated. "If what you are doing with your character makes sense to you, if it is coming from a true place in you, then I think it will come across that way to the audience. If it is not true to you, it's not going to be true to the audience. The audience [and] the camera pick up a lie faster than anything you have seen."

Jeter seemed to like VQT's feedback, and always said so, whether on a panel or accepting a Quality Award (he received two for playing Herman Stiles in *Evening Shade*). "Those of us who come from theater backgrounds are used to having an immediate reaction from the audience to our work. Viewers for Quality Television is the only group that I know of that actually gives us feedback on what we are doing. Otherwise we [just] get a bunch of statistics and a bunch of graphs from people we don't know."

I asked these panelists what makes the characters they play special to the audience. Most credited the writing. Amy Aquino explained: "I think one of the things that makes the writing good is the specificity. What's frustrating is when it's just general, when it's some sort of stereotype—when they're not thinking."

Wendy Phillips's reply to my question "How much of the force of your own personality contributes to your character being who he or she is?" was that she didn't think you could keep that part out. "I will leave a stamp of my own on every character I play, no matter what I try and do."

Alley Mills added that in television there are two different kinds of performances.

One is where you play yourself, and I don't need to name names, but there are personalities on television who are always themselves, and they are fabulous and you always love them. Most of the people here are character actors from the theater. I think we are really lucky to play characters that are not ourselves. I love the fact that I'm playing someone I know absolutely nothing about—a docile, domesticated woman.

Mills added that "hopefully, as promised five years ago, she is going to break out some day." (Norma Arnold was always viewed from her son Kevin's perspective on *The Wonder Years,* so she only got to play, and we only got to see, that dimension of the character.)

We were discussing the restraint sometimes put on characters when Jeter expounded on the general constraint that is in the television business. He said it involved us, the audience, as Elizabeth Ashley said the networks perceive us, "the unwashed masses." He told us again what Linda Ellerbee had told us years before, that

the show itself is not the product. Network television is run on money that is spent by advertisers, and they are not paying for the show. They are paying for the size of the audience of the show. When a script is written and the network people sit down, they actually send copies to the advertisers. And the advertisers say, "We want you to take that out or change that or constrain her," because they are scared to death they might offend someone out there in that gray mass of the unwashed. I think it is an insult to you the audience. It makes it sound like you're a bunch of five year-olds who can't think for themselves, can't be challenged, can't hear something that might make you think, that might challenge your point of view.

Jeter explained that the constraint does not just come from writers, it comes from the economic fear that

we are going to alienate you and you won't want to watch us anymore. I think that groups like yours can help effect a change in this. You, by showing them and telling these people that you are not threatened by seeing something a little different—you are not going to all of a sudden change the channel just because you're seeing that. You can help effect a change in that constraint yourselves by being an active participant.

That was one of our most spirited panels. They did not want to leave. They wanted to keep talking. Michael Jeter told us that night at the Quality Awards banquet that he and Grant Shaud were so stimulated by the questions that they continued the discussion by phone after they got home.

Another great panel, with Paul Reiser, Teri Hatcher, Kathy Baker, Judith Light, Mimi Kennedy, and Swoosie Kurtz, is lost forever. Because of an audio-tape glitch, there is no audio. Instead of paying for a professional audio engineer, we relied on a volunteer. She meant well. The actors all look great on the video, but they are speaking in silence. They had so many interesting things to say. I miss that lost record of their words.

Unless there is a reversal of fortune, the 2000 Conference on Quality Television will be the final one. While these gatherings lasted, they brought viewers of quality television together and educated them about this business called television. We brought the makers of quality television programs and viewers of quality television programs together in a unique, intimate forum.

Every producer, actor, writer, and director who attended any of VQT's conference events lent their names and their presence to our organization and thus heightened its credibility and influence. Everyone who said no or did not respond hurt us. Every studio, network, or personal publicist who understood this organization's mission and responded to that contributed to our success. They know who they are: Maryann Ridini, Diann Shaw, Paul Gendreau, Neil Schubert, Jennifer Freeland, Leah Krantzler, Pat Schultz, Sue Binford, Chris Ender, Terri Corigliano, Tom Tyrer, John Wentworth, David Stapf, Heidi Trotta, Tracy Harper, Carla Princi, Richard Hoffman, Troy Nankin, Cynthia Snyder, Nan Sumski, Kim Sandifer, and Audrey Davis, Kim Conant, among others. I cannot thank them enough.

THE SINCEREST FORM
OF FLATTERY

As VQT grew, I was surprised at how many different skills I would be expected to master. Overseeing this grassroots organization, I read and assimilated large volumes of mail from VQT members nationwide and from the general viewing public. I had to grasp trends from that mail, and then articulate those views in the newsletter and to the media. I taught myself computer skills and necessary software programs that included word processing, desktop publishing, database management, and custom-made survey programs. As Hollywood and New York publicists called, I had to remember the show that each individual, studio, and network represented, as well as how most VQT members felt about a given show and what we could or could not do to help. I learned how to give a coherent interview, and became deft at the sound bite that I knew they wanted—and then to subtly beg the interviewer to print VQT's address in the article. I discovered, and am still learning, the art of public relations.

These endeavors tapped all my energies and skills. Luckily, I was surrounded by smart and talented volunteers who were always ready to assist and help me improve.

Had any number of VQT members—almost too many to name— attempted to take over the leadership of VQT or form a rival organization, I would not have been shocked. The intelligence level and charm of many VQT members have always been extraordinary.

But what follows is, to me, still an inconceivable chapter in VQT's history. If I gathered all VQT members in a hall, the last one I would guess might think she or he had the knowledge, skill, or talent to take a run at me personally, and finally form a splinter viewer group, was Sharon Rhode of West Allis, Wisconsin. But in 1991, this is exactly what she did.

I said in 1984:	Sharon Rhode said in 1996:
I'm not a television watcher. I really can't explain what happened to me, but I got hooked on [*Cagney & Lacey*].[1]	I never was that much of a TV watcher. I just got hooked on *Cagney & Lacey*.[2]

At VQT's second Los Angeles convention in September 1989, and again a year later, a small group of zealous VQTers gathered under the auspices of organizing a greeting committee. They were led by Sharon Rhode. The greeting committee was her idea.

At some point, either at the convention or later, a few discussed how surely anyone could do it if Dorothy could. Anyone could create a respectable and successful viewer group, anyone could present awards and the winners would come, anyone could write press releases and speak credibly to the press, anyone could write an articulate and readable newsletter containing objective opinions that journalists, television studios, and networks would quote—anyone could do that. This small group, headed by Sharon Rhode, eventually laid the groundwork for what would become their own dissident, copycat viewer organization. There were red flags from Rhode all along; I was too preoccupied with keeping VQT afloat to notice what she was doing.

It began with a letter from Barney Rosenzweig in December 1988, in which he suggested that VQT support quality shows in their network afterlife (in syndication). He encouraged communication with local stations. Intrigued, I announced a VQT Affiliate Program in the newsletter, asking members to contact me if they were interested in heading such a program in their local area. Some came forward, willing to supply the necessary names and addresses of their local stations. The ultimate goal was to appoint qualified VQT members in local markets to head small groups that would approach the network-affiliated stations about discussing the airing of current quality network series and quality series in syndication. It wasn't long after this announcement that Sharon Rhode called me to say that executives at her local stations wanted to meet with her. It did not occur to me at the time to ask her how they had learned of her. All she was supposed to be doing was compiling addresses. Yet, I reported in VQT's January/February 1990 newsletter that "Sharon Rhode, Affiliate Captain in Milwaukee, has been contacted by the ABC, CBS, NBC and Fox affiliate stations there to gather local VQT members and meet on a regular basis to discuss programming." I cautioned in the newsletter: "There are guidelines as to what can be discussed within the VQT forum, dictated by our by-laws and by our petition to the IRS for tax-exempt status. These guidelines must be explained to you before any meetings are scheduled. The affiliate representatives will be chosen based on their understanding of VQT's goals and purposes." I was hesitant to authorize just *anybody* to be a VQT spokesperson. I had worked too hard to establish and maintain VQT's outstanding reputation.

Rhode asked for my guidance in her endeavor; I urged her to comply with VQT's agenda. From this moment on, the Milwaukee Affiliate Program took on a life of its own.

The Milwaukee group consisted of fewer than five VQT members from the area, including Karla Johnson and Deborah Schroeder, who was the VQT Sponsor Program coordinator. As such, and vital to this story, Schroeder was receiving mail, and therefore addresses, from VQT members around the country who wanted sponsor lists of our supported shows in order to write positive letters.

Very early, Rhode called to request a copy of VQT's bylaws and articles of incorporation. Although these are available to anyone upon request, I found her reason curious. She told me that the station managers wanted proof that VQT was legitimate. This seemed a reasonable explanation at the time, but in retrospect, our many press clips would have provided ample proof of the organization's credibility. I would later realize that Rhode had wanted these copies for other reasons.

The Rhode group met monthly with various affiliate station executives, and Johnson submitted regular reports to me. At one point Johnson confided in me that she felt the affiliate station managers were humoring them and weren't taking them seriously.[3] I did not have a problem with this revelation. It was a pilot program, after all, and I did not feel that its success was crucial to VQT. From her correspondence, it was clear to me that Sharon Rhode did.

A November 2, 1989, article for the *New Berlin Citizen/Greenfield Observer/ West Allis Star* raised a red flag. In discussing Rhode's involvement with *Cagney & Lacey*, the writer said, "When the network decided to cancel *Cagney & Lacey*, Rhode decided to do something about it. She joined Swanson's network of fans."[4] I was astounded to read this, and wondered if Rhode was changing the facts to suit her own agenda. Rhode was never a part of my "network of fans"; in fact, we didn't meet until five years *after* the *Cagney & Lacey* campaign. Another red flag rose when the writer identified her as "regional director" (of VQT).[5] When asked about both discrepancies, Rhode said that the writer had misunderstood her. For the moment, I believed Rhode. But I became wary of what was unfolding.

I regularly urged Milwaukee area VQTers to join Rhode's group. She was very eager for more members. I did not understand why; she could only take a few people to the affiliate station meetings. I refer to these promotions for her group because she would later grow increasingly angry at me for what she perceived was a lack of support.

When Rhode informed me that she hoped to write and distribute a local VQT newsletter, I felt overwhelmed by her acceleration of events and by the fact that she was taking this project in directions that had not been discussed or approved.

That November the group's report included the fact that Rhode, Johnson, and Schroeder would appear on a Jones Intercable public access show in West Allis on January 23. There was also a notation in the report that the group intended to help local quality programming. This differed greatly from VQT's stated purpose. It was not VQT's mandate to "help" quality programming, whether national or local; rather, we were to educate viewers on how to "recognize and advocate" quality programming. It had been made especially clear that we would not become involved with local programming, because the potential for pressure to be applied would be too great. Rhode was adamant about doing it, and began trying to persuade me to come to Milwaukee so we could all appear on the local "Milwaukee Talking" show. The show did not want to feature the local group without a larger "hook," and according to Rhode, wanted me, a local TV critic, and a Nielsen representative.

In September I announced to VQT members in the newsletter that Rhode's group had been asked to produce their own public access show for Jones Intercable in West Allis. It would be called the "Viewers for Quality Television Show." The acceleration mounted. Rhode called me regularly with questions about content and format. I suggested a discussion format in which the trio (Rhode, Johnson, and Schroeder) would talk about quality scenes on quality shows to educate viewers on how to recognize quality. They could perhaps show clips from the shows. I remember one phone conversation between Rhode and Pat Murphy as Murphy literally outlined the first show for Rhode and her costars.

It became necessary to reeducate Rhode on the necessity of staying within the guidelines of VQT's articles of incorporation. I asked that only VQT-endorsed series be promoted on her show so that no misunderstandings would result. She felt that this restricted her; she wanted access to more shows. Fine, I said. Just don't call it the Viewers for Quality Television show.

The first half-hour Viewers for Quality Television Show for the local public access cable station introduced, with clips they had solicited, material from the as yet unseen *The Trials of Rosie O'Neill*, Steven Bochco's *Cop Rock*, and the entire Fox lineup (supplied by the local affiliate station). The second show featured clips from *Designing Women* (no problem there), and David Jacobs's *Paradise*.

It began to alarm me that Rhode was following her own agenda while representing VQT. It was apparent that her focus as VQT affiliate captain was to secure celebrity interviews for her public access show, not to further affiliate communication or viewer education. I told her that this was not the direction we wanted to take, nor was it something we felt comfortable with, as it would give the incorrect impression of who we were. I asked her to discontinue her pursuit of interviews with producers and stars because it could compromise future funding for any affiliate program—and for VQT.

This was a very busy and important time for VQT. We had just received our 501(c)3 tax-exempt status the previous December. Compiling information on which foundations might supply us with grants was of paramount concern. Seeking funding was uppermost in my mind, but Rhode wanted her local endeavors to be my priority, and told me so almost weekly. I was also preparing for our fourth national convention; this alone was a full-time project. Rhode's needs and problems were extremely distracting to me.

Our annual convention that September was punctuated by Rhode's anger. Indeed, it was a constant, noticeable undercurrent. She arrived sour and remained sour. I did not understand why. I gave her her own panel discussion to tell the group about their affiliate program, during which her associates spoke mostly about problems they were encountering. I included her in all staff meetings. I gave her a dedicated table at our registration center to sell auction tickets for items her affiliate stations had given her to raise money for VQT, such as a toaster and a camera. I recall that VQT collected about $200 from raffle tickets for those items. I gave the money to Rhode to use for expenses she had incurred on behalf of the "affiliate program."

After our staff party that closed the weekend's activities, which Rhode nearly ruined with her acerbic attitude, Pat Murphy and I asked her to remain in our suite so we could talk. We asked our two assistants to stay. They sat at a table across the room while Rhode railed at us for imagined wrongs and omissions. It was incredible. Listening to her speak and watching her, I wondered how I could have ever allowed her to represent VQT. How could I have been so blind to her raw ambition?

As if Rhode wasn't already ill-tempered with me, I had asked Karla Johnson, *her* associate, to assist our convention coordinator and thus have some of her expenses covered. Rhode maintained that she should have been consulted before I chose Johnson. I begged to differ with her, insisting that I had a right to choose my own staff from among VQT members. Nothing was resolved during this very heated exchange. The next morning I ran into Rhode in the parking lot of the Beverly Garland Hotel as we were both leaving. I informed her that I would not be coming to Milwaukee, that I did not want to appear anywhere with her. I was annoyed with her for her divisive behavior, and wanted nothing more to do with her. She had ruined an otherwise spectacular convention, one that saw the participation of Sharon Gless, Burt Reynolds, Dana Delany, Delta Burke, Scott Bakula, Steven Bochco, Marg Helgenberger, Park Overall, Robert Picardo, Barney Rosenzweig, Fred Savage, John Sacret Young, Marilou Henner, and more. She begged me to reconsider, offering to refrain from going to the "Milwaukee Talking" studio if I would just make the trip. I was appalled by her desperation.

During this convention, Karla Johnson spoke with Pat Murphy and me forthrightly and revealed that what Rhode wanted was her own group, and that she was using VQT as her platform. I feel foolish now for not heeding this warning. Johnson also expressed the opinion that Rhode did not represent VQT well, which had already become my impression. She assured us that her own loyalty lay with VQT.

I was not satisfied with the Milwaukee local newsletter. It bore VQT's logo, but it was amateurish and contained an inexcusable amount of grammatical and spelling errors, as well as unattractive multiple typefaces. It was not consistent with VQT's standards and agenda. Rhode had written in March 1990 that she hoped I didn't mind that she had mailed her newsletters before she got my okay. I did mind. It had been our agreement that nothing with the VQT logo on it, not even the Milwaukee newsletter, would go out without prior approval. Interestingly, their newsletter already boasted (and included) a letter from Barney Rosenzweig touting his new show for the following season, *The Trials of Rosie O'Neill*, starring Sharon Gless. He addressed it to "Sharon Rhode" and ended it, "Thanks in advance for the support and encouragement of all your VQT members. We hope and expect to be worthy of your praise."[6] "*Your* VQT members?" "Thanks in advance?" I rightfully had never been thanked by anyone in advance of a viewing, nor had I ever assumed ahead of time that a show would be of quality caliber. Obviously, Rhode had written him offering her support on behalf of VQT—before VQT had voted on the show's merits.

In March 1991 the situation came to a head in what turned out to be an embarrassing public confrontation. The first I knew a serious problem existed was when a reporter with the *Los Angeles Daily News* called to ask me if I knew why Lucie Arnaz had said, on *The Arsenio Hall Show,* that Viewers for Quality Television had gotten in touch with her to help save her show—the low-rated and critically drubbed *Sons & Daughters.* The reporter knew that VQT had not expressed interest in Arnaz's show. Not knowing what had happened, I told her candidly that I did not understand how Arnaz could be under that impression because I (along with local VQT staff) had picked *Sons & Daughters* as one of the worst pilots we had seen that season. The reporter printed that comment. (The lesson being, if you don't want to see it in print, don't say it.) Arnaz had now been embarrassed twice, once on *The Arsenio Hall Show* and now in print. I don't remember how I finally traced this public-relations disaster to Rhode, but I did. I asked her what she had done and with whom she had spoken. She gave me the name of Dana Freedman at Paramount (now Dana Walden, president of Twentieth Television), but denied any wrongdoing. I called Dana, who was a publicist with the Los Angeles firm of Bender, Goldman and Helper, and got the full story. I took notes as Freedman told me that she was glad to have the opportunity to relate to me her conversation with Rhode so that I would be able to take "corrective measures." Rhode had called CBS, Paramount, and Bender to find the *Sons & Daughters* producers because she wanted to promote the series on her TV show. Freedman told me that she had been misled by Rhode into believing she was offering her support to the show on behalf of VQT in her area. Freedman told me that she had even asked Rhode at one point, "Are you speaking on behalf of the organization?" and that the response had been that she was speaking on behalf of the Milwaukee group of VQT; that she did not always agree with Dorothy Swanson and would be able help *Sons & Daughters* on her own. Encouraged by Rhode's interest and her self-described influence in the organization, Freedman called the producers of the show and told them of VQT's support. They told Arnaz, who was going on *Arsenio* that night, and she happily announced VQT's support. The more I learned, the more mortified I became. My patience and trust were finished.

When I asked Freedman what I might do to placate the producers and Arnaz, she suggested that I call the producers and write to Arnaz. Dreading it, but recognizing the need for damage control, I called the office of Eugenie Ross-Leming and Brad Buckner, reaching Ross-Leming. I told her that I was sorry this had happened, but that Rhode had no authority to encourage producers on behalf of VQT. Ross-Leming thought it was wonderful that Rhode wanted to feature clips from *Sons & Daughters* and asked why *I* would not support her show. I told her that it just had not captured the interest of VQT members. She responded, "Don't you realize that people's jobs are at stake?" I had to tell her that it was not *my* job to safeguard *her* job, and tried to explain to this disinterested and now cross producer just what VQT's "job" was. She angrily suggested that I keep a tighter rein on my "representatives." It was a disastrous conversation, and my lasting impression is that Ross-Leming and Buckner have never forgiven me.

I wrote an apology to Arnaz and received a handwritten, gracious response from her dated March 15, 1991, that thanked me for my kind letter of explanation.

After a pointless telephone conversation in which Rhode insisted that Paramount, Freedman, Buckner, and Ross-Leming all jumped to the "wrong" conclusion, I wrote Rhode on March 9 ending our association. I told her that, effective immediately, her public access show could no longer be produced under the auspices of Viewers for Quality Television and that in any future calls to Hollywood production offices, she was to make it clear that she was no longer affiliated with VQT. I ended, "I have worked for five years to maintain VQT's integrity and reputation and I will not have it damaged by one misguided individual, no matter how well-intentioned you might have been at one time." I sent copies of the letter to her Milwaukee cohorts.

Regrettably, I felt obliged to clarify the matter publicly. Wanting to insure that Rhode could no longer use VQT's name, I wrote Milwaukee television journalists and affiliate station managers that Sharon Rhode was no longer representing VQT. Both local television journalists found this interesting (it must have been a slow news day) and interviewed the two of us; both articles were "she said/she said" stories. A local VQT member told me she thought it was interesting that neither TV critic took the side of their local activist, choosing to remain objective.

The *Milwaukee Sentinel* wrote of Rhode on March 19, "Her own interest in *Sons & Daughters* led her to telephone the producers and publicists for the show to get clips of it."[7] Rhode responded to Duane Dudek's statement that I claimed she had "misrepresented herself" when she said that VQT endorsed the show. Dudek wrote, "Rhode said she told the show's producers that *she* was 'interested' in the show. 'I never said VQT supported them.'"[8] Rhode failed to comprehend that if you say you are "interested," that is taken as a sign of support. Freedman had told me that VQT is considered a "lifeline out here." We had a responsibility not to misuse that perception. Dudek wrote, "Rhode has responded by forming her own group, Viewers Choice." (That name was already taken; they would rename it Viewers Voice.) "She will continue to host her weekly cable show under the auspices of the new group that, she said, will concentrate on local affiliates rather than on letter campaigns [like those] that VQT launched on behalf of programs."[9] This was contradictory to what she told the other Milwaukee paper, and would soon prove not to be her intention.

The *Milwaukee Journal* wrote on April 7 that "Dorothy Swanson said that Sharon Rhode of West Allis had overstepped her role giving the impression that VQT was ready to lend its support to the endangered show."[10] Rhode either exposed her ignorance or misspoke when she told Joel McNally that "I was always under the impression that we could help shows even if they weren't on the endorsed list."[11] Here, Dana Freedman recanted the term she had used with me, "misrepresented," and chose to state instead that "people associated with the show had misunderstood and passed the incorrect impression along to Arnaz."[12] I was quoted: "We decided Sharon is not ready to be a spokesperson if people are going to get what she says that mixed up." Rhode finally admitted in print, "It's a good opportunity for us to take off on our own, which we'd been talking about anyway." Dudek reported that "She [Rhode] and other members of the Milwaukee group were reorganizing as Viewers Choice Television, which also is the new name for the cable show." Dudek wrote that the group would continue to meet with local TV stations *and* would "campaign on behalf of network shows—starting with *Sons & Daughters.*"[13] Which was it, local or national? Whichever it was to be, I felt that Rhode had been deceitful.

Johnson and Schroeder stayed with Rhode and became secretary and vice president respectively of the new organization. Pat and I felt betrayed by them both, especially Johnson, who had worked with us at the convention.

Baffling me, both Rhode and Schroeder sent deposit checks that April for VQT's 1991 convention the following September. I was more than a little suspicious about why they would want to attend and decided it could only be to further their new group, which would need industry contacts and members to be successful. After talking over the situation with David Masterman, VQT's attorney, I returned their checks with a brief note.

I discovered that the splinter group had incorporated on April 19, 1991, as Viewers Voice, Inc. This was extremely quick action, unless they had been planning it for some time.

On April 28, David Masterman faxed me news of a phone call he received from Rhode, in which she suggested that VQT's bylaws did not permit me to exclude a "member" from the convention. She wanted me to reconsider my decision to bar her from the convention.

Two weeks later Schroeder called Masterman, saying basically the same thing. David advised me to publicly clarify the notion that VQT "members" have inherent rights to participate in actions, and asked me to keep in mind Article 4 of the Restated Articles of Incorporation (1988) that require that the corporation "shall be a nonmember, nonstock corporation." We had been using the term "member" somewhat loosely, in a nonlegal, nonbinding sense, because it is more welcoming. But legally, VQT was a corporation, not a club. It had no "members"; it had participants. Therefore, neither Rhode nor Schroeder had any stated "right" to attend the convention, which was essentially a private function. David advised that from now on we call our dues "newsletter subscriptions" and refer to our "members" by some other term. We chose "participants," and to this day interchange that term with "members." The distinction has not caused any further problems.

Almost immediately, Rhode began sending mailings to VQTers she hoped to sway to her group. On her mailing list were people with whom she had exchanged addresses and phone numbers at VQT conventions and those who had written Schroeder for sponsor information. I know this to be a fact because some of them forwarded those packets to me. The first page of the packet contained a flyer that stated the group's purpose. "Low ratings for your favorite show? Afraid you'll never see it again? Here's your chance to do something about it! Join Viewers Voice. Viewers Voice is a non-profit organization established to provide viewers with the means to help keep their favorite programs on the air. Join us! Let your voice be heard!"[14] It was like reading early literature on VQT, only the defining term was missing—quality. The next page was more plagiarized VQT material: "We are a non-profit group with no moral, religious or political agenda. We are not a censorship group. We do not try to take programming off the air."[15] Except that I was outraged, it was laughable. She was using me, my knowledge, and my ideas, and there was nothing I could do about it. Also included in the packet were both Milwaukee newspaper articles on the *Sons & Daughters* incident, my letter to the program director of channel 12 stating the severance of the national organization from Rhode, and his response to me supporting her local work. Some VQTers just forwarded the packet for my edification; a few requested explanations. And a very few chose to leave VQT and align themselves with Rhode's new group. There happened to be some discontent at this time among the die-hard Sharon Gless fans in VQT, sparked by what was perceived by them as my lack of support for her new show, *The Trials of Rosie O'Neill*. (See "Misunderstandings, Misconceptions and Manipulations".) Rhode was able to turn some of this discontent to her advantage.

To make matters worse, I heard from a few Hollywood production assistants and publicists who also were in receipt of Rhode's packet promoting the upstart group. One of them, then vice president of publicity at Lorimar, called to ask what I thought. But I asked him what *he* thought, and he replied that it looked like a "complete rip-off" to him. He went even further by saying that he was skeptical of someone with their own public access TV show, because what they usually want is to advance their own agenda and get picked up by other stations.

Most in Hollywood who contacted me about the situation (not all did) were sympathetic and unimpressed. But some were intrigued at the thought of another viewer group that might be able to help them. Heidi Trotta, the former Warner Bros. publicist for *China Beach* and with whom Pat and I had become close during that campaign, put it into perspective when she said, "Maybe they'll like some of our shows you don't like." Indeed they would. Any organization that lists the Three Stooges Fan Club and Sandra Dee's official fan club as resources in their publication is certainly ecumenical.

On July 25, 1991, the *West Allis Star* gave the group ink again. I was insulted by one paragraph that altered VQT's history and my own: "Rhode became an active viewer advocate for the first time when the television show *Cagney & Lacey* was threatened with cancellation. The producer of that show, Barney Rosenzweig, put Rhode together with Dorothy Swanson, another vocal viewer, to form VQT and subsequently save the police show, according to Rhode."[16] What? Whether this is what Rhode really told the reporter, or how the reporter interpreted it, it was a totally inaccurate account of the *Cagney & Lacey* campaign and of VQT's formation. Infuriated and offended, I wrote to journalist Mary Balistreri disputing her version and enclosed press clippings from the past that documented the truth. I asked for a correction, if not a retraction. I felt it was important, because Rhode was disseminating this article to the public. But I never heard from the writer. Farther into the article, Rhode stated her group's purpose and talked about VQT. "The new organization will campaign for the continuance of shows in which the public displays an interest. It will also rally for local shows as well as for network fare."[17] Quoting Rhode, Balistreri wrote, "VQT never let us back the local people. The question is who decides what is quality? Quality is in the eye of the viewer." And "We're advising people to write the networks."[18]

Further duplication of VQT's goals and purpose was in an article by Barb Falk in the *West Allis Enterprise*'s September 22–28, 1991, edition.[19] "Viewers Choice, Inc. fights for the return of television programs that have been cancelled. The organization is dedicated to providing viewers throughout the nation with the means for communicating effectively with the television industry."[20] Another paragraph got my attention: "Viewers Voice encourages its members and the general public to write to the sponsors, informing them of their likes and dislikes with the network's choices in programming."[21] Of course, why wouldn't they imitate our sponsor program? And of their TV show, Falk wrote, "The program is designed to educate viewers on what can be done to keep their favorite television program on the air."[22] Exactly—just like Pat Murphy had advised. Further, "It also supports local programming. This month the program is airing behind the scenes of 'The Wisconsin Lottery Money Game.'"[23] You can't get more local than that.

It was apparent that Viewers Voice would differ from VQT in two obvious and significant ways. (1) They would have no identifying criteria or standards. Quality television was not their concern; they backed any TV shows people liked or that were pitched to her by Hollywood publicists. (2) They would not be grassroots. By June 1992 Sharon Gless's personal assistant would be listed in their newsletter as head of a California "chapter." (This was *not* Beverley Faverty, who had returned to her home state of Tennessee once *Cagney* had wrapped.) This same individual with ties to the television industry would later be listed in their newsletter as "Supervising Editor and Set-up Editor" and would ultimately hold a position on their board of directors. She also accompanied Viewers Voice officers to a few meetings with producers in Hollywood. It apparently did not occur to Rhode that some of the above was contributing to journalists' dismissal of her organization.

It does not end here. Rhode and her colleagues were not content to just build their organization based on their own merits and accomplishments; they felt the need to diminish VQT.

On November 18, 1991, Deborah Schroeder, vice president of Viewers Voice, Inc., registered a complaint about VQT to the Commonwealth of Virginia Division of Consumer Affairs. David Masterman, as our attorney, was sent a copy of the complete file, which he forwarded to me. We were asked in a cover letter to inquire into the matter and keep the complainant and the office of Consumer Affairs informed of our findings and to inform them of any actions taken to resolve the complaint. Schroeder had officially complained to the state agency that allows VQT to do business that the organization had denied her her rights by refusing to let her attend our convention. Her explanation was less than candid. Schroeder wrote on the complaint, "The reason given was that there was a conflict of interest since I am now involved in a similar organization. Since I belong to many organizations that share similar goals with each other and have always been welcome at any of their functions, I find this exclusionary practice of VQT extraordinary and unacceptable." Masterman wrote the manager of the Office of Investigations at the State Division of Consumer Affairs and stated that "the complaint does not provide you with all of the details concerning Ms. Schroeder and her relationship with VQT. When all of the facts are provided, her complaint does not withstand scrutiny; therefore, VQT requests that it be dismissed without further investigation or referral." Masterman provided the missing details and explained,

> One may reasonably question Schroeder's motivation in filing this complaint. She is now the vice president of an organization which in many respects is attempting to duplicate VQT and which, in order to be successful, needs to develop ties with members of the television industry and to locate members of the general public who care enough about television to make financial contributions to a proactive television advocacy group. In that sense, Viewer's Voice and VQT are competitors. The complaint from an officer of a competing group should be evaluated most carefully for possible bias or a potential hidden agenda, such as the desire to use VQT as a platform to further her competing group. Finally, I note that Ms. Schroeder did not take this matter up with your office before the convention, rendering her motivation even more suspect.

Schroeder's action was quickly dismissed by the Commonwealth of Virginia.

In June 1992 another Viewers Voice member and former VQT participant registered a complaint about us to the same state agency. The agency sent this complainant a curt letter advising that her grievance appeared to involve a "dispute among members of an organization or interest group rather than a retail sales establishment. Such disputes are not under the purview of this office." Enclosed to her was a form containing the investigator's findings. Unfortunately, the official findings named Sharon Gless, for in the complaint some of her fans in Viewers Voice had made false accusations that VQT had promised Gless's attendance at our 1991 convention. The handwritten note from the investigator: "A conference is being advertised as featuring Sharon Gless, actress, who can't be there, and [they] hope to get people's registration fees, which they won't refund. Read complaint. This is bickering of a personal nature. No action required by DCA (Department of Consumer Affairs)." How embarrassing for Sharon Gless. I hoped she didn't know how she had been used.

This latest file was thick and, to me, illuminating. Allegations were made by the complainant that were totally baseless and malicious. Under "Description of Complaint," the person wrote "See Attachments," which turned out to be copies of letters to me from various VQT members who were now Viewers Voice members; copies of some of my letters to Viewers Voice members at the time they were still with VQT; Sharon Rhode's deposit check to VQT's convention, which I had returned; copies of Deborah Schroeder's earlier unsuccessful complaint *minus* the official letter of dismissal; a copy of a letter sent to Schroeder from the agency dated December 6, 1991, informing her that her complaint was a civil matter rather than "an area regulated by the State [and] we are unable to pursue a desirable conclusion on your behalf." There was even official correspondence from VQT attorney David Masterman. Also included, and ultimately important to VQT, was a copy of a letter from Mary Louise Miller of Camp Hill, Pennsylvania, telling us why she left VQT for Viewers Voice.

Through more phone calls from producers' assistants, I learned that this entire packet—*minus* the evidence of the official dismissal of the complaint— was anonymously sent around Hollywood. One assistant to a producer with whom VQT had enjoyed a good relationship assured me that her boss would never see the packet of materials that was mailed from Michigan. Rhode's scheme—or Viewers Voice members acting with her knowledge—was being dismissed on face value. Still, I worried. While I could never prove that this had hurt us, it seems logical that it must have.

Referencing the above letter from Mary Miller, Pat Murphy and I had answered her strongly worded June 4, 1991, letter. We had met Mary, and did not feel that the letter sounded like something she would write by herself. We wrote and asked her if Rhode had anything to do with it. In December 1991, six months later, Miller wrote back a sincere letter of apology and regret, and provided us important insights into Rhode's behavior and motivation.

> It was at [Rhode's] urging that I wrote that letter to you. The truth is, I was first made aware of [Rhode's] plans to start her own group very shortly after your 1990 convention. She told me she was disgusted with your organization. Over the next few months, she started getting her group together. Even before she was "fired," the new group was already in the process of being formed. I asked her why she was so upset about leaving VQT when she would soon have her own group. She told me that the press would be [unfavorable] for her in recruiting members, so she had to point this in her favor.

Mary continued, "When you rejected her bid [to attend convention] she was enraged. It was a smart move on your part because she only wanted to attend for her own group's furthering." Mary then explained that Rhode had painted a distorted picture of VQT to her. "She said she was mailing packets of information about her new group to VQT members she felt she could trust and ones she felt she could win over. All this time, she was verbally attacking you in every way she could."

Mary also told me about a disastrous visit to Milwaukee.

> What I found when I got there was a very hostile group. They weren't Viewers Voice, they more reminded me of the "Let's get Dorothy and VQT" group. I was subjected to a constant barrage of how awful VQT was, and the ways they were going to get even with you. I actually heard them say on several occasions, when they approached someone about Viewers Voice [they were recruiting members at a local carnival], and the person asked if it was affiliated with VQT, that their group was formed as a result of the unethical ways of VQT, and this group was going to be more powerful than VQT. She said she planned on becoming more powerful than you and she was going to contact producers who she said you had burned and try to sway them to her group. Her motive for Viewers Voice was simply to overtake you and force VQT into oblivion.

Mary added that "I also know that she has been determined to undermine you to Barney Rosenzweig and Sharon Gless." Mary summarized, "Sharon Rhode had an agenda of her own; she wanted to have what you had and she was willing to destroy you, me and VQT to accomplish it."

The group has received little if any press other than locally that I am aware of, except from *Milwaukee Journal Sentinel* TV critic Joanne Weintraub. She gave the group space (along with VQT) in her column about letter-writing campaigns on May 4, 1997.[24] Weintraub wrote about Viewers Voice again on July 1, 1997. In mentioning the Fox series *Party of Five,* Weintraub found it significant to mention that "cast members throw their arms around group representatives who make it to the set for a visit."[25] While I've been greeted affectionately by "cast members" of shows we have championed, I would never mention that to a journalist writing about VQT. There were always weightier things to discuss and report.

The reasons for Viewers Voice's lack of national press recognition might be obvious. In April 1992 Viewers Voice decided to launch a campaign for the ABC series *Anything But Love* starring Richard Lewis and Jamie Lee Curtis. VQT had campaigned for this series the year before with success; to this day Richard Lewis is among VQT's greatest admirers and calls or faxes occasionally. But this time, the *network* did not cancel *Anything But Love;* the *studio,* Twentieth Television, did. President Lucie Salhany had decided that the show was not strong enough to ever make it into syndication, which is where the studio would have finally made money on it. Without a studio, a show was as dead as it could get. I understood this, and accepting reality, so did Richard Lewis.

But Rhode did not grasp the situation. Thinking she had an opportunity to save a show and get publicity for her new group, she wrote journalists announcing her campaign. Not only did her appeal fall on deaf ears, it also irritated several journalists enough that they devoted negative columns to it. Her action contributed to journalists' growing impatience with letter campaigns and it brought unfortunate publicity to a fine show. Greg Dawson's story in the *Orlando Sentinel* ran under the headline "Whine–o'grams Won't Save Shows."[26] In it, he complained about letter-writing campaigns for "the rottenest of shows" and used Viewers Voice as an example: "Like this one from Viewers Voice, Inc., a Viewers for Quality Television wannabe: 'The show *Anything But Love* has been canceled as of January 13. It's time for us to get out our pens and pencils again and start writing letters.'" Dawson responded, "With all due respect to a pretty funny show—Not!"

Viewers Voice attempted their own conventions starting in 1992. The first few years, Sharon Gless fans who had bolted VQT attended, until Viewers Voice no longer provided access to the star. It is my understanding from members who have left the group that there has been little participation in their conventions from the industry overall. In 1994, while VQT hosted Dennis Franz, Kathy Baker, Helen Hunt, Paul Reiser, Julia Louis-Dreyfus, Brett Butler, Dean Cain, Sharon Lawrence, the Thomasons, Chris Carter, Tom Fontana, David Lee, Lynn Marie Latham, Beth Sullivan, David Hyde Pierce, and others, Viewers Voice hosted two producers and an actor. Their banquet featured a dance by a member and a "pat ourselves on the back speech" by another member.[27] Mostly, the small gaggle of fans visit various sets. I remain concerned, however, because too often it has been apparent to me that industry people confuse the two groups.

Through the years, Viewers Voice's newsletters occasionally referred to VQT in a negative way, prompting me to respond in our newsletter. I was particularly disappointed when I read an interview with Barney Rosenzweig in their August/September 1992 issue. Among their questions to Rosenzweig was "What do you think is the most effective action that viewers can take to keep a favorite series on the air?" His response was the usual, until he added,

They must avoid what I see happening in Viewers for Quality Television, which is to get so cozy with the establishment that they naïvely
begin to "buy" the various network executives' rhetoric. I was stunned
to read in a recent VQT newsletter an editorial advising members not
to protest the cancellation of a [particular] series as it would be a waste
of time. I, for one, am certainly glad there was no such advice given by
one of our own when I was out there against all odds in 1983 trying to
save *Cagney & Lacey.*[28]

I, too, was stunned. One, by Rosenzweig's interpretation of my editorial;
two, by what was either his failure to understand the nature of my amicable
relationship with the networks or his deliberate rejection of the necessity to
establish and maintain a nonadversarial relationship. It's called "public relations," and Rosenzweig knows it. It's his forte.

The editorial he referred to was from our May 1992 issue. It was a reality
check about all our endangered shows: *Life Goes On, Anything But Love, Brooklyn Bridge, I'll Fly Away, Reasonable Doubts,* and Rosenzweig's *The Trials of Rosie
O'Neill.* I had written that "I have never in the seven years of VQT's existence
encouraged viewers to fight for a show that didn't stand a chance of benefit-
ting from that fight." I added that it was not my function, as spokesperson
for VQT, to be "loyal to any particular person or show." This statement was
in reference to the heat I was taking for being realistic and objective about
Rosenzweig's show and printing the views of members who were disappointed in it. I continued, "To what extent will VQT direct its resources and
energies to the resurrection of each of its lost shows? To the extent that each
is realistically 'savable.'" I cautioned that we would not issue a blanket statement that promises that "this show can be saved if you just work hard
enough." Without getting into the whole *Rosie O'Neill* dispute here (see "Misunderstandings, Misconceptions, and Manipulations"), I was frank with my
readers about which shows were likely to benefit from letters and which were
not. By now I had developed instincts, I had gained experience, and I had
sources at the networks whom I trusted and believed and who were direct
with me. The argument for the renewal of *Rosie* was weak. I quoted my CBS
source, who had implied that the decision had already been made, by saying
simply, "Your energies would be well directed elsewhere." I added that "VQT
is not saying to give up; even a slight ratings increase might do it; but I am
very guarded about its chances."

There were many quality shows in danger that May. I wanted to guide
VQT members in how best to direct their energies. Right or wrong, it was per-

ceived by those with *Rosie O'Neill* that I had abandoned the show. Viewers Voice embraced it and launched a futile campaign. As a producer, which viewer group would you have favored? This time it was not Viewers for Quality Television. Rosenzweig got even with me in the Viewers Voice newsletter.

The group's May/June 1993 newsletter, still with Sharon Gless's assistant on staff and on the board of directors, definitively differentiated them from the agenda of VQT. In her editorial, Rhode criticized quality television. "Quality—a word that lately is very overrated. Who's to say what quality is? It's almost like being back in school and the teacher tells you that you must read a certain book because it's a classic. The word entertaining doesn't carry the prejudice that some people seem to put on the word quality." I was relieved that they had finally distinguished themselves in this way.

Yet, on September 26, 1996, you guessed it: the *West Allis Star* wrote another piece on the group. Again Rhode took credit for *Cagney & Lacey*, altering television history and mine.[29] Nan Bialek quoted her, "I was never that much of a TV watcher. I just got hooked on *Cagney & Lacey*."[30] The writer added, "When rumors circulated that CBS was going to cancel the show, Rhode got off the couch and into action, organizing a letter-writing campaign to try and save the series."[31] Irked that this appropriation of my ideas and accomplishments was still going on, I compiled a packet of information for Bialek and the *West Allis Star* publisher that again included documentation of the facts, including my earlier letter to their journalist. I never heard back from either the writer or the publisher.

There were further misrepresentations. For several years, the home page of the Viewers Voice Web site listed *Cagney & Lacey* among the shows they "actively supported." As we know, *Cagney & Lacey* left the air three years before Viewers Voice was formed.

By 1999 it was apparent that the group's focus was their cable access TV show in West Allis; their newsletter was published only quarterly. While Viewers for Quality Television, still pursuing quality television, openly criticized the networks for their methods and mediocre programming, Viewers Voice promoted network shows for West Allis cable viewers. This ability—to provide free publicity—gave them entre to television industry publicicsts, producers, and executives.

The sincerest form of flattery was still evident in their publications in 1999. I am not flattered; I am hurt and disgusted.

MISCONCEPTIONS, MISUNDERSTANDINGS, AND MANIPULATIONS

Misconceptions

Agenda

W HAT'S in a name? By its very title, Viewers for Quality Television is often conceived to be driven by a moral agenda. Even Dana Delany told me, after meeting Pat Murphy and me and hearing about VQT directly from us, how relieved she was to realize that VQT was not going to monitor *China Beach* for material deemed unacceptable or inappropriate for public consumption. The assumption exists that "quality" can only mean clean, nonoffensive family fare. VQT always had to clearly define "quality."

VQT member Sue Chapman found it necessary to clarify VQT's purpose in a guest editorial published in our January 1995 newsletter. She was concerned that so many journalists persisted in defining VQT as a "watchdog" group.

> The dictionary defines "watchdog" as a person or group that takes action to prevent something from happening; while an "advocate" is one who takes positive action on behalf of something. I fail to see why the media cannot make that distinction when they characterize View-

ers for Quality Television. At no time has VQT ever attempted to have a television show removed from the air as some of the self-proclaimed watchdog groups have done. On the occasions when VQT speaks as a group, it is always in a positive manner as an advocate of what a majority of its constituents believe to be quality programming.

Sue felt that in labeling us a "watchdog" group, *TV Guide* had perhaps scared readers away from us instead of drawing them to us, as had been the magazine's intention. I agreed with her, and from then on was sure to use the term "advocate" in all future informational press releases about the organization. Soon, the word "advocate" appeared in most mentions of VQT.

Function

The misconception still persists that, like television critics, VQT responds to pitches from publicists. There are certain network or studio publicists who know exactly when to call to alert me to something special and send a tape to preview. Warner Bros. publicist Heidi Trotta knew this with *China Beach,* although she was not the first to contact me about that show; rather, she didn't miss a beat as she picked up the ball from the publicist who immediately preceded her. David Staph of Warner Bros. knew when to contact me and when to not. Paul Gendreau always knew (my association with Paul began when he was with Warner Bros., and continued through his tenure at Fox). He alerted me to the potential quality of *Party of Five.* Terri Corigliano of CBS had the same eye for quality that I did; we invariably loved the same shows. Those publicists knew that quality is found, or not found, in the product that airs, by viewers who respond to it. From some publicists, I endured season after season of pitches and pressure.

Misunderstandings

Sharon Gless, Barney Rosenzweig, and *The Trials of Rosie O'Neill*

The very thing that first united Sharon Gless and me—my passion for her show and her performance—would damage us seven years later. My mail had reached Sharon back in 1984 because I gave her a truthful, insightful read of her performance in *Cagney & Lacey.* The same truthful read on *The Trials of Rosie O'Neill* tore us apart.

Pat Murphy and I viewed the first episode of Sharon's new series in Barney Rosenzweig's office while in Los Angeles on business in 1990. Written by Beth Sullivan (who went on to create *Dr. Quinn, Medicine Woman*), it was compelling and interesting. It had a downbeat, realistic ending—Rosie with her head cast downward after losing an emotional court case. Barney said he was going to add another scene to make it more upbeat because he knew the network would not accept this kind of dispiriting ending with a first episode. We had high hopes for this series.

In the September/October 1990 newsletter, I included *Rosie* under "Worth Your Quality Time," reviewing new series I had previewed. "If you liked *Cagney & Lacey,*" I promised, "you'll love *Rosie.*"

But my enthusiasm waned as I saw more episodes and received letters from other viewers expressing disappointment with the quality. I wrote Barney a letter that fall expressing this dissatisfaction. I told him that I felt the scripts were not serving Sharon's talent. I also was so bold as to remind him that the messages in *Cagney & Lacey* had been subtle and woven through the storylines, suggesting that in *Rosie* they were obvious, and wondered if this might be off-putting to viewers. He called me, not to discuss the concerns I had expressed, but to defend the show. In this call, Rosenzweig tried to convince me that *Cagney & Lacey* wasn't as terrific as I had thought it was. When I suggested that the quality of *Cagney & Lacey* was superior to that of *Rosie O'Neill* because the issues were not preached in *Cagney* as they were in *Rosie,* Barney offhandedly remarked that *Cagney* hadn't really been that great, and seemed to take pleasure in revealing, "We fooled you." I was too astounded to reply. I felt, sadly, that he had lost respect for *Cagney* and maybe for his audience, too. Frankly, I was offended and confounded. What fan of *Cagney & Lacey* wouldn't be? I set down the phone believing that Barney hadn't known what he had in the show he had fought so hard and so brilliantly and successfully to resurrect.

Still, VQT voted *The Trials of Rosie O'Neill* the Best New Drama in our New Season Opinion Poll of March 1991, because "the people creating it care deeply about doing an intelligent, quality drama, and it shows."[1] Ellice Orveck of Elmira, New York, added in the same issue, "She [Rosie] makes you hurt right along with her. Now, if they'd only let her smile." Elizabeth Doree from Englewood, New Jersey, suggested in the same issue that they "play down the stereotypes a bit. There's one of every type at the P.D.'s office (the Irish, upper-class woman; the black, defiant lawyer; the Jewish boss). The diversification of people is fine, it's just that the show tends to get preachy and confines its characters by relegating them to their stereotyped roles."

I had a dilemma. Should I print honest criticism and risk the relationship

I had with Barney and Sharon? Or should I print only the positive comments? There was only one honest choice: I felt I had an obligation to print both points of view; I also had a duty to be objective.

Barb Mangels from Bloomington, Illinois, a *Cagney* fan, wrote in the November 1990 newsletter about *Rosie:*

> The biggest disappointment of the season. Sharon Gless really does quite well with the material she's given, but she hasn't been given much. There hasn't been an original idea in this show yet, and the supporting characters are one-dimensional stereotypes. Points for originality are not given for peppering Rosie's speech with more colorful language. Get some new writers on this show or kiss it goodbye, quickly.

In retrospect, that comment was harsh, but there were so many like it that I felt it should be printed. The problem was that VQT members were predisposed to love the show, and assumed that they would. Cindy Henderson from Bluefield, Virginia, said in VQT's January 1991 newsletter: "She [Rosie] is distinctly different from that New York detective we grew to love, but somehow comfortably familiar. Rosie is vulnerable and lovably grumpy, but possesses compassion and an inner strength that she has not yet fully discovered. Sharon Gless is undoubtedly giving us another unforgettable character."

Some were appalled when the episode about an AIDS patient aired that showed Rosie sitting near the ill man's bed fully gowned and wearing protective gloves. Many thought that was overkill—and careless. VQT members said so.

It was felt by many that the show would benefit from more humor. Michael Smolinski of Grand Rapids, Michigan, wrote in the January 1991 newsletter, "Imagine *The Trials of Rosie O'Neil* with a little more humor, a little more vulnerability. Rosie needs to loosen up. She should be allowed to fail. Let her have a good laugh."

Sharon Gless was on our newsletter mailing list as a courtesy; her copies went to the attention of Carole Smith in Barney's office. I did not realize she read them until she returned the issue in which Michael made the above comment, along with a letter reminding me that she and Barney had helped me start VQT. She had made notations over the *Rosie* comments in the newsletter that clearly and sometimes profanely expressed her anger. Under the comment about being in gown and gloves with an AIDS patient, she defended that practice as sometimes being required. Her letter expressed her disbelief that my mail about her show was so qualitatively different from hers and the network's, and suggested (correctly) that the choice of comments printed represented an editorial judgment. She was disappointed at what she felt was ignorant criticism being leveled against the show. I had upset her, I had hurt her feelings, and I felt terrible! After a letter of apology, I received a thoughtful, four-page typewritten letter in which she explained how confused she had been that *Rosie* had done so well in our surveys and polls yet sustained so many critical comments in the newsletter. It was a point well taken; she did not understand that the critical comments were from fans who just wanted the show to be better, mostly because they felt that she deserved better material. I could understand why fans would write me those sentiments and not Sharon or Barney.

Longtime *Cagney & Lacey* fan and VQT board of directors member Judy Samelson of Bayside, New York, wrote an objective view of *Rosie O'Neill* for our March 1991 issue, where she, also, criticized the depiction of unnecessary caution in the AIDS episode. In a mostly positive article, Judy wrote about the attempts *Rosie* was making to explore the "portrait of a woman coming into her own." Judy felt that Rosie's character was "wonderfully written." However, she admitted that the writing was less successful when it turned to Rosie's work.

> Although dealing with all the politically correct legal issues, the scripts lack a certain toughness in execution that render them without dramatic conflict in this area. Why make her a public defender if not to dramatize the complex ideals that are part of the job description—how it can demoralize its most ardent practitioners, how we are made more civilized by its very concept. If *Rosie O'Neill* wants to be taken seriously in terms of its legal themes, these questions must be tackled more convincingly. Have they made mistakes? Of course. No one visiting an AIDS patient has to put on full surgical garb.

To summarize its first season, Judy purported that "[the show] has made good on 50 percent of its promise," and suggested that the show was "strong enough to take the criticism, and if anyone should have the patience to stick with a series that exhibits the slightest glimmer of intelligence, humor and thoughtfulness, VQT members should. Rosie is just beginning to lighten up on herself. We ought to be able to do the same."

Unfortunately, those associated with the show were not "strong" enough to accept the criticism. And viewers were running out of patience waiting for the show to fulfill the promise Judy had suggested.

Lacey Wood of Canaan, Connecticut, commented in the February 1991 issue that "Rosie is in danger of whining herself right out of my sympathy." Carm Gottuso of Utica, New York, commented in the same issue that "the show's plots and characters are very predictable." "While [Sharon Gless's] character develops further, the plots remain behind, uninspired," wrote Donna Kaye of Vancouver, British Columbia, also in the February issue. Ellen Kagan felt that *Rosie* "lacks humor and seems to take itself too seriously. It's hard to sympathize with her when she has so much materially." Lynn Yanagihara, of Cerritos, California, a staunch Gless supporter, wrote for the March 1991 newsletter, "The characters and relationships are not yet as fully developed as we'd like them to be." C. J. Bonfig of Havertown, Pennsylvania, felt that "while Sharon Gless's talent is still outstanding, the scripts are not. Gless breathes life into her character, but the supporting cast seems weak and clichéd."

CBS pulled *Rosie* in January of its first season and put *Northern Exposure* on Monday nights after *Designing Women*. The network could no longer air *Rosie* there; they said they needed something stronger. I understood that. Sharon's fans did not. I urged letters for *Rosie* in the April 1991 newsletter, as well as for our other endangered dramas. Feeling guilty and pressured, I pushed for *Rosie* long after I and many in VQT had ceased to find it significant.

In our newsletter, I continued to print both positive and constructively critical comments, feeling I owed it to both sides of the controversy to present a balanced view. However, the debate did not appear totally balanced, as the negative comments far outweighed the positive. For a while I saved letters that were too strongly worded to publish. One suggested that Barney view his tapes of *Cagney & Lacey* to remember what quality really was. The objective fans were frustrated and wanted to nudge the producer and writers to do better; the "diehards" constantly castigated me for publishing anything negative. The fact that I agreed with comments like the following by D. Joyce Reynolds of Baltimore, Maryland, in the October 1991 newsletter, did not affect my editorial decisions.

The characters don't sound like they're having conversations, they sound like they're giving lectures. I'm sure some viewers are turned off when they are constantly being told how they should think and feel. Why does every case have to be so heavily issue oriented, and why does Rosie have to yell at the top of her lungs to protest life's injustices? I think *Rosie* can remain a quality show and become a more widely appealing show if it would get off the political soapbox. Tell good stories, develop interesting characters, and have things happen that viewers can care about.

Reynolds added in the November/December issue,

> My comments in the October issue may have left the impression that I
> have a negative attitude towards the show. Actually, I love the show and
> watch it avidly every week. I tried to look at the show objectively and
> consider why it doesn't attract more viewers. I still think that the heavy
> emphasis on the message may be the factor. The episodes that have taken
> a more subtle approach have been more effective than those that *shout*
> the points it wants to make. I just want more viewers to like the show.

But objectivity was not appreciated. By now Barney Rosenzweig and Sharon
Gless were married. It was pointed out to me once that to criticize the show
was to criticize Barney, and that was unacceptable to Sharon.

I was called regularly by television journalists, asking for comments about
Rosie. Gless fans, unaware of how interviews with newsmagazines and newspapers are conducted and how sound bites are chosen, rose in anger over a
comment of mine chosen to be aired by *Entertainment Tonight* on November
6, 1991. *ET* ran the piece in response to Barney's ad, which would run that
week in three major newspapers; it was an open letter to viewers urging them
to watch the show on November 15, 1991. I was interviewed by *Entertainment
Tonight* for twenty minutes. Knowing that my comments would be carefully
scrutinized by the fans, I chose my words carefully, being sure to state that
Rosie was a quality drama endorsed by Viewers for Quality Television, and
that it deserved a full season pickup by CBS (the network had ordered only
eighteen episodes). I responded to each of the questions put to me in a positive way, not representing the contingent of VQT that felt *Rosie* had already
had a fair chance. One of the questions put to me was "What does *The Trials
of Rosie O'Neill* need?" My answer was, "What *The Trials of Rosie O'Neill* needs
is several million more viewers and a network to support it." Well, you might
guess. What aired was only the first half of that sentence, "What *The Trials of
Rosie O'Neill* needs is several million more viewers." Which was *exactly* the
point of Barney's open letter, about which *ET* was reporting! You would have
thought I had pronounced a death sentence, based on the responses of those
fans who lived to ingratiate themselves with Barney and Sharon. They wrote
me scathing letters that they copied to Barney. They wrote *TV Guide*. They
wrote *ET*. There was no explanation that placated them. To them, I was attacking the show, and, therefore, I was attacking Sharon.

Still, I persisted in giving honest assessments to the press, and they persisted in choosing sentences from my interviews that would further inflame

Rosie loyalists. *TV Guide* reported in its December 14–20, 1991, issue that although VQT urged viewers to write letters for *Rosie,* many VQT members were hesitant.[2] "I think the show appeals to a narrow group," Tim Carlson quoted me. "It takes the risk of offending those who may not be of the political persuasion that *Rosie O'Neill* espouses."[3]

The fans who were incensed over my remarks completely disregarded my advocacy efforts on behalf of *Rosie,* including a *USA Today* article of February 18, 1991, in which I named *Rosie* as a show deserving of letters,[4] a March 6, 1991, article in *USA Today* that reported *Rosie* VQT's Best New Drama for the season,[5] and a segment on CNN's *Showbiz Today* where I named *Rosie* one of five endangered shows worthy of viewer backing, resulting in several clips being shown from the show.

What was becoming clear to me was that an increasing number of viewers, in and out of VQT, wished, like me, that *Rosie* would appeal to a broader audience and thus be more successful. We also wanted the show to be more interesting, to focus more on character and less on conspicuous message. We felt that although there was nothing wrong with the message, it could be delivered more skillfully and with more subtlety and, therefore, more successfully. I felt that I presented a balanced view of what VQT thought of *Rosie*—the unconditional support *and* the constructive criticism.

The commentary continued as the show experienced viewer erosion. fourteen million had strayed since September. "We have enjoyed Sharon Gless for many years and would like to continue with *Rosie O'Neill,* but we object to her habit of sermonizing and always having a chip on her shoulder," wrote Mrs. Lee Werner of Webster Groves, Missouri.

In January 1992, Jeff Sagansky (CBS Entertainment president) said that *Rosie* would get one last six-episode tryout when he found the right time slot, once the winter Olympics were over. I went against the tide of VQT when I again urged letter writers to plead for the best time slot possible. I felt that each time the show seemed to be on the verge of finding its rhythm, its schedule had been interrupted.

Pat Everson of Gold Canyon, Arizona, expressed how she felt in our January 1992 newsletter: "Despite weak plots, shallow characters, and much sermonizing, watching *Rosie O'Neill* is still a pleasure, if only to be in the receiving line when Sharon Gless so skillfully [acts]."

A polarizing point for viewers seemed to be the opening sequence that showed Rosie with her psychiatrist—played by Barney (only the back of his head showed). VQT member Marjorie Cummings of St. Catharine, Kentucky, commented in the May 1992 issue, "I wish *Rosie* would do away with the very

unrelated opening—Rosie's monologue to her shrink. It has no relation to the
body of the story and actually has probably turned off many first-time viewers." Barney knew that it did. Jeff Sagansky had shown him the audience statistics, minute by minute, that showed exactly where people turned off the
show.[6] But Barney liked the bit, and kept it at the beginning of the show.

Barney's assistant, Carole Smith, gave me some insight into the confu-
sion of those associated with the show when she expressed the opinion, as if
it were fact, that when VQT first formed, it was just an upscale Sharon Gless
fan club. I was dismayed to learn that this is how VQT had been perceived by
those I had admired most. VQT never was a Sharon Gless fan club, "upscale"
or not; I resented the implication.

Barney and the people at *Rosie* dismissed VQT's opinion of the show
because it was not indicative of the glowing mail he was receiving. It seemed
logical to me that their hard-core fans would not criticize them directly.

D. Joyce Reynolds from Baltimore, Maryland, summarized it in our January 1992 newsletter:

> I'd like to blame CBS for [the show's] low ratings, but the truth is,
> while they may not have been enthusiastic about the show, they've
> certainly given it a fair chance. I can't blame viewers who did indeed
> sample the show. No, it seems to me the blame rests mostly on the
> shoulders of Barney Rosenzweig. I still believe he should have attracted
> and built his audience first, then gradually injected his messages.

Apparently a Gless admirer, Reynolds added, "I feel that Ms. Gless succeeded
in making Rosie a believable person, but that success may be lost or overlooked in the general disregard for the show."

Sharon Gless admirer Marsha Campbell, a VQT member who had successfully bid for a Day on the Set of the show at one of our auctions, raved
about Sharon Gless in our August/September 1992 issue even after the series
was canceled. "She [Gless] triumphed over the mediocre writing, mostly
stereotypical characters, preachy plots, and even the failure of the writers to
completely develop her own character."

CBS aired the last six episodes on Saturday nights at 10:00 starting April
11. In Matt Roush's review for *USA Today,* he gave it two stars (out of four)
and concluded, "While CBS may have done little to help it out, there's no
compelling reason why it should."[7]

Just before the airing of the last six episodes, any remaining patience with
me from Barney and Sharon came to an end. Monica Collins interviewed me

for "The Collins Report" in *TV Guide* that she would call "The bloom is off this long fading 'Rosie'." It would run the last week in March 1992.[8] I did not know what her slant was going to be, which is not an excuse for having given her further ammunition for her story. Collins openly criticized Barney for "shamelessly and persistently" promoting the series, "crying out for critics and fans to save the show." Collins wrote that this time, Rosenzweig was "crying in the wilderness" and claimed that *Rosie* was "better off gone and forgotten."[9] Collins seemed to agree with many VQTers when she described the arc of the last six episodes where "the emphasis shifts from her professional life as a humorless, beleaguered public defender to her personal life as a humorless, beleaguered mistress."[10] Taking no prisoners, Collins reminded readers that of the twelve episodes broadcast so far that season, only the first two broke into the top 60. Enter Dorothy Swanson, who admitted to Collins for the interview that *Rosie* was a "hard sell." In all honesty, and in print, I said, "With a show that consistently drops off, it's just hard to argue it."[11] Collins ended her column by telling Barney it was time to stop, that "his campaigning is just one trial too many in the many trials of *Rosie O'Neill*."[12]

That column would haunt me. Months later I came to realize how livid Sharon was over this. A disgruntled Gless fan sent me an audiocassette of a radio interview with Sharon and Barney. In it, Sharon mentioned how Monica Collins and I had obviously gotten together to trash the show. She made sure that the listening audience knew, contrary to what Collins had said in describing me, that VQT had *not* saved *Cagney & Lacey;* that I and VQT had not even existed at the time (I did exist at the time, but of course, VQT did not) and that Barney had saved *Cagney & Lacey.* I felt sad listening to the tape, and realized that my relationship with Sharon and Barney was truly over. I did not feel that anything could ever heal their feelings toward me. But time did apparently heal to some extent. Sharon Gless and I made our peace a number of years later without ever talking about what had happened. In response to a letter I wrote her in which I suggested that perhaps there had been enough "water under the bridge and over the dam and through the woods," she called, responding with characteristic graciousness and good humor. In that call and one other, we talked of many things. Like old times. Only not quite.

Except for written conditional permission to quote from his early notes and letters to me for this book, Barney Rosenzweig and I have not communicated. He told a gathering of TV critics in 1994 that we had had a falling out over comments I'd made about *Rosie* to the press. He relayed to journalists his perception that he had invented VQT.[13]

Not until July 1996, in a Los Angeles–based magazine called *Lesbian News,* did Sharon Gless offer some insight in print to the *Rosie O'Neill* story. In examining her character, Gless said, "I wanted her to be something so far away from Christine Cagney, but I fucked up. I lost some of the joy that I bring to the project by trying to be so unlike Cagney. She [O'Neill] was serious and not irreverent."[14] But Gless still blamed the network, not the show, for the demise. "In the second year, it had five time changes. Yes, it was politics."[15]

The Thomasons

"The VQT Award simply comes from the hearts of all you viewers who care so much. And it means a lot to me that you recognize us. Whatever success we achieve with *Designing Women,* we feel that you are truly partners of ours and our success also belongs to you."[16] It's a sadly similar story. VQT loved their first show (*Designing Women*), liked their second (*Evening Shade*), and rejected their next two (*Hearts Afire* and *Women of the House*). While those two added to the distancing, the rift began while *Designing Women* was still on the air, during a highly publicized feud between Delta Burke and the Thomasons. Delta went public with accusations that she had endured verbal abuse from the Thomasons, and the Thomasons countered those accusations in what became a war of faxed press releases. Delta was ultimately written out of the show.

The feud tore viewers apart. They resented having to take sides and they resented the intrusion of the conflict upon the course of the series. As Cindy Henderson of Bluefield, Virginia, said in the February 1991 VQT newsletter,

> To all those involved in the feud, please wise up. Evidently somewhere in your genteel Southern upbringings, someone forgot to inform you that private business is not conducted in a public forum. You have forced friends to choose between friends. You have weakened an integral part of your show. You are risking everything in this clash of egos. Sit down and work this out like the mature adults you all are reported to be so that you can fully concentrate on continuing to be the best sitcom on television.

Disenchantment with the show evidenced itself as early as mid-1991. Cindy Thompson from Pittsburgh, Pennsylvania, wrote in the May issue, "I stay in the room while *Designing Women* is on the air in the vain hope that it will recall its former standards." Trish Elliott of Oakland, California, agreed, submitting for the June 1991 newsletter, "It saddens me to say it, but there is nothing unique or special about *Designing Women* anymore. I find myself agreeing with those who call it shrill and silly. The plots are not being written true to the characters. It is a tribute to the outstanding cast that they rise above the material to the extent that they do."

It was probably expected that VQT would never publicly say anything critical about *Designing Women,* the show it had helped resurrect and that gave the group its credibility. I imagine the producers were bewildered—in retrospect, perhaps rightfully so—to read comments such as the following by Stanley Hocevar of Euclid, Ohio, in the November/December 1991 newsletter: "It is as if someone stripped these women of their intelligence. For me, the one thing that has always set this show apart from others is its focus on the conversations among the four distinct and distinguished women of Sugarbaker's. But now it's only trivial chatter." Ann Raymont of Indianapolis added to that issue, "The stories have just lacked heart lately, and miss the funnybone more than they used to."

When the 1991 season began, *Designing Women* had lost three of its original women—Delta Burke, Jean Smart (who chose not to renew her contract), and Linda Bloodworth-Thomason, who relinquished creative control of the show. The loss was too sudden and too great.

A slight and inadvertent misquote in *TV Guide* stung me and had to have hurt the Thomasons, as it gave the impression that I had taken Delta's side in their feud with her. By October 1991, Jan Hooks and Julia Duffy had replaced Burke and Smart with characters that many found "shrill, poorly conceived and generally unsatisfactory."[17] *TV Guide* reported that the show's producers and the cast were happy with the show, but that despite high ratings (the show was still nestled between *Murphy Brown* and *Northern Exposure* on Monday nights), longtime fans were not.[18] Responding in a telephone interview to how I felt Delta's departure had affected the show, I was quoted almost 100 percent correctly: "Suzanne was a character who started out hard, but Delta made her likable. She was the comedic center of the show."[19] In the interview, I had been certain to state that *Suzanne*—the character, not the actress—had been the comedic center; the way it ultimately read it could be construed that I had meant that *Delta* had been the comedic center. As soon as I saw it, I faxed an attempt at an explanation to the Thomasons; I do not think they ever saw it. I was told some years later that it had indeed been perceived that I had taken Delta's side. This incident began a long period of silence between the Thomasons and me.

Other viewers agreed, however, that Suzanne was sorely missed. *TV Guide* quoted another fan: "Delta was a star with real impact. That spark is gone."[20] And VQT member Marjorie Cummings of St. Catharine, Kentucky, remarked in VQT's newsletter, "Suzanne was the indispensable dash of seasoning."

VQT gave "qualified support" to the Thomasons' next project, *Evening Shade,* and over the life of that show bestowed its Quality Award to Burt Reynolds once and Michael Jeter twice. *Hearts Afire,* the next vehicle, was never embraced by VQT. Yet, that show reunited us with Harry and Linda. In 1993 Harry and John Ritter attended a Meet 'n' Greet at our Conference on Quality Television at the Hollywood Roosevelt Hotel, and Harry, Linda, and numerous cast members from *Hearts,* including Markie Post, attended our tenth anniversary luncheon there as part of our 1994 convention.

Linda and Pat Murphy had hit it off like old high school classmates when they first met in 1987; their birth dates are only a few days apart. There had been subsequent correspondence and phone calls between the two, and every time they met, they picked up where they had left off. Pat sat at Linda and Harry's table at this luncheon. Pat told me later that Linda had said to her with her usual enthusiasm, "We're so glad you love the show (*Hearts Afire*)!" Honest as always, Pat looked at her kindly and responded, "But Linda, we don't." "Oh, really?" Linda said, surprised, then added with a laugh, "Oh, that's all right, you're gonna *love* the next one!" She hadn't even known that VQT did not care for *Hearts Afire.*

The "next one" would be *Women of the House,* developed by the Thomasons for Delta Burke, effectively ending their feud and resurrecting the character of Suzanne Sugarbaker. It lasted less than a season. Critics did not embrace it, VQT did not endorse it, and I let VQT members express why in our publication.

After a couple of months of reading the negative, but hopefully constructive comments, Harry Thomason sent me a one-line fax politely asking that he be removed from our mailing list. I should not have been surprised. I wondered how he had lasted as long as he had. First, the loss of interest in *Designing Women,* then the cool reception to *Hearts Afire,* now rejection of *Women of the House.*

Harry had taken umbrage earlier at some of the comments in the newsletter about *Hearts Afire* and called to tell me so. He sounded impatient and upset and wanted me to know that Linda was doing her best writing ever on *Hearts.* Instantly recalling the brilliant, beautiful writing on *Designing Women*'s "Dash Goff, the Writer" and "Killing All the Right People," I asked Harry, "Do you really believe that?" He said that he did. There was nothing more to say.

In *Women of the House,* Linda again had four women for whom to write, and perhaps unknowingly and unintentionally repeated herself. Aside from the fact that many jokes were recycled from *Designing Women* (one viewer wrote me that she got the feeling we were supposed to think of Julia Sugarbaker when Nattie gave her "we aren't hookers" speech[21]), she even created a situation where the four could be in bed together—in the Lincoln bedroom of the White House—apparently trying to repeat the hilarious scene from *Designing Women* where Julia, Mary Jo, Suzanne, and Charlene all ended up in a motel room bed together when they caught the flu while traveling.

There was also a basic conceptual problem with *Women* that a VQT member pointed out in our February 1995 issue. Ruth Darmstadter, a student of the Constitution from Bethesda, Maryland, called our attention to the fact that "no one can be appointed to fill a House vacancy, as in the premise of this show. Unlike the Senate, either a special election must be held or the seat remain vacant until the next regular election." Ruth quoted from the text of the Constitution and suggested that "the Thomasons of all people should know this." I printed the comment, after pondering long and hard about criticizing the Thomasons in this way. I hated to do it, and probably would not do it again. I lost their regard over a technicality, albeit an honest one.

After receiving Harry's fax, I wrote an editorial for our newsletter that thanked the television producers and publicists who understood and respected the necessity of VQT being objective. I stated that VQT "does not give unconditional support depending upon who the producer (or star) is." I reiterated that VQT's Members' Forum in the newsletter reflected the opinions of individual VQT members, and when numerous comments come in about a show, whether positive or critical, those opinions will be published "in the hope that any criticism will be taken constructively." I explained, without revealing any names, that when a producer requests that his or her name be removed from our mailing list, we feel badly, especially when the association has been one of long standing. "It is a loss. It is deeply felt." I ended that editorial with words from Pat Murphy that Harry Thomason would never see because he would not receive the newsletter: "We regret that occasionally a rare but valued few think we will cheer always because we did once."

Although Linda had told us once that our judgment about her show meant more than anyone else's[22], the reality was that they expected our judgment to always be positive.

When the Thomason association fell apart, Pat and I felt for the first time that VQT was not worth it. We had hurt people we cared about, and apparently had lost their friendship. Yet, ironically, we could never have even known them without VQT. What I had done in both instances was choose the business over the friendship. If VQT was to remain credible, objectivity had to be maintained. But the cost had been high.

Not until I sought permission from Harry Thomason to publish the photo in this book showing Pat and me with Linda and the women was communication reestablished. An assistant relayed Linda's love to both Pat and me, and Harry sent his best wishes, warm regards, and the hope to meet again, along with his permission to use the photo. It felt good. I allowed warm, real feelings for this amazing couple to resurface.

A conclusion may be reached in analyzing the Thomason, Rosenzweig, and Gless relationships: producers and actors may be peeved for the moment, but they often come back as time passes and circumstances change. Or it may just be that some people are willing to forgive and forget and others are not.

Manipulations

The potential for manipulation of this organization has always been tremendous. For the most part, I have been successful at avoiding being manipulated. It isn't always easy when you're walking the fine line between maintaining credibility and maintaining good public relations.

Too many times I agreed to let a production company or a studio fund a special mailing to VQT members so they could reach them to tout their show. In reality, they wanted to influence; I saw it as an attempt to inform. I never sent anybody VQT's mailing list; I always prepared and mailed the communication from VQT headquarters. Numerous VQT members would always let me know they resented this, and that they felt manipulated. In my defense, we used these funded mailings as opportunities to communicate with our members between newsletters, and always included other material of immediate interest to our members. Funding was always a problem, so we rarely turned down an occasion to contact our readers.

The manipulations are not to be confused with the networks and studios using the results of our polls and endorsements to try to increase awareness for shows valued by them and by us. This was why we existed. This served to increase awareness of VQT and of a quality show.

Valerie Harper

Two different Valerie Harper representatives called me in August 1987 when the star was fired from *Valerie* over a salary dispute. Twice in one week I was asked to muster my troops and start a campaign demanding Harper's return to the show (her character had been killed off). I had to refuse. The issue was her salary, not the quality of the show, and it would have been highly inappropriate for VQT to become involved.

I don't remember how the *Washington Post* got the story, but on September 2, 1987, the newspaper ran a "Giving Thumbs Down to 'Valerie'" story along with my photo. It was a big story at the time, as Lorimar had sued Harper for breach of contract when she held out for higher wages. I told *Post* writer Elizabeth Kastor that "what was disconcerting was that they [the publicists] called twice and didn't get the message," and that they didn't seem to understand my limitations.[23] Harper's publicist, Monique Moss, told Kastor she was hoping I could help and that "we didn't know what the group was, exactly what the ramifications were."[24] Kastor went on to report that I not only told them I couldn't help, but advised them not to attempt such a campaign, that "public opinion would not be on the side of Valerie Harper in the middle of a contract dispute. I'd question how grass roots this campaign is if it starts in Hollywood."[25]

Ken Wahl and Stephen J. Cannell

The executive producer, Stephen J. Cannell, claimed that Ken Wahl, the star of the show, quit *Wiseguy;* Ken Wahl said that Cannell fired him. I do not pretend to know the whole story, nor am I prepared to say who was right and who was wrong. But I became involved, and learned a valuable lesson: never take sides in any controversy involving television personalities.

CBS announced that *Wiseguy* would not be returning in the fall of 1991, but would be a midseason replacement with Wahl "probably returning for the first two to four episodes before leaving the show as Stephen Bauer inherits the lead."[26]

Wahl called me from Mexico where he was filming a movie. He made my acquaintance, said how much he admired the organization, and that he wanted VQT members to be given a message from him. I took it down, and printed it in our July/August 1990 newsletter—but not before I faxed the statement to television journalists who I presumptuously thought should know Wahl's side of the story. It was a disastrously inappropriate move on my part. I had taken sides without having all the facts. Wahl said, and I let the world know,

> Under no circumstances did I dump the show. It's been near and dear
> to me. It appears that I just wasn't wanted anymore. I am not doing
> the first two to four episodes as reported; my heart is not in it because

the only reason they want me to do it is to introduce the new character so there will be a smooth transition. I want to thank David Burke, head writer and executive producer, and Les Sheldon, executive producer, for all their hard work and determination to make the show the best it could be. We've never been afraid to fail; we've always given it everything we had to make it the best it can be.

Journalists used parts of Wahl's statement in their columns, effectively disputing CBS and Cannell's version. John Carmody wrote on June 4, 1990, "Wahl told the *L.A. Times* and Viewers for Quality Television that he had been dumped and was not going to do the early episodes and now there's talk that Wahl's agent and Stephen Cannell are having further talks."[27] Knowing Wahl was notoriously press phobic, I came to realize that I had probably inadvertently and momentarily become Wahl's publicist.

USA Today reported on the same date that Wahl disputed CBS's statement that he would return to just "make a clean transition."[28] Wahl told Peter Johnson that it was Cannell's fault.[29] Johnson quoted Wahl: "He [Cannell] told me he didn't like what I or the writing staff had done with the show. He said, 'Why don't we just shake hands and go our separate ways?' So I agreed. I wasn't going anywhere where I wasn't wanted."[30]

The *New York Post* also reported information from my fax, quoting Wahl, thereby giving ink to his account. According to the *Post*, VQT's campaign for *Wiseguy* had become a campaign for "the restoration of the *Wiseguy* that viewers knew and loved."[31]

Stephen Cannell called me the day after those news stories appeared and cast doubt on the truthfulness of Wahl's statement. He told me Wahl was using me, insisting that he did want out of *Wiseguy,* and that he had letters from Wahl and his attorneys proving it. Cannell faxed me a handwritten note from Wahl dated January 31, 1990, that did indeed request release from any obligation to render further services. The reason given had to do with what Wahl felt was an unreasonable expectation to complete a current episode on time, despite a painful ankle injury.

I received several more calls from people I knew in the industry. Each warned me to steer clear of any controversy involving Wahl. Yet, two people close to Wahl, a publicist and a producer, backed his version of the story. I was confused, and felt foolish. Either way, I had allowed myself to be manipulated. I never did have contact with Cannell again, although VQT members would meet Wahl at three future VQT conventions. One of the executive producers and the series' show-runner, David Burke, addressed us at our 1990 convention and talked at length about *Wiseguy*. I asked him if he thought it was the focus on characterization that had made *Wiseguy* so unique among all the other "cop" shows. Burke's reply, published in our January 1991 newsletter, corroborates Wahl's interpretation of the problem, that there had been extreme disagreement between himself and Cannell about the direction of the show:

> For me as a writer, it was never a cop show. It was a show about hidden agendas and political motivations and the struggle for power, and that struggle for power finally got translated to policing. The closest thing I had to a cop in my mind was when I wrote the Frank McPike character. There was constant disagreement between myself and the company [Cannell Productions]; it never really mattered to me if we caught anybody. In the third year, we had an arc that took place in Washington, and I didn't want to catch the bad guy. Stephen Cannell just flat out over-ruled me and made me catch the bad guy. I wanted Vinnie to be vanquished from his authority in Washington and wander around the real world for seven or eight episodes and then find his way back to Washington to defeat this man who had defeated him. But it didn't work out that way, because there was a rule that could not be transgressed, which is you must catch the bad guy at the end of the arc.

Burke insisted this "rule" came from Cannell, and described Kim LeMasters, head of CBS Entertainment, as "incredibly open to new approaches." He added, "If you look at Kim's tenure, you can see *Wiseguy* and *Designing Women* and *Frank's Place*" and "you can almost see Kim's ghost in your monthly newsletters. He was real supportive of doing things differently."

In the same interview, Burke confirmed VQT's role in the *Wiseguy* story by saying, "You guys were incredibly important to that show. It helped Kim [LeMasters] justify renewing it; it literally helped keep us on the air."

Ken Wahl appeared on a panel discussion in September 1991 with Jill Eikenberry, Neil Patrick Harris, Robert Picardo, and David Clennon. He painted a picture of an embattled show—his, David Burke's and Les Sheldon's vision for Vinnie Terranova versus "the people here in L.A." (meaning Cannell). He revealed, "We fought constantly." I asked how the producers in Los Angeles envisioned the show, and he said, "As a very typical kind of cop show. The whole reason I left *Wiseguy* is because the bosses wanted the show to become more visceral as opposed to cerebral, which is a fancy way of saying that he wanted more shoot-outs and car chases. And so I said, 'You can do that, but not with me.'" He added that "it was a miracle it was on as long as it was because there was so much opposition, not only from the producers, but from the network as well. Because they always want the guys in the show to be like the hunky guy, the whole *US* magazine stuff. And I flatly refused to do that, because we had something decent and asked, 'Why do we have to cheapen it?' I don't think the promotion for the show should be more important than the show itself."

Wahl's contention that the network attempted to cheapen the show by the way it promoted it was disputed at the time by the CBS publicist who had taken the show to her heart. Terri Corigliano stood in the back of the room that day in September 1991 when Wahl told VQT and any journalists present how inappropriately CBS had sold the show, and approached me afterward wanting to correct the impression Wahl had given of the network's publicity efforts. She walked in step with me as I hurried toward a crisis I had to deal with. I couldn't address her concerns at the time, but now, years later, want to.

When asked for her recollections for this book, Corigliano told me, "*Wiseguy* was my baby, my reason for wanting to get to work in the mornings."[32] She fell in love with the show at the same time I did, during the Steelgrave arc. "No one," Terri recounted, "not the television critics, myself or any other CBS executive, could have foreseen where Ray Sharkey, Ken Wahl, Jonathan Banks, Jim Byrnes, and this amazing collection of guest actors were going to take the story of Vinnie Terranova and Sonny Steelgrave, the mobster he came to love and respect, but had to bring down."

In fact, Terri recalled, most critics had dismissed the pilot once they saw a helicopter explode. "They thought Cannell was doing the *A-Team* again." When CBS "rested" the show for November sweeps, promising to bring it back after the holidays, Terri asked to work on the drama and for $10,000 to promote it.

> I had this idea—to edit the entire Steelgrave arc into a one-hour compilation reel. My boss gave me leftover money from that year's budget. And so there I sat, in the pitch black editing room with Jeff deRome, another publicist and *Wiseguy* aficionado [now at Fox]. He kept me company for two days and really long nights. It was easy to do, because the words and the performances were there. It was a labor of love. The reel ended with one line on the screen: "In January, the story continues."

Terri was heartened when critics responded to the tape by writing about it, admitting they had been too quick to judge the show. Viewers who already knew, among them many VQT members, persuaded people who didn't watch already to give the show a try. "We did put *Wiseguy* back on the air, starting with Kevin Spacey as Mel Profit—and we never looked back," Terri said.

Terri feels this back story is important because "for me, the only way to sell *Wiseguy* was to let the show speak for itself. I pitched the show one way: please watch this, and I guarantee you will want to write about it. It always worked. And I never changed the way I did business in four years, and I was never asked by anyone at CBS to do anything differently." Contrary to Wahl's assertions that he was asked to do publicity that would diminish the show, Terri insists, "We did no Vinnie the hunk T-shirts, we didn't set up any Ken Wahl *Tiger Beat* contest." Terri did recall the interviews that ran in *Rolling Stone*, which rarely covered TV, the *New York Times, Time,* and *Newsweek.* "Ken told me what he wanted and what he didn't, up front. Look, he was a nice-looking guy, and the media always wants to showcase that. But I respected his point of view, and we never exploited him. When we did publicity stills, we only shot him in character. No 'beefcake' stuff. When I looked at what Ken was doing on the screen, I thought 'good actor.' Period."

Today, Terri can still remember lines of dialogue from the show. She counts Banks, Byrnes, and Spacey as friends, and she is haunted by one last conversation between herself and the man who played Sonny. "Before he died, Ray Sharkey told me that when he was feeling lost, he'd take out that Steelgrave reel and sit in the dark, all alone, and watch it. To remind himself that the work was good, that something he did counted."

Terri is, to this day, disquieted by Wahl's assertions back in 1991.

His memories to the contrary, Ken Wahl had no enemies at CBS. The producers tried to make him happy, but they had to try to build the show's ratings. I do recall discussions about catching the bad guy, and "to arc or not to arc." We had to draw more than a cult audience, which was all we had, and that was not enough. We wanted it on the air, quality undiluted. It's insulting to the people at CBS and Cannell Productions, who worked their butts off on this show, to suggest otherwise. It was disheartening then and it's disheartening to me now to hear what he's saying. No one was happy when Wahl left. I'm sorry he can't look back and feel proud of what he left behind. The work is there—and it's good.

Elaine Batterby of Macedon, New York, responded to Wahl's departure in VQT's September/October 1990 newsletter:

I find it very hard to believe that Ken Wahl would arbitrarily and in that fashion opt out of a critically acclaimed series. I find it equally

hard to believe that Stephen Cannell would arbitrarily dump the central player in his series in a fit of pique. It is unlikely we will ever know
the real truth behind all this, but I think it's safe to say that some portion of the blame rests with each one of them. Unfortunately, the real
losers are going to be the viewers who want quality television.

VQT members did not care who was to blame for Wahl's departure from
the show; they only cared that the show was less without him.

NYPD Blue

NYPD Blue began its life on network television trying to overcome initial negative campaigning from fear mongers with a religious agenda who had never
seen the show. Immediately recognizing its quality, VQT advocated and countered the special-interest groups who campaigned to influence sponsors to
stay away and affiliate stations to refuse to air it. (See "Growing Campaigns".)

There was some pressure on me from the publicity firm representing
NYPD Blue in its second season to launch a "campaign" to further quell any
possible effects of boycotting and to interest bigger sponsors in the show.
Although I was interested in furthering viewer awareness in this quality show,
I was hesitant to throw VQT resources into a successful show when others at
that time needed those resources—and my time. The publicist I spoke to was
charged with *increasing* the success of the show, and wanted my assistance.
She told me over the phone that although *NYPD Blue* was certainly successful, it had the potential to make even more money. I was uncomfortable with
this from the start, and told her I needed a more compelling reason to continue to campaign, and asked that she supply me with one. More affiliates
had signed on to the show (only nineteen still refused to air it, compared with
fifty-seven the season before), and sponsors were not pulling out. I asked her
to better define the problem. After working with this very pleasant and well-
meaning individual for a number of months, and finding a disproportionate
amount of my time was being spent on what I determined to be an unnecessary endeavor, I had to tell her that VQT was not in business to help ABC
or Steven Bochco Productions increase their revenues; we had shows in danger of cancellation, and that was where our energy and funds must go.

In my opinion this "second-season campaign" was not necessary, and to
my knowledge it never happened. *NYPD Blue* became the hit it deserved to
be because it was *good,* not because of any gimmicky campaign.

"FAMILY" TELEVISION

BEFORE we analyze family TV, we must agree on its definition. Is "family" television about a family, or is it one that a family can comfortably watch together? For the purposes of this chapter, I'll assume the latter definition. *Touched by an Angel* is not about a family, but it can be enjoyed by all family members; *The Sopranos* is about a family, but the situations are of an adult nature.

Over the years, VQT has endorsed its share of family-friendly series, while rejecting others. The endorsement—or the dismissal—always had to do with the quality content of the show, not its moral content. The misconception exists that just because a program does not offend any member of the family, it must be "quality." That all "family" programs are "quality," and if it is not family oriented it cannot be quality. This is just not the case.

Merely the fact that a show is about a family and is wholesome, does not make it quality. One should ask: Is it substantive? Does the dialogue ring true? Is the dialogue memorable or trite? Would you talk like that? Would people react that way? Are you inspired? Are you stimulated? Are you involved? Are you bored?

Actor Stephen Collins (*Seventh Heaven, Tattingers, Sisters*) answered the question in VQT's one hundredth issue newsletter in May 1997. "Just because a show is trying to be a family show does not mean it is going to be a quality show. What makes a family series a quality program is the same thing that makes any series a quality program—careful writing, having a head writer with a strong point of view and a strong desire to tell a story a certain way."

Elaine Davis of Fairfield, Connecticut, clarified the issue in our June 1997 newsletter when she wrote: "I find as much quality in "family" programs such

199

as *Dr. Quinn* and *Touched by an Angel* as I do in programs such as *EZ Streets* and *NYPD Blue*. If the program enlightens, enriches, challenges, involves, and confronts me; if it dares to take risks; if it is honest, illuminating, and intelligent; if characterization is explored and if it is thought-provoking, it gets my endorsement regardless of whether it is family fare or adult entertainment."

A good quality drama must be about something. Just being about a family is not enough. The story must be compelling, the characters interesting. A quality drama is *not* simplistic, manipulative, predictable, contrived, condescending, or sappy, as too many family dramas tend to be. I've tried to encourage VQT participants, as critical, discerning viewers, to fine-tune their standards and continue to differentiate between the brilliant and the bland.

VQT member Gary McCloy offered in our November/December 1993 newsletter, referring to family programs: "I am concerned that many VQT members feel that if a series ends with a positive message and leaves you with a warm, fuzzy feeling all over, then it must be quality. Certainly quality has to show us more than strong moral values."

In an editorial for our April 1994 issue, I asked, "If it's a 'family drama,' it must be quality television, right? Not necessarily." I contended that the same standards set by VQT members themselves when they compiled the definition of a quality program must apply: that it must be involving and challenging; it must take risks; be honest and illuminating, appeal to the intellect, and touch the emotions. It should provoke thought. Characterization should be explored. Most of all, it must be *interesting*. As I said in *TV Guide* about *Party of Five*, Fox's drama about five siblings trying to raise themselves after the death of their parents in an automobile accident, "What sets this show a notch above the others are the substantive stories and moving characters."[1]

Pat Murphy wrote about two family dramas, *Byrds of Paradise* and *The Road Home,* which aired during the spring of 1994, neither of which survived. The networks, producers, and viewers appreciative of that genre questioned why. Both shows were touted and advertised as "family" dramas that everyone would love. Murphy attempted to explain the "why" in VQT's April 1994 newsletter.

> If these shows were on life-support, it would be one long line—flat, no blips, no ups or downs. Nothing happens that isn't predictable, except for the pre-teen vomiting immediately after a first kiss. I never would have predicted or expected that. And the next week she's putting laxative in the family cake; is this the first digestively-challenged teenager in primetime? Where does this come from? This kind of unexpected, I can do without.

Murphy referred to an episode of *Byrds of Paradise* where an annoying teenager lets the family car roll off a cliff after taking it without permission, and comments that the producers perhaps expected that viewers would be so happy she was safe that they wouldn't wonder how this accident might affect the family's insurance rates. "The child wrecks the family car, yet Dad is in trouble with the child for not understanding! By the time the family had their special moment at the rim of the volcano, I was wondering if the writers had thought of human sacrifice as a way to handle the daughter." Murphy questioned some scenes in *The Road Home*. Preparation for dinner seemed to take twenty-four hours in one story as kids prepared the laxative cake, grandpa came home for dinner, grandma sent him away, the son spent the night in jail, grandpa sold his boat but had time (before dinner) for fishing and sex with grandma, then they all played on the swings, then they had dinner. Murphy wrote that both shows felt to her like they were patronizing their audience, "as if they are setting up that 'ahhh' moment to be felt by all." Murphy admitted she was more judgmental about "the waste of resources and lack of attention to detail" because *Road* was produced by Bruce Paltrow and *Byrds* by Steven Bochco, both attached to earlier quality series. She challenged that "families are living, changing, breathing, volatile, emotional entities, not plastic formula people and cut-out plots."

Mike Antonucci of the *San Jose Mercury News* interviewed me at the time and referred to each show as a "driblet of tenderly scripted and heavily hyped 'family' shows."[2] I told him that "these producers and networks assume that if they call a show a family drama, it's going to be quality. And it's not necessarily so. We're supposed to accept something as quality because it has beautiful sunrises and sunsets, and birds and water and hand-holding."[3]

While some VQT members found the shows appealing, most did not and articulated why. Lucy Micik of Poughkeepsie, New York, asked in the May 1994 newsletter, of *Byrds of Paradise*: "Are the Matsons supposed to be a normal family, or Hollywood's idea of normal? Perhaps when the show stops trying so hard to be all things to all people it will get better." *Byrds of Paradise* and *The Road Home* each broke one basic rule: they were not interesting. How do you involve the whole family if the show is uninvolving?

When Brandon Tartikoff's New World family drama *Second Noah* was introduced by ABC midseason 1995, it was generally assumed it would appeal to all family members. After all, it had a multiethnic cast, adopted kids, adopted animals, and attempted to tackle modern-day problems. But in trying to appeal to everybody and offend no one, it captured the interest of only a few. It was not absorbing drama. John Levesque of the *Seattle Post-Intelli-*

gencer called it "sappy and unimaginative."[4] Critic Monica Yant reported that although fans were chatting among themselves on computer bulletin boards about the show, "they've yet to launch a full-scale viewer campaign."[5]

Brandon Tartikoff called me about the possibility of VQT getting behind *Second Noah*. I had to tell him there just wasn't enough interest. He was intent on starting a campaign to save the show, rumored to be on ABC's cancellation list. Ratings were consistent but mediocre, most weeks reaching about 13 percent of the audience.[6] It ranked 58th of 100 prime-time series, reaching 7.4 million households. "Family shows are notoriously slow starters," Tartikoff told Monica Yant.[7] But Tartikoff had the support of Parents Television Council, which lobbied for family-friendly programming. Pam Long, the series' executive producer, and Tartikoff, ran their own campaign. Monica Yant reported that "Long wrote 15,000 letters to priests, ministers and rabbis in the 50 biggest TV markets across the country, urging them to watch the show and encourage it among their congregations."[8] Tartikoff went on Oliver North's radio talk show twice and arranged a *Second Noah* marathon on the Disney Channel. Kathie Lee Gifford plugged it, as did Oprah Winfrey and Larry King.

But the passion was not there. Nor were television journalists with their critical acclaim. Yant reported that ABC received only a half-dozen letters from fans.[9] I responded to her, "It's passion that saves a show; you want people up in arms." I added, "I wonder if the people who watch *Second Noah* are that passionate, or if they're just glad to watch this nice little show. You're not going to rile people up just because it's nice. People want more than a nice family show."[10] Yant said that the show had not been endorsed by VQT perhaps because of its "attempt to please everyone without offending anyone."[11]

VQT is all for family dramas—as long as they are quality dramas. The two do not necessarily go together. When both are combined, they can be extraordinary, as in *Brooklyn Bridge, A Year in the Life, I'll Fly Away, Touched by an Angel, Dr. Quinn, Medicine Woman, Party of Five, Seventh Heaven, The Cosby Show, Family Ties, The Wonder Years, Life Goes On, My So-Called Life, Our House, Almost Grown*—all family shows supported by VQT in their network lifetime.

Once the networks figure out how to make shows wholesome *and* involving, they'll have more success in that genre. There is no formula. The bottom line remains for family *or* adult television: it must be interesting.

A DAY IN THE LIFE OF VQT

No two days are ever the same. There are, however, cycles of days: the frenzy of a campaign and all the letters that result; the hectic, often frantic preconference planning and postconference duties; the never-ending writing and editing of the newsletter; the periods when viewer survey information must be tabulated in the computer; and the "slow" days of just trying to catch up. There is one constant throughout. There is no paid staff, no clerical assistance, no one else to answer the phone; there are only occasional volunteers with limited time.

When I first moved to Virginia, I ran VQT from a finished basement room. I moved and have since run the organization from an upstairs bedroom. On a shoestring budget I might add. Because our cause is only television, and adult television at that, no foundation or corporation has been interested in funding VQT's work.

Because of the lack of funds, there has never been a budget for paid clerical help. Therefore, on a typical day, I am the only person in the office handling every task, whether talking on the phone to a network representative or television journalist or opening the mail. There are always interruptions, sometimes of a minor nature, sometimes so important that the task at hand is abandoned.

Let me try to describe a typical day with no campaign going on, no convention to plan, or no newsletter mailing scheduled. One might call this a low-key day. The mail must be retrieved from the post office and opened. Depending upon what is going on at the time, the mail can vary from a dozen letters to several hundred. As I open it I sort it into piles: what is suitable for the newsletter, new member and renewal forms, inquiries from viewers seeking more information, and surveys or ballots that have come in. I read every piece of mail myself. I place potential newsletter material in the next month's newsletter file. If there is time that day, I enter the renewals, new members, and inquiries into my database.

The newsletter is a full-time project by itself. I feel it should be monthly to keep the group glued together and to constantly keep our information out there. If finances do not improve, *The Viewer* may have to go back to an every-other-month issue. Roughly 70 percent of the newsletter is compiled information of opinions, observations, and thoughts of VQT members who have written me. Perhaps 30 percent is original writing by me or VQT members of an explanatory, informational nature. Sometimes I write opinion in an editorial format.

If viewer surveys are piling up for a particular viewing period, I begin entering that information. It is a tedious job. I have on occasion had help with this, but it takes more time for me to train someone to use the survey program than it does for me to do it myself. The program is old and unique and I understand its foibles. Besides, there is not a local volunteer who does not hold a full-time job that is comfortable or skilled at a computer.

During a typical day I might receive several calls from television journalists seeking comments on a particular subject. These are especially heavy when a new season starts. They are my favorite calls. I enjoy relaying VQT opinion for the general public to see. I just wish more journalists would tell their readers that they can participate in VQT. I've heard from many viewers who said they didn't know they could join.

Then there are the calls from publicists wanting to tell me about their current shows. Often these are welcome calls because the show is one VQT members have become interested in. Sometimes the call is a waste of the publicist's time—and mine. They just don't understand that it isn't the pitch that counts, it's the quality of the show.

Add a letter-writing campaign to the mix and the result is chaos. Often the daily work has ground to a halt because of the volume of letters arriving about a particular program. This happens less frequently now that there are fewer shows that provoke passion in viewers.

Throw in conference planning, which happens every summer, and you have nonending tasks. Some days every moment is spent preparing letters that I hope will persuade an actor or a producer to participate in our conference. One round goes out and the next round is being prepared for when those in the first round decline to participate. After the Quality Award winners are determined, I write letters to every one of them notifying them and inviting them to attend, again attempting to convince their personal publicists, who will invariably be the first to read the letter, that it will be beneficial for the winner to appear. There are name tags to prepare, informational packets to compile, questions for panel discussions to be formulated, details to be worked out with the hotel.

Local volunteer, VQT patron and longtime member Janet Harding wrote "Views of a Volunteer" for the March 1993 newsletter that described a typical newsletter mailing day. It was written so other VQT members might appreciate what went into the preparation and mailing of their newsletter.

> Once a month, we gather at the home of Dorothy Swanson to prepare your newsletters for mailing.
>
> We are a diverse group, mostly women, who arrive mid-morning ready to tackle a massive task. We wear comfortable clothes—sweats, sneakers, etc.—and usually bring our lunch, a 15 minute break at best. We have often worked through lunch, but we don't care because it is a labor of love. If there are no inserts or stapling to be done, we can finish in about four hours. If there is an insert, the task often goes into a second day.
>
> Because of United States Postal Service regulations, we must be constantly mindful of zip code order. If your mailing has a little round sticker on it, your newsletter or letter was the top one in the bundle. In addition, we need to be alert to "flags" on the address label. We may need to add a label alerting participants that they need to renew, for example.
>
> Bundles are secured by heavy rubber bands. Each state bundle is put into a mail sack (a filthy, dusty old mail bag). Each sack must have a label and an accurate count of its contents. In addition, about 20 percent of your newsletters are mailed first class and they are handled differently.
>
> As we do all of this, the phone is ringing and the fax machine is running. By mid-afternoon we get a bit giddy. If we don't have a good handle on the process, we can "lose it." Often, Dorothy is the first one to lose it. After all, she has written, compiled, and edited the newsletter, sent it to the printer, printed the labels, "flagged" the labels that need attention, and organized the mailing process before we arrive on the scene, so she feels totally responsible.
>
> When all 15 (or 18 or 20 or 30, depending on the weight of the newsletters) sacks are full, counted, and properly labeled, they must be hauled ("taken" doesn't quite cover it) to the Merrifield Bulk Mail

Acceptance Unit. If they are ready on a Saturday, local volunteer Chuck Adams usually takes over here. But if they happen to be ready mid-week, this task also falls on Dorothy and a volunteer with some residue of energy. Once at Merrifield, the mailing is verified and begins its journey to you.

Dorothy is all business about her work (and ours) and *always* is concerned that you get your mailing in a timely manner. We do our best to help. It is work and it is fun! A good, soaking bath or shower is our reward (and necessity) after a day spent preparing your mail. As my muscles relax, I think, "Yes! We did it again!"

In summer 1994, Trish Elliott visited the area from Oakland, California; I arranged for a newsletter day to coincide with her visit, and she wrote about it for the July 1994 issue. Only relevant portions that show how the reality of being at "VQT headquarters" differed from the expectation are reprinted here.

I was greeted at the door by Dorothy herself, who showed me around, after reassuring herself that the rest of the troops were proceeding diligently with the task at hand. Upstairs, the heart and guts of VQT, revealed the computers, the files, the chair in which Dorothy opens the numerous letters she receives—and of course, Tabitha the cat, comfortably curled up on her cushion next to the computer. I took a twirl in Dorothy's computer chair and it felt like being on the bridge of the Enterprise. The room is compact, cluttered, and impressively organized, with a fascinating gallery of pictures on the walls. I was very aware of the sense of VQT history that enveloped me when I entered that room.

Downstairs, the volunteers (Wendy Held, Janet Harding, Jean Hall, Tony and Rosie Ricciardi) were busily sorting, labeling, counting, and squeezing in tidbits of conversation as they worked. As Jessie dashed around barking for my attention, Dorothy settled me into the dining room group and explained my assignment—affixing labels and keeping the zip code in order, remembering to merge in complimentary copies from a separate pile of labels. It's straight-forward work but requires concentration. Once I'd demonstrated a grasp for that assigned task, she moved me into the living room where a pile of newsletters awaited first class stamps. The entire floor hummed with activity and purpose, and it was clear that everyone knew their task and worked on automatic pilot. I couldn't help being impressed with the dedication and familiarity they all brought to the work.

After lunch Dorothy moved me once again, into the kitchen to assist her in counting and bundling. This, she explained, was tedious, but the most important part. Based on the accuracy of our counting and bundling, the post office would either accept and mail the bulk rate newsletters or send them all back to be redone. I could feel my tension mounting, but soon I fell into the rhythm with my co-workers.

People began to leave as other duties called, and Janet and I stashed all the bags on the front porch for Ken Herst, who would stop by later and haul them to the bulk mail acceptance center. We had finished the job!

VQT member Don Schwartz from Mill Valley, California, envisioned a fully successful VQT in the June 1997 newsletter. We would have the funds and the help needed for VQT to fulfill its potential and realize its visions.

What would Viewers for Quality Television look like and what would it accomplish if it had all the money it needed to fulfill its mission? Here's my vision from specific to general. All VQT needs is funding or donations.

• There would be an announcement in each week's *TV Guide* alerting readers to VQT, explaining what it is, what it does, and how to join. There would be advertising in various entertainment magazines that include television. This level of advertising would facilitate increased editorial coverage of VQT's activities.

• Websites and other kinds of information would inform the potential participant in detail about the values and mission of the organization and how to participate.

• Membership would grow to a minimum of 50,000 viewers.

• There would be frequent polls of the membership evaluating the full range of available television programming.

• Results of polls would be available quickly on the website, through e-mailings and regular mail.

• There would be an industry liaison office to handle all industry communications.

• There would be a VQT handbook for all members exploring in depth the mission and values of VQT, the role each member plays, and the role VQT plays in the television industry.

• There would be an industry handbook including all information in the members' handbook, and clarifying how producers, distributors, advertisers, and broadcasters can best relate with VQT.

• There would be an annual televised awards show honoring the highest-rated shows, benefiting VQT.

• There would be a cornucopia of VQT-sponsored seminars, workshops, conventions, and conferences on specific and general topics within the television industry.

• As a result of all this activity and communication, the industry—and advertisers—would have an invaluable conduit of information about what viewers really think, how viewers make decisions, and what viewers really want from televised entertainment.

• Many more quality programs would be saved. And the overall quality of entertainment programs would be enhanced by this group of people who have decided to vote with their hearts and minds in addition to their pocket books.

In Don's dreams, or a possibility?

WHAT'S WRONG WITH THE SYSTEM?

The Networks

SIXTEEN years after its inception, VQT is fighting the same battle for quality television; only the players change from year to year as network executives come and go. Does this continuing battle mean there is something wrong with the system? Or is the problem simply the notion that viewers expect a say in what they see on the public airways? What is it about viewers that makes them want to participate? What is it about the industry that it refuses to change, to make allowances for that smaller and smaller piece of the pie, to continue to blame the quality show and the audience because "only" 9 million people tune in? Moreover, why do they shoot themselves in both feet with the preoccupation with the youthful audience, dismissing everybody over fifty-five? Viewer frustration mounts as year after year, quality show after quality show, good taste and intelligence conflict with a decrepit system that kills good shows because of networks' shortsightedness, misguided scheduling, and advertisers' insistence on an unreasonable percentage of "product"—viewers.

Viewers feel disenfranchised from the system that seeks them. VQT member Marilyn Gingrich from Laguna Niguel, California, complained to Matt Roush in 1993, during the *I'll Fly Away* letter campaign, "The networks aren't targeting audiences like me. They're targeting those who watch anything."[1]

Actress, television writer, and author Mimi Kennedy asked the VQT membership once, "How much time and passion can you devote to television you really love and get something good from before the return diminishes, even if the programs stay on? Can you begin to tell the network executives about your lives, and the importance of habit to brand loyalty, of shows and products?"[2] She also challenged the validity of a system such as Nielsen by asking, "When you know your habits are being monitored, do they stay the same as when they are not being monitored? When I am given a 'voter''s responsibility, I react differently to things. I keep thinking that this must affect the TV viewing of the Nielsen families. I consider the power of the Nielsen ratings, and wonder if the sophisticated psychological thought that has illuminated so many other aspects of our work and family has anything to contribute to considering the efficacy—or distortion—of this system which so affects our public discourse."[3]

With few exceptions, VQT members throughout its history strongly believed that there is indeed something wrong with the system, and that if network television as we know it is going to survive, the system has to be more accommodating to low-rated but high-quality shows. Viewers who care have been telling the networks for years, through VQT and individually, that there is a problem; I have printed many of the comments in our newsletters; I have conducted dialogues with network entertainment presidents.

Rosie Geonotti of Maricopa, Arizona, shared "Five Ways to Kill a Series" for our May/June 1993 newsletter. She was referring to NBC's treatment of *Quantum Leap*, but her mockery can be universally applied.

1. Move [the program] randomly throughout the schedule with little or no notice.

2. Fail to promote it. And when you do promote it, focus on things that have little or nothing to do with the context of the episode or program.

3. Never let the series garner much of an audience before moving it yet again.

4. Interfere with the creative process by making demands of the series' producers by asking for silly plot lines.

5. Make promises you never have any intention of keeping.

Speaking of "silly," VQT member Toni Snellback of Kailua, Hawaii, wanted the networks to know that "vulgarity is not wit."[4] Too often, coarseness on sitcoms becomes a lazy substitute for good writing. Lee Ann Gradwell agrees, saying, "I am so tired of pathetic comedies that only center on crude comments and sexual innuendo. If they can't be funny without being lewd, then they have no business being on the air."[5]

A prime example of the state of quality television in 1997 was ABC's puzzling treatment of its quality dramas. Canceled were Steven Bochco's *Murder One*, Andrew Schneider and Diane Frolov's *Dangerous Minds*, and Ed Zwick and Marshall Herskovitch's *Relativity*, all of which were victims of the worst possible network scheduling. ABC claimed they had no ratings-friendly place to put these high-quality dramas. (Of course they didn't—ABC was overloaded with prime-time newsmagazines.) *Murder One* had been mistreated from the beginning, first by Ted Harbert, then by Jamie Tarses. Harbert sealed the fate of *Murder One* from the start thinking he could challenge NBC's solid hit *ER* with something so new and innovative. Although perhaps overreaching and expecting too much of the audience (*Murder One* was to follow one trial for an entire season), VQT endorsed it and critics embraced it. However, that didn't prevent ABC from continuing to mishandle the show.

When David E. Kelley's 1997 midseason replacement *The Practice* (see "Growing Campaigns") was iffy for renewal despite better-than-average ratings, Kelley wrote me after he saw my advocacy ad in *Daily Variety* and gave me some insight into what was happening in network television. ABC executives had told him in meetings that while they loved the show, they could not commit to ever again airing it. While he expressed confidence to me that *The Practice* would make the fall schedule (it did), he felt that the message he received from the executives was "very unfavorable for the state of television. Whereas network executives were once inclined to stick with quality programs (perhaps for a full season or two) despite marginal ratings, now they are unwilling to even *sample* them sufficiently if the ratings are not immediate. As a result, character-driven series may become dinosaurs on the networks." Kelley made me feel that VQT was accomplishing something positive after all when he added, "Your letter served to remind us that people out there not only do care about content, they can even be passionate about it. I am hopeful ABC will feel passionate about *The Practice*. But it will have nothing to do with our content. Only our numbers."

Longtime VQT member Susan Lempke of Chicago, Illinois, feels that every time a network promotes a new show that captures the interest of millions of people, then cancels it after a few episodes, "they convince more television viewers that there is no point in watching new shows."[6] Lempke asked, "Who would want to tune in and begin to sort out the plot lines and the characters, then have it disappear just as you're beginning to enjoy it?" She was not surprised that the new shows trotted out midseason 1997 generated little interest. She surmised, then, that "the network honchos become convinced that they just haven't found the right formula, when the real problem is they've broken faith with us too many times, and now we don't trust them to keep a show on the air."

Another longtime member, Trish Elliott, recalls challenging CBS executive Maddy Horne at VQT's 1989 convention about *Frank's Place*. Horne assured the VQT audience that *Frank's Place* was renewed for the following season and expressed the hope that the show would find its audience if given a little more time. Never one to mince words, Elliott stood up, took the microphone, and insisted to Horne that *Frank's Place had* found its audience: "It is us."[7] When asked what she would say now to a network executive if asked, Elliott offered: "If you continue to reject 5 million people, casually commenting that a show failed to find an audience, that very audience will turn to cable. Just continue to repeatedly tell us that we don't count and you will continue to see us defecting. This is what people do who feel invisible. In no other medium are 5 million people discounted so thoroughly."[8]

That is precisely what I wrote in *USA Today* as a guest columnist on December 13, 1988. For that column, I adopted the misleading notion that viewers are consumers. I argued that no industry except the television industry routinely dismisses the opinions of millions of consumers and "spends vast sums on a new product, basks in critical acclaim, then pulls it off the market after a few weeks because it is not an instant success."[9] I declared that money and talent are wasted and viewers are cheated as new series are destroyed "before their promise is fulfilled."[10] I suggested that the networks adopt the practice of making a one-season commitment to every new show and consider a better system for measuring success. I also challenged viewers to become less passive and communicate their opinions about what is shown on TV. "If the networks cannot commit to the shows they present, if viewers sit idly by while intelligent, sophisticated series are cancelled, shows of substance will continue to be denied a chance to build and grow, and network TV will never reach its potential for excellence."[11] And as of 1999, they have not. Nothing has changed.

VQT member John Doucette of New York City told me that one of the most frustrating things to him about the current system is the tendency of the networks to relocate shows. He understands the reasons behind the practice, but he deplores it. He believes that a more constructive approach to boosting ratings for a low-rated quality show would be to "increase advertising for the show, targeting time periods where many viewers are watching, particularly viewers for whom that show is likely to appeal."[12] He also stated what is obvious to viewers but which escapes the networks, that what would really benefit a show is "to give it time to acquire a loyal audience. While I understand that the financial realities of television today make it difficult for network executives to have such patience, I feel that waiting may be a better long-term strategy than giving up on a show too early. When the show is abandoned, it may just be replaced with another show of lesser quality that may ultimately prove to be equally disappointing" in the ratings.[13] Doucette agrees that there are exceptions to this. Certainly CBS's transfer of *Everybody Loves Raymond* to Monday nights near the end of the 1996–97 season was logical, as was moving *Chicago Hope* out of the way of the instant hit *ER* a few years before.

Heidi Sanchez of Bethpage, New York, accepts that the networks are in business to make money, and that they get this money from advertisers who don't want to spend dollars for time periods where "nobody" is watching. "The only way anyone can tell who is watching is by a flawed ratings system."[14] Sanchez echoes many when she says, "I don't think you can use a few thousand randomly chosen families to gauge what America is watching." She asks, "What about people, like those who join VQT, who want something better, something above average that doesn't cater to the lowest common denominator? Is there no place for us?" Sanchez wants the networks to make a commitment to carrying a few quality shows no matter what the ratings. Sanchez says, "Make the money up on the big number shows. Use the lower-rated but quality shows to attract a certain audience and to provide [prestige] for the network. Have a few shows to be proud of."[15] Sanchez dares the networks to take a financial hit and have the courage to present quality shows that are not and never will be ratings winners. She dares sponsors to spend money supporting lower-rated quality shows. She believes that ultimately "perhaps supporting quality in this way would result in financial benefits for both the networks and the sponsors because of the quality-minded consumers they would be reaching."

As for the exodus of viewers from network television, Sanchez feels that it is "more a matter of increased choices than anything else." She doesn't think there is anything the networks can do about that, other than "make their choices more attractive to viewers than what is being offered elsewhere." And that the networks must accept a smaller share of the viewing audience.

Sanchez also suggests that PBS can do more to support quality American programs. "I'd rank *EZ Streets* right up there with *Prime Suspect* in terms of quality. Must actors have British accents for Mobil to support a show? Why can't corporations support quality American programming for the same reasons they support the marvelous British imports we see on *Masterpiece The-*

ater and *Mystery?* American television is capable of producing just as high quality a product as the BBC."

Rhea Baldino of Charlottesville, Virginia, believes that it is probably impossible to stop the erosion of viewers from the major networks unless cable and satellite companies price themselves out of business.[16] She adds that "the networks need an attitude adjustment if they really want more quality programming" that will require "much more patience in nurturing new shows." She chides network demand for "instant gratification" in lieu of long-term quality.[17]

VQT board member Laurie Strollo asks the networks not to underestimate the audience, claiming that "if you provide product that is intelligent, does not talk down to the audience, and attempts authentic emotion, dialogue, and characters, the audience will find it (provided it doesn't move too much)."[18] She suggests ceasing the practice of copying what has worked in the past. "*Seinfeld* worked, that must mean any situation comedy with a stand-up can't miss!" She also claims that "formula" shows and "stringing a bunch of gag lines together" are sure ways to annoy an audience. Strollo cites *M*A*S*H* as an example of how to win an audience with its "ton of funny quips" and "its perfect tone in irony as it explored the themes of war, suffering, and duty." She advises executives, in buying and cultivating product, to "keep in sight the bigger picture: what the show is about, what tone it wants to strike, and what the characters are about."[19]

Strollo warns the networks that they cannot expect the audience to "follow a show to the ends of the earth or endure frequent reruns," and that allowing reruns too early in the season or "double-pumping already-aired episodes creates overexposure." Strollo is another who understands that "the financial and business constraints that produce reruns are understandable and probably unavoidable," but that "common sense should be used so that a show that is just beginning to find its momentum can keep building audience before decelerating into reruns."[20]

Leon Czikowsky of Harrisburg, Pennsylvania, believes that innovation is a leading ingredient toward improving quality and attracting viewers.[21] Television executives should not lose sight of the fact that any art "requires time to develop an appreciation." That is, if television is to be considered an art form. He asks a valid question: "There are four major networks along with a few emerging networks. If there are few outlets for so many talented people and ideas, why is it that the major networks fail to present [superior] television programming over and over again?" Answering his own question, Czikowsky guesses that "the idea for the basis of a show is likely the result of a committee established to create a certain type of show to attract a prede-termined viewing population. This idea is then likely presented to a com-mittee of writers who may be more closely defined as dialogue writers than the show's creative engineers. Actors and directors then work within narrow confines of the resulting script."[22] Czikowsky feels the lack of quality when a show is predictable, does not tell us something we don't already know and of which we do not care to be refreshed, and insults us. He believes that quality shows emerge when an innovative idea breaks through the "cautious indus-try process." Unfortunately, the television industry's process of creating shows often results in a narrow category of shows that avoid risk and innovation. He wants the television industry to recognize that innovation, while risky, will be its salvation. "Rather than a group-think process in creating a show, wasn't it better to let Jerry Seinfeld and Larry David operate creatively by themselves?" He urges the industry to "be creative, be innovative, strive for quality, don't be afraid to challenge us with new ideas and new presentations, and don't insult our intelligence."

To win back viewers, Czikowsky advises the networks to look closely at what has appealed to the public, television critics, and the VQT membership. He finds consistent themes. "Good comedy exists where the joke surprises us in a believable even if ridiculous situation. Bad comedy is when we're not sur-prised, either because we've seen the same joke or the same situation before and it's so telegraphed that the joke is lost. Comedy can engage in outrageous situations if it remains believable." As for detective and mystery shows, Czikowsky asks that he be kept in suspense. "I never understand the detec-tive or mystery show that reveals the guilty party at the beginning of the show and then bores us with watching someone else figure it out."

Robert Black of Pasadena, California, agrees with Czikowsky. "Too many TV series are being developed by committees of marketing experts instead of by individual writers and producers. Writing by committee muddies any kind of individual creative vision."[23] Black feels it is obvious that basing a series format on marketing strategies instead of artistic sense produces a group of shows that all look the same. Black also criticizes executives who are "all look-ing for instant smash hits instead of shows that grow and develop at a slower but steadier pace. They want home runs, not base hits." He blames it on the enormous amount of money being spent on each series. The executives "don't want to wait around for a return on their investment. With the high turnover rate in most Hollywood jobs, those executives may not keep their positions long enough to see a profit if it does not come quickly."[24]

Black does not see the erosion of network television's audience as a negative. "Quality TV shows frequently are the product of one person with a strong artistic vision," and he cites Rod Serling, Gene Rodenberry, and David E. Kelley. All had "fresh ideas and the ability to present them in entertaining ways." He fears that most have a difficult time getting through the maze of mainstream Hollywood and that they are too often rejected by executives afraid to take chances. More and more often, their ideas are rewritten by a marketing committee.

Black concludes that unless the fabric of American society makes a drastic change, we cannot look to the "big" networks as the sole means of bringing quality to the American TV set. "There's simply too much money involved. Too often, it's either easier, safer, or faster to be mediocre." Black challenges viewers themselves to encourage quality programming wherever it is found, and suggests that viewer support can make an executive more willing to take a chance. "In a survival of the fittest free market, it is up to us to ensure the fitness of a quality product."

TV Guide's J. Max Robins blamed it on Madison Avenue in 1997. "NBC's fall schedule reflects a problem plaguing the industry as a whole—that programming decisions are increasingly based on business and marketing concerns rather than simply on finding the best shows."[25]

Newsday's Verne Gay had a solution for the networks in a 1998 column. "Exercise taste and discretion. Bad shows hurt a network in the long run. Conversely, good shows with weak ratings deserve a very long leash."[26] He praised CBS for keeping *Everybody Loves Raymond* on the air even though the numbers did not soar.

TV Guide's "couch critic," Jeff Jarvis, took his shot in April 1996 when he lamented that too many good shows go unnoticed. "Out here in the audience, watching TV has come to feel like working as a nurse in intensive care: you don't want to get too attached to a patient in case he dies."[27]

VQT members Sue Chapman and Don Schwartz both believe there is nothing wrong with the system. "Technology is progressing. There are new media," says Don Schwartz from Mill Valley, California. "The networks, which are of course big businesses, by virtue of their size lose the flexibility to change with the times." And declares: "They have paid the price."

Sue Chapman elaborates, stating that except for public television, "American television is market-driven and as such it will always be influenced by some form of rating system."[28] She believes that the Nielsen measurement is the most effective means of gauging the public's viewing habits. She even believes that demographics provide the decision makers with a remarkably, if frighteningly accurate, profile of who is watching their programming.

Chapman's argument is directed at the advertisers rather than the networks. "I resent advertisers who insist on limiting their scope to a target audience of 18–49 year-olds. I doubly resent advertisers who self-righteously attempt to inflict their own narrow-minded moral standards on me by withdrawing their commercial support of a program that they deem to be in conflict with their own world view." While resenting it, Chapman defends their right to do so in a free market system.

Chapman explains that because characters in television series come into our homes each week, we know them and personally care about them, and therefore feel very passionately about our favorite shows. "Because of that relationship, viewers are offended when a show is cancelled, moved, or recast." And the first target they see is the network. Chapman believes that none of the networks make their decisions capriciously, that considering the enormous cost of producing a show, it is in everyone's best interest to see the show succeed. "Rescheduling is an effort to make that success happen, providing there is sufficient promotion announcing the move." She notes exceptions. "There is no question that *Frank's Place* and *A Year in the Life* deserved more time to succeed."

Chapman acknowledges that with the proliferation of cable channels, the networks have become increasingly competitive. "The 'little three'—Fox, UPN and WB—can afford to stay with a marginal show for a longer period of time. However, the 'big three'—NBC, CBS and ABC—are hard hit by so much alternative programming; they are in a constant fight for survival to retain their viewers." She feels that "audience erosion" is an ugly term. "We haven't so much eroded as we have diversified our interests." But it means the same thing: the loss of audience for the "big three."

Chapman laments, but acknowledges, that today a show must be successful right out of the gate, that high ratings are necessary to justify high advertising fees, "which are necessary to pay high licensing fees which are necessary to pay high production costs." She knows this is how the system works. "That's why it's called show *business* or television *industry*." And she does not see this as a negative. "The competitive nature that exists in television today is compelling the networks to continually offer a variety of product. There should be something for everybody on TV. It won't all measure up to a given individual's or group's criteria of quality." As examples of audience diversification, "*The Dukes of Hazzard Reunion* is not going to attract the same audience as *Masterpiece Theatre*. Those viewing the A&E/BBC production of *Ivanhoe* are probably not going to tune into *Men Behaving Badly*." But Chapman praises the system that allows that wide range of variety, and echoes what has been said many times: "We get the television we deserve."

Despite Sue Chapman's understanding and acceptance, producers of television programs have shared viewers' frustrations for years, and some have expressed it to VQT. Jacqueline Zambrano, executive producer of *Under Suspicion,* the short-lived CBS detective series starring Karen Sillas, told me in an interview for VQT's February 1995 newsletter: "If I had the power, I would not choose a different time slot; I would choose a different method, or a different madness, by which we put dramas on the air and then decide to keep them there, and commit to them for a certain amount of time."

Deborah Joy Levine, creator of *Lois & Clark: The New Adventures of Superman* and *Courthouse,* said at our September 1995 Conference on Quality Television: "The system to a certain extent is based on fear. They're [network executives] fearful that they're not going to get ratings and they're not going to get a big hit show."

Judith Paige Mitchell, who developed *John Grisham's The Client* for CBS's 1995–96 season, explained that "the executive producers are answerable to a studio, and the studio is answerable to a network." And "from their point of view, they're [the networks] investing huge sums of money. From our point of view, it's not enough money to make the show. So we're being asked to substitute imagination for money."[29]

Peter Noah, an *Anything But Love* producer who tried and failed to garner acceptable ratings for two shows in a row (*Dweebs* and *Mr. Rhodes*), offered some perspective at VQT's 1995 conference: "The blinding revelation to me is what do these [Nielsen] numbers mean. If you get a 30 share, you are a raging hit. You are probably in the top ten; you could be in the top five. What a 30 share [really] means is that seven out of ten people who are watching television that night are watching something else."

Ron Cowen and Daniel Lipman, cocreators of NBC's *Sisters,* told me in an interview for VQT's newsletter in 1993 that "the problem is the *expectation* the networks have of dramas in tough time slots; the solution is *not* to get rid of the dramas and replace them with shows that will appeal to a lower common denominator."[30]

Ron Koslow suggested in an interview for VQT's newsletter that "a network owes the public a certain amount of good will," and thought that a certain number of television shows could be made as "something to give back to the people."[31] Koslow liked the idea of the networks "doing something to enrich the public consciousness," and suggested that if a show such as *Beauty and the Beast* or *The Days and Nights of Molly Dodd* is performing at all, if it has any kind of audience, "a network lets a show like that run. I think the good will that a network creates by allowing a show like that to run comes back many, many fold." (This is the man who had written a fairy tale, remember.)

CBS's Kim LeMasters told VQTers while he was the network's entertainment president that "the bottom line of my job is to simply produce hits. That's what we're supposed to do. We are *commercial* television, and our companies are driven by ratings that translate into dollars." He added, however, that "ratings success at the cost of all other standards is not right."[32] LeMasters cited pressure from affiliates as a factor in the decision to cancel.

Brandon Tartikoff said at the same panel discussion that "no one sets out to make bad television. The road to cancellation is paved with good intentions."

At a 1993 panel discussion with VQT, Ted Harbert defended the need to cancel low-rated shows. "There just comes a time when we say, well, the people who watch it love it, but there are a lot of other folks that don't. So it ends up being my job to make the terrible decision to say, well, I've got to go find something that maybe more people will watch." (And that will make more money.)

At the same panel discussion, Robert Singer, creator and executive producer of NBC's *Midnight Caller,* responded to the network's moving of his show from Tuesday night at 10:00 (where it successfully anchored the night) to Friday night where it did not work. Because it was Friday night, NBC wanted Singer to "inject more action."[33] He felt the networks could be more attentive to the content of a show and "pick their time periods more based on that."[34] Harbert responded, "I don't know what the explanation could have been as to how it made sense to take a time period leader like *Midnight Caller* and make it a loser in another time period. The most precious asset you have is a successful show and if you end up diminishing that asset by a scheduling move, you get your scheduling stripes taken away."[35] Harbert had his stripes taken away in late 1996.

Singer had a solution that nobody has yet tried. "The first 13 weeks [of a season], let everybody concentrate on making the show better. Let the advertisers have some faith in the show and open [the Nielsen numbers] up at the end of 13 weeks. You could see a trend: the audience is finding the show; the audience is rejecting the show; we're flatlining here; it appeals to them. So that way you're not changing bolts on a car." It sounded like a wonderful idea to me.

Marvin Kitman told the networks to "stop blaming alternative media" for the loss of audience.[36] He questioned, "Why don't they [the networks] face up to the fact that they are causing 'the vanish'? Why don't they make decisions the old way, based on their own convictions about what entertainment is or should be? The old giants of show business always operated that way. They knew what the people wanted, not what the numbers told them so inaccurately."[37] I asked the network entertainment presidents to respond to this at our 1997 panel discussion. Littlefield answered: "Marvin and a number of the other critics think that most of the decisions we make are based on research. [But] we make decisions based on what our instincts tell us is good work, believing in the people—it's a huge gamble." Based on this response, Kitman is right, the "old giants" of the TV business had better instincts than the present ones.

It seems inevitable that the networks will continue to lose viewers if they don't change their criteria for presenting and keeping programs of quality. Network executives continue to determine that 9 million viewers are not enough—10 million are not enough—5 million are not enough. Now they are gone—customers, whether consumers or product, who were turned away. *That's* the problem. The result is loss—of product, of program, of viewers.

To make matters worse for themselves, the frenzy to satisfy advertisers and program for young viewers reached a pitch for the 1999–2000 TV season. The *New York Times* counted eighteen of thirty-seven new shows on the six broadcast networks looking at the world "through youth-colored glasses, joining more than a dozen returning series with similar skews."[38] Writer Stuart Elliott noted that "the broadcast networks will be diverted from an audience they ought to be pursuing: the aging baby boomers, the 76 million consumers born from 1946 to 1964 whose incomes for the most part dwarf those of younger viewers."[39] Elliott quoted Stacey Lynn Koerner, vice president for broadcast television research at TN Media, the media services arm of True North Communications: "A broadcaster is exactly that, a 'broad-caster.' Broadcasters can't narrow themselves to one audience and remain viable. They have to in some sense be all things to all people."[40] Elliott makes the case that if broadcasters "narrow their focus to fixate on youth" they "run the risk of becoming clones of cable networks, which most commonly aim their programming at smaller, specific targets. That would then weaken the strongest argument for advertising on broadcast TV."[41]

Michele Greppi of the *New York Post* warned in her June 9, 1999, column on this subject, "Those who think smaller are doomed to be smaller."[42]

VQT member Leon Czikowsky said to network programmers in the July 1999 newsletter, "If you program for a narrow audience, do not be surprised when you lose *total* audience. If you concentrate on producing quality programming, you will attract more viewers. All age groups recognize quality. If you produce inferior programs aimed at a select audience, you usually insult the intelligence of the select group and lose the rest of the audience."

The big news for the 1999–2000 season was that the successful new shows featured and appealed to grown-ups. Most of the new series about teens and people in their twenties failed. Hits *Family Law, Judging Amy, Now and Again, Once and Again, Law & Order: Special Victims Unit,* and *The West Wing* are hopefully the beginning of a new trend. They certainly revitalized the drama.

Nielsen Ratings System

It is a certainty that some kind of ratings system will always be necessary to gauge the success of television programs. Even Viewers for Quality Television uses one. In 1998, the networks were challenging the validity of the system it has relied on all these years, the system that has been allowed to kill the quality shows mentioned in these pages. The major networks were challenging the Nielsen system because it did not report sufficient audience for them. They want a system that will report a larger audience so they can demand higher advertiser rates. *Sacramento Bee* TV columnist Rick Kushman believes that both the networks and Nielsen Media Research are right.[43]

The business of television continues. What is known about the current Nielsen system?

In his April 20, 1997, article, Rick Kushman reported some common but little-known findings.[44]

The Nielsen ratings come from Nielsen Media Research, which is the only company that measures viewers of the American broadcasting networks, cable channels, and syndicated series. Kushman reports that over one year, a single rating point, approximately 1.5 million viewers, is worth $100 million.

Nielsen has three different kinds of surveys. All of them pick households scientifically at random, "if that doesn't sound like an oxymoron."[45] The major ratings, those with demographic information, come from five thousand households spread geographically. "Nielsen researchers identify blocks of houses reflecting the makeup of the country, then computers randomly pick a household from each group."[46] Then recruiters visit, and if the family agrees to participate, equipment is hooked up for two years. If the family declines, another home is chosen the same way, but it must have the same cable status and the same number of kids as the first.

From three hundred to four hundred new households are added every month as two-year terms expire.

Extensive wiring is installed. Each television set inside the selected home is monitored to show whether it is turned on and to what channel. VCRs are also monitored and register as they record. There is also an electronic pad, called the people meter. Each person in the household is assigned a button to punch when they're watching TV and when they stop watching. Regular visitors are also given a button, and other visitors are asked to punch in and give demographic information.

If a set is tuned in to the same channel for seventy minutes in a row, a light flashes on the meter asking if anyone is still there. A "yes" button confirms that.

Every morning about 3:00, each monitored TV downloads information through a telephone line to Nielsen's central computers. Those results are available by the next afternoon and are reported weekly in the press.

To get the "overnights," only TVs are monitored; demographics are not measured. Five hundred homes are wired without people meters in each of the country's thirty-six largest markets for about five years each.

The third survey is taken during the sweeps months of November, February, May, and July. Five hundred thousand homes get diaries to record their viewing for a week. About 2 million diaries are sent out through the year and are divided among each of the country's 211 media markets. This is considered by many an unreliable method, as it is so easy to fabricate viewing.

There are obvious problems, Kushman reports.

• Viewing is not measured in nursing homes, college dormitories, restaurants, bars, hotels, or airports.
• The sample seems to be weighted toward people who watch TV, for who else would endure the inconvenience?
• Equipment failures mean a house does not get counted, and this drives participation rates down. Equipment fails the most in homes with multiple VCRs and cable hook-ups—precisely where people watch the most television.
• It would be illogical to assume that the Nielsen families follow all the rules all the time.

Marvin Kitman found it strange that the networks would turn on the system they treated as gospel. "When the numbers turned on them, they don't believe in the system anymore. It's incredible how people can finally see the light."[47] Kitman pointed out that the networks were not blaming their own scheduling gimmicks, quick cancellations, boring programming, increased program interruptions, more commercials, more promos, or infantile shows. Instead of asking if the show is fresh or exciting, Kitman reported, the networks are only asking what the ratings are. He thought that this might be funny if it were not so pathetic and predictable. Kitman asked the obvious: "If the numbers are inaccurate, why are they still used to cancel shows?"[48] And he named some of the wonderful shows that were canceled using "inaccurate" ratings: *Brooklyn Bridge, Shannon's Deal, Alien Nation, TV Nation, Homefront, Under Suspicion, Due South, The Equalizer, Wiseguy, Crime Story,*

I'll Fly Away."[49] He felt that all of the shows canceled under the flawed system deserved another chance. "In a court of law, when the evidence is found tainted, a new trial is granted. If what the networks say is true, and all of these shows were executed by the Nielsen electric chair on the basis of factually incorrect evidence, then all of the canceled shows so executed deserve a reprieve."[50]

Advertisers

I believe that as long as network television is driven by advertisers' demands for "the most bang for the buck," quality television on the networks will be fragile and fleeting. If the system is to change anywhere, it has to begin with advertisers' expectations.

Through the years, VQT members have been outspoken about advertisers. The following comments are all from the May/June 1993 newsletter, responding to my article about my encounter with Jack Myers's Worldwide Marketing Leadership Panel. (See "Quality TV—An Oxymoron?")

"I'm starting to believe that we as a society are becoming desensitized to the message of commercials, and I know that will shock the [advertisers]. Now it's so easy to zap through commercials if you've taped a show, or hit the mute button on your remote," wrote Ken McManus of Orlando, Florida.

Denise Brophy of North Hollywood, California, wrote, "I don't remember most commercials. Unless it's extremely clever, it's just dead air time as far as I'm concerned."

"If a show is a no-brainer, we may have the television on, but we're doing something else at the same time—homework, paying bills, whatever. With the quality shows, we know we'll be completely absorbed, so we don't even try to have anything around to distract our attention. So I would say with certainty that we notice commercials *less* on mindless sitcoms and/or reality shows than we do on the thought-provoking, heart-warming series endorsed by VQT," added Ann Raymont from Indianapolis, Indiana.

Nancy Orenstein of Appleton, Wisconsin, wrote, "I think we are advanced enough to just tune out what is not important to us. You learn to ignore. I know this is not what advertising companies want to hear, but it is the truth."

"If the companies really want their product to be remembered and purchased, they would do well to fully fund a program such as they did in the 50s. I still remember the Philco Hour, Lux Video Theatre, and Texaco Star Theater. Product identification was automatic and I would guess, effective. Is there anyone who doesn't know who is responsible for the Hallmark Hall of Fame?" asked Sue Chapman, of Johnson City, Tennessee.

"Although I understand that the advertisers want to know the multitudes are watching the shows for which they paid a lot of money for advertising time, demographics are more meaningful than mere numbers. People with intelligence who care about what they watch, as opposed to having noise in the background, also care about what they buy, and they tell their friends. Discerning people are discerning people, whether it's television and how they spend their time, or how they spend their money. If you have a quality product, it behooves you to advertise it to the people who are in the market for quality. This makes more sense to me than scattering bread crumbs to the winds, crossing your fingers, and hoping something lands somewhere with someone," suggested Trish Elliott of Oakland, California, for the August 1993 issue.

I've always thought that advertisers should give more consideration to *who*, not *how many* viewers they reach. Matt Roush quoted one of his readers in 1993, after the cancellation of *I'll Fly Away*. Bruce Davis in Santa Fe, New Mexico, wrote him that "advertisers ought to consider [that] the people they'd most like to sell their products to have lives a little too interesting to bother with TV."[51]

Conclusion

If we accept that the networks will become dinosaurs, then the argument that there is nothing wrong with the system can be considered valid. However, if the networks are to survive as we know them and as they perceive themselves, there *is* something wrong with the system as has been put forth in this chapter.

David Bianculli concluded in *Teleliteracy: Taking Television Seriously* that "something is wrong if nothing on television excites us at all. Blaming television for that no longer works, because the quality and quantity is there for the viewing. So the fault, dear Brutus, is not in our TV sets, but in ourselves."[52] While I almost completely agree with that, the fact exists that most quality shows cannot sustain life on the networks. I fault the networks as much as the viewers who stay away in droves from quality shows such as *Brooklyn Bridge, I'll Fly Away, EZ Streets, Murder One, Dangerous Minds, Relativity, Under Suspicion, The Bonnie Hunt Show, Due South,* and *Nothing Sacred,* to name just a few recent losses. It is the responsibility of both the commercial networks *and* viewers to insure the survival of quality on network television.

As Sam Waterston said to Matt Roush in 1993 when *I'll Fly Away* was canceled, "If TV is to change, it's going to be a result of viewer demand and citizen revolt."[53] It is not too late. I call for a viewer revolt, and I offer to lead it.

EPILOGUE

DAVID Bianculli wrote in *Teleliteracy: Taking Television Seriously,* "I believe, unapologetically, the best way to play an active part in improving television is to seek out, acknowledge, and support its most important and impressive efforts."[1] This is exactly what Viewers for Quality Television has tried to do since late 1984.

In his speech to VQT members at the 1992 Quality Awards banquet, producer Gary David Goldberg said,

> I think there are basically three myths which are falling away in American life today. The first myth is: these are the cars we've always wanted to drive; the second myth is: these are the politicians we've always wanted to vote for; and the third myth is: this is the television we want to watch. I think what's demonstrated here, and the yearning that's out there across the country, is for better television, more complex television.

He encouraged us to seize the day and take back the media. Viewers can do that. VQT can do that—with enough united viewers.

I believe that VQT's original goal can still be accomplished. If enough viewers band together under an accredited organization such as VQT—like all fifty thousand people who ever came through the group either as a member of the organization or to inquire about saving a particular show—the imprimatur of this organization, of those viewers, could assure the longevity of quality television programs.

In thanking VQT for his Quality Award for *Ally McBeal* in 1998, David E.
Kelley reminded viewers to speak out:

> I was here a couple of years ago [when] Dean Valentine lectured you all
> [that] you have no power. I don't know whether you have power or
> not, but you certainly do have influence. We're reading your mailbags,
> and we know what you're thinking, and we do know that it is coming
> from an intelligent and informed source. So while I can't stand here
> and say that you can change the face of television, I can say that you
> very much can influence the people who are in television—and maybe
> occasion us or cause others to try to change it.

In a letter published in our July 1996 newsletter, actress and author Mimi
Kennedy said to all of us in VQT, "You have changed television—no less than
that. You demanded conscience from creators and purveyors, had enough
faith that significant numbers of people agreed with your goal, and went
ahead and announced your presence in the audience, which, up until your
advocacy, had existed to network executives only as that pathetic handful of
Nielsen households." She praised VQT for forcing the decision-makers in television to realize that "their mandate is to get smarter or die. *You* were the
wake-up call."

I truly have tried to be, and encouraged all VQT members to be, as Mimi
says, a "conscience" to the television industry. We say, "But you can do better; we deserve better." We expect more series of the caliber of *Hill Street Blues,*
Cagney & Lacey, St. Elsewhere, Homicide, NYPD Blue, Designing Women, Frasier,
ER, China Beach, The Practice, and will not accept less with any enthusiasm.
The networks continue to read the Nielsen numbers but they also covet the
imprimatur of "quality." This is VQT's accomplishment. This is my story.

Appendix
Notes
Indexes

APPENDIX
VQT-Endorsed Series, 1984–1999

Ally McBeal
Any Day Now
Beauty and the Beast
Brooklyn Bridge
Buffy, the Vampire Slayer
Cagney & Lacey
Cheers
Chicago Hope
China Beach
Cosby Show, The
Dangerous Minds
Designing Women
Dharma & Greg
Dr. Quinn, Medicine Woman
ER
Everybody Loves Raymond
EZ Streets
Family Ties
Frank's Place
Frasier
Friends
Golden Girls, The
Grace Under Fire
Hill Street Blues
Homefront
Homicide: Life on the Street
I'll Fly Away

Kate & Allie
L.A. Law
Law & Order
Life Goes On
Mad About You
Masterpiece Theatre
Miami Vice
Moonlighting
Murphy Brown
Murder One
My So-Called Life
Mystery!
Newhart
Northern Exposure
Nothing Sacred
NYPD Blue
Once and Again
Our World
Party of Five
Picket Fences
Practice, The
Reasonable Doubts
Remember WENN
Quantum Leap
Roseanne
Seinfeld
Sisters

60 Minutes
St. Elsewhere
Sopranos, The
Sports Night
Star Trek: The Next Generation
thirtysomething
Touched by an Angel
Tour of Duty

Trials of Rosie O'Neill, The
Under Suspicion
West Wing, The
Will & Grace
Wiseguy
Wonder Years, The
X-Files, The

NOTES

Cagney & Lacey & Me

1. Julie D'Acci, *Defining Women: Television and the Case of Cagney & Lacey,* (Chapel Hill: Univ. of North Carolina Press, 1994), 93.
2. Alan L. Gansberg, "'Cagney & Lacey' on for Seven More Episodes," *The Hollywood Reporter,* Dec. 7, 1983.
3. Jay. Sharbutt, "'Cagney & Lacey' Going Back to Work," *Los Angeles Times,* Dec. 2, 1983.
4. "'Cagney & Lacey' Return Thanks to Public Demand," *Jackson Citizen Patriot,* Feb. 9, 1994.
5. Beverly Payton, "Back from the Brink," *Emmy,* Nov./Dec. 1987.

Humble Beginnings

1. Jo Griffin, "One-woman Fan Club Fights for 'Cagney & Lacey'," *Jackson Citizen Patriot,* Apr. 25, 1984.
2. Michael Duggan, "Viewers of the World, Unite," *San Francisco Examiner,* Dec. 18, 1984.
3. Ibid.
4. Ibid.
5. Judy Mann, "TV Ratings Rebellion," *Washington Post.* Mar. 8, 1985.
6. Mark Lorando, "Viewers Group Keeps Eye on Quality Programs," *Times-Picayune,* Nov. 15, 1985.
7. Ibid.
8. Michael Duggan, "Backing Quality TV," *San Francisco Examiner,* Dec. 10, 1985.

Victory at CBS: The Rescue of *Designing Women*

1. Judy Flander, "'Designing Women' Returns Today on CBS," *Los Angeles Times,* Feb. 1, 1987.

2. "CBS Cuts Women," *Salem Oregon Statesman Journal,* Dec. 16, 1986.

3. Liz Smith, "Mail Call for 'Designing Women'," *New York Daily News,* Dec. 17, 1986.

4. Jill Brooke, "Grant's Fury Spurs CBS Kitchen War," *New York Post,* Jan. 9, 1987.

5. Ibid.

6. Matt Roush, "Women Return," *USA Today,* Jan. 9, 1987.

7. Matt Roush, "'Women': A Will and a Way," *USA Today,* Jan. 12, 1987.

8. George Maksian, "'Designing Women' Returns," *New York Daily News,* Jan. 12, 1987.

9. Ibid.

10. Ibid.

11. Bob Brock, "VQT Had Its 'Designs' on 'Women'," *Dallas Times Herald,* Jan. 14, 1987.

12. Mike Duffy, "Viewers Speak Out," *Detroit Free Press,* Feb. 1, 1987.

13. Ibid.

14. Ibid.

15. Barbara Miller, "Her Pen Is Mighty Ally of Quality TV," *Los Angeles Times,* Apr. 4, 1987.

16. Ibid.

17. Ibid.

18. Ibid.

19. Yardena Arar, "Viewers for Quality TV Co-founder Deen Quits" and "Take a Letter, Mr. Network President," *Los Angeles Daily News,* June 22, 1987.

20. Ibid.

21. Ibid.

22. Ibid.

23. Ibid.

Our World: Not in This World

1. From testimony of Thomas S. Murphy, chairman and chief executive officer, Capital Cities/ABC, before Subcommittee on Telecommunications and Finance, U.S. House of Representatives, Apr. 30, 1987.

2. John Carmody, "The TV Column," *Washington Post*, May 28, 1987.

3. Mark Schwed, "'Our World' Not Yet out of TV's Orbit," *Pittsburgh Press,* Oct. 4, 1987.

4. Ibid.

5. David Freedman, "A Chance to Save 'Our World'," *Philadelphia Daily News,* May 28, 1987.

6. Mark Schwed, "'Our World' Not Yet Out of TV's Orbit."

7. John Kiesewetter, "It's the End of the 'World'," *Cincinnati Enquirer,* July 9, 1987.

8. Ibid.

9. Don Freeman, "Battle for 'Our World' Has Its Microcosmic Ramifications," *San Diego Union,* July 12, 18, 1987.

10. Ibid.

11. Ibid.

12. Ibid.

13. Victor Valle, "Viewers Protest End of 'Our World' with Big Letter Campaign," *Los Angeles Times*, June 23, 1987.

14. John Carman, "Bring Back the Good Old Days," *San Francisco Chronicle*, June 25, 1987.

15. Mark Schwed, "'Our World' Not Yet out of TV's Orbit."

16. Bob Davis, "This TV Fan Wages Campaigns to Rescue Her Favorite Shows," *Wall Street Journal*, Aug. 4, 1987.

17. Ibid.

18. Ibid.

19. David Bianculli, *Teleliteracy: Taking Television Seriously* (New York: Touchstone, 1992), 157.

20. Michael Ryan, "The Housewife the Networks Can't Ignore," *Parade*, Apr. 17,1988.

21. Ibid.

22. Ibid.

23. Ibid.

Quality Television—An Oxymoron?

1. David Bianculli, *Teleliteracy: Taking Television Seriously*.

2. Ibid.

3. Matt Roush, "Emotions Run Deep in Wrenching 'Homicide'," *USA Today*, May 9, 1997.

4. Brian Lowry, "The Medium Is the Messenger," *Los Angeles Times*, Apr. 13, 1997.

5. VQT newsletter, Apr. 1987.

6. Judy Samelson, "Quality Characters," VQT newsletter, Dec. 1986.

7. Ibid.

8. Rick DuBrow, "Missing Elements for Real Chemistry?" *Los Angeles Times*, Dec. 1, 1992.

9. Ibid.

10. Ibid.

11. Ibid.

12. Ibid.

13. VQT newsletter, Nov. 1992.

14. Sigrid Weingold, VQT newsletter, Dec. 1994.

15. Cecile Hamermesh, VQT newsletter, Dec. 1994.

16. Teresa Gardner, VQT newsletter, Dec., 1994.

17. VQT newsletter, Mar. 1997.

18. Ibid.

19. Ibid.

20. VQT newsletter, June 1987.

21. VQT newsletter, July/Aug. 1990.

22. Robert P. Laurence, "'Frank's Place' Adds Wit, Spice to the Rich Stew," *San Diego Union*, Sept. 14, 1987.

23. Yardena Arar, "'Frank's Place' Serves Up a Tasty Alternative to Southern Stereotypes," *Los Angeles Daily News*, Aug. 27, 1987.

24. Ibid.

25. David Rosenthal, "'Frank's Place' Is 'Place' to Be Tonight," *New York Daily News,* Sept. 14, 1987.

26. David Gritten, "A Sitcom with Character," *Los Angeles Herald Examiner,* Sept. 14, 1987.

27. Monica Collins, "The Trouble with Tartikoff's Tart Tongue," *USA Today,* Jan. 21, 1988.

28. Gordon Walek, "'Frank's Place' Has All the Right Ingredients," *Daily Herald TV Magazine,* Sept. 13–19, 1987.

29. Robert P Laurence,. "'Frank's Place' Adds Wit, Spice to the Rich Stew."

30. Tim Reid, VQT newsletter, Oct./Nov. 1988.

31. Ruth Butler, "It'll Be Murphy vs. McMurphy," *Grand Rapids Press,* Apr. 1, 1990.

32. David Gritten, "Women at War," *Chicago Tribune,* Dec. 4, 1988.

33. Ibid.

34. VQT newsletter, Aug./Sept. 1991.

35. Ibid.

36. VQT newsletter, June/July, 1989.

37. VQT newsletter, Feb./Mar. 1991.

38. Robert Goldberg, "The Demise of a Sad But Lovely Series," *Wall Street Journal,* Dec. 24, 1990.

39. Robert J. Thompson, *Television's Second Golden Age* (New York: Continuum, 1996).

40. Miriam Ford, VQT newsletter, Jan. 1992.

41. VQT newsletter, Nov. 1990.

42. VQT newsletter, June 1991.

43. VQT newsletter, Nov./Dec. 1991.

44. VQT newsletter, Jan. 1992.

45. Ibid.

46. VQT newsletter, Aug./Sept. 1992.

47. Ibid.

48. VQT newsletter, Aug. 1993.

49. Ibid.

50. VQT panel discussion, Sept. 1991, published in VQT newsletter, Nov./Dec. 1991.

51. Ibid.

52. Ibid.

53. VQT newsletter, Feb. 1991.

54. Ibid.

55. VQT newsletter, Mar. 1991.

56. VQT newsletter, May 1991.

57. VQT newsletter, Jan. 1992.

58. VQT newsletter, Aug./Sept. 1992.

59. VQT newsletter, Aug. 1993.

60. Bill Carter, "Tracking Down Viewers till They're Captured," *New York Times,* Feb. 19, 1997.

61. Ibid.

62. VQT newsletter, Mar. 1997.
63. An NBC slogan in the mid-1990s.
64. Robert J. Thompson, *Television's Second Golden Age.*
65. Ibid.
66. VQT newsletter, Nov. 1994.
67. VQT newsletter, Dec. 1992.
68. Ibid.
69. VQT newsletter, Aug./Sept. 1995.
70. VQT newsletter, Feb. 1993.
71. VQT newsletter, Aug./Sept. 1995.
72. VQT newsletter, Feb. 1995.
73. VQT panel discussion, Conference on Quality Television, Sept. 1995.
74. "Producing a Quality Series" panel discussion, Sept. 23, 1995, published in VQT newsletter, Feb. 1996.
75. VQT newsletter, Jan. 1996.
76. David Bianculli, "Gettin' A Fenced-In Feeling," *New York Daily News,* Apr. 21, 1996.
77. VQT newsletter, Aug./Sept. 1995.
78. Ibid.
79. VQT newsletter, July 1996.
80. VQT newsletter, Jan. 1997.
81. Ibid.
82. Jefferson Graham, "Winning Over Affiliates and Viewers," *USA Today,* Oct. 26, 1993.
83. Ibid.
84. VQT newsletter, Aug./Sept. 1995.
85. VQT newsletter, Mar. 1996.
86. Robert J. Thompson, *Television's Second Golden Age.*
87. VQT newsletter, Nov. 1994.
88. VQT newsletter, Jan. 1995.
89. VQT newsletter, Mar. 1995.
90. Robert J. Thompson, *Television's Second Golden Age.*
91. VQT Newsletter.
92. VQT Newsletter.
93. VQT newsletter, Dec. 1994.
94. Ibid.
95. Ibid.
96. VQT newsletter, Nov. 1994.
97. Ibid.
98. VQT newsletter, Apr. 1995.
99. VQT Conference on Quality Television, Sept. 24, 1994.
100. Ibid.
101. Robert J. Thompson, *Television's Second Golden Age.*
102. Tom Shales, "TV's Sept. Song," *Washington Post,* Sept. 20, 1998.
103. Ibid.
104. Ibid.

After Grassroots: The Growth and Development of VQT

1. Steven Cole Smith, "They Just Want Quality Shows," *Fort Worth Star-Telegram,* Dec. 12, 1992.

2. Peter J. Brown, "The Fight for Viewers' Rights," *OnSat,* Jan. 1993.

3. Ibid.

4. Mike Antonucci, "A Former Teacher Leads a Crusade for Better TV," *San Jose Mercury News,* Oct. 1, 1993.

5. Ibid.

6. Ibid.

7. Ibid.

8. Ibid.

9. Diane Haithman, "VQT"—A Rising Voice in the TV Wilderness," *Los Angeles Times,* Sept. 23, 1988.

10. Lon Grahnke, "Turbulence for 'I'll Fly Away'," *Chicago Sun-Times,* Nov. 26, 1992.

11. "Power 101," *Entertainment Weekly,* Oct. 30, 1992.

12. "Mail," *Entertainment Weekly,* Nov. 20, 1992.

13. VQT newsletter, Jan. 1994.

Growing Campaigns

1. Peter M. Nichols, "Tilting at Networks: A Group Tries to Save 'Quality' Series," *New York Times,* Jan. 17, 1993.

2. Ibid.

3. Rob Owen, "These Days, When a Favorite TV Show Is Canceled, Viewers Don't Want Sympathy–They Fight to Save It," *Pittsburgh Post-Gazette,* Apr. 4, 1999.

4. Ibid.

5. Ibid.

6. Anita Gates, "You Loved the Show? We're Sorry, It's History," *New York Times,* June 4, 1995.

7. Ibid.

8. Ibid.

9. John Carmody, "The TV Column," *Washington Post,* Oct. 5, 1988.

10. Ibid.

11. Greg Dawson, "*Frank's* Deserves Better Than Death," *Orlando Sentinel,* Oct. 10, 1988.

12. DeWayne Wickham, "The Loss of more Than a TV Show," *Des Moines Register,* Oct. 17, 1988.

13. Ibid.

14. Alec Harvey, "Is there a Glimmer of Hope for *Frank's Place?*" *Birmingham News,* Nov. 3, 1988.

15. Ellen Gray, "Quality Reaches Critical Mass on This Channel," *Philadelphia Daily News,* Dec. 4, 1996.

16. Gary Mullinax, "A New Lease on 'Life?'" *Sunday News Journal* (Wilmington, Del.), May 15, 1988.

17. Ibid.

18. Joe Stein, "Fighting for Quality TV," *San Diego Union,* Aug. 31, 1988.

19. Ibid.

20. Ibid.

21. Ibid.

22. Martha Bayles, "A Cancellation That Hurts," *Wall Street Journal,* July 11, 1988.

23. Ibid.

24. Ibid.

25. Kay Gardella, "NBC's Classy 'Year in the Life' Deserves to Live," *New York Daily News,* June 27, 1988.

26. Ibid.

27. Rob Owen, "In Search of Excellence on the Screen," *Albany Times-Union,* Mar. 3, 1997.

28. John J. O'Connor, "An Urban Fable Goes Beneath the Surface," *New York Times,* Nov. 22, 1987.

29. Ibid.

30. Ibid.

31. John J. O'Connor, "'Beauty and the Beast' on CBS," *New York Times,* Sept. 25, 1987.

32. Don Merrill, "Review: 'Beauty and the Beast'," *TV Guide,* Dec. 26, 1987.

33. Ibid.

34. David Zimmerman, "The Beast Women Want to Paw," *Philadelphia Daily News,* Dec. 18, 1987.

35. Ron Koslow, VQT newsletter, Aug./Sept. 1989.

36. Gene Seymour, "Monster Smash," *Philadelphia Daily News,* June 2, 1989.

37. "Beauty and the Beast's Third Season Delayed—or in Danger?" *Pipeline,* June/July 1989.

38. Ibid.

39. Ibid.

40. Gene Seymour, "Monster Smash."

41. Tom Feran, "'Beauty and the Beast' on Hold, 'Equalizer' to Bite the Dust," *Cleveland Plain Dealer,* June 21, 1989.

42. Jerry Krupnick, "'Beauty and the Beast' Is Back," *Newark Star-Ledger,* Dec. 10, 1989.

43. Ibid.

44. John Kiesewetter, "'Beast' Viewers Roar Frustration at CBS," *Cincinnati Enquirer,* June 20, 1989.

45. David Freedman, "Bringing Out the Beast," *Newsday,* June 16, 1989.

46. VQT newsletter, Aug./Sept. 1989.

47. VQT newsletter, Aug./Sept. 1989.

48. Rick Kogan, "Adieu, Beauty," *Chicago Tribune,* Dec. 12, 1989.

49. Jerry Krupnick, "'Beauty and the Beast' Is Back."

50. Elizabeth Wilson, VQT newsletter, Aug. 1993.

51. Jefferson Graham, "A Successful 'Leap' of Faith," *USA Today,* Mar. 5, 1991.

52. *Quantum Quarterly,* no. 13.

53. Ibid.

54. Interview with Heidi Sanchez, May 14, 1997.

55. VQT newsletter, Feb./Mar. 1994.

56. Robert J. Thompson, *Television's Second Golden Age.*

57. Marvin Kitman, "'China Beach' Enters ABC Quagmire," *Newsday,* Apr. 16, 1990.

58. Ibid.

59. Rick DuBrow, "'Peaks,' 'China Beach' Make Prime-Time Cut," *Los Angeles Times.* May 22, 1990.

60. Jerry Krupnick, "Eye on TV," *Newark Star-Ledger,* May 22, 1990.

61. VQT panel discussion with network entertainment presidents, Sept. 20, 1991, published in VQT's Oct. 1991 newsletter.

62. Ibid.

63. Robert Goldberg, "The Demise of a Sad But Lovely Series."

64. Ibid.

65. Ben Kubasik, "VQT Battles," *Newsday,* June 5, 1991.

66. Matt Roush, "TV Watchdogs Lose Hope as Programming Loses Bite," *USA Today,* July 9, 1991.

67. Ibid.

68. Jonathan Storm, "Quality TV Shows on the Line," *Philadelphia Inquirer,* Dec. 6, 1992.

69. Susan Stewart, "Complex Series Flies Back to Prime Time Tonight," Syracuse *Post-Standard,* Feb. 28, 1992.

70. Ibid.

71. Ibid.

72. Lon Grahnke, "Turbulence for 'I'll Fly Away'," *Chicago Sun-Times,* Nov. 25, 1992.

73. Steve Hall, "Do Viewers or Networks Kill Quality Shows?" *Indianapolis Star,* Jan. 7, 1993.

74. Jonathan Storm, "Quality TV Shows on the Line."

75. Jerry Krupnick, "Critically Acclaimed Series Gain Reprieve with Their Inclusion in NBC's Fall Lineup," *Newark Star-Ledger*, May 19, 1992.

76. Steve Hall, "Do Viewers or Networks Kill Quality Shows?"

77. Ibid.

78. Ibid.

79. Jonathan Storm, "Quality TV Shows on the Line."

80. Ibid.

81. Ibid.

82. Mike Duffy, "Soapy 'Heartbeat' Pumps Enjoyment into Silly Tale," *Detroit Free Press,* Feb. 8, 1993.

83. Tom Shales, "Can PBS Give Wings to 'I'll Fly Away'?" *Washington Post,* Mar. 4, 1993.

84. Ibid.

85. David Bianculli, "At NBC Quality Flies Away," *New York Post,* Feb. 5, 1993.

86. Dennis Byrne, "NBC Fumbling Kills Great Show," *Chicago Sun-Times,* Feb. 4, 1993.

87. Ibid.

88. Ibid.

89. Michael McWilliams, "'Quality' TV Stands on a Middle-Class Soapbox," *Detroit News,* Feb. 6, 1993.

90. Deborah Starr Seibel, "The Winged Victory," *TV Guide,* Oct. 2, 1993.

91. Ibid.

92. Rick DuBrow, "Video Shows Set to Take on '60 Minutes',"*Los Angeles Times,* June 15, 1993.

93. Daniel Cerone, "Separation Anxiety in Prime Time," *Los Angeles Times,* May 20, 1993.

94. Ibid.

95. Mike Duffy and Susan Stewart, "Operation TV Rescue," *Detroit Free Press,* Apr. 11, 1993.

96. Ibid.

97. Rob Owen, *Gen X TV* (New York: Syracuse Univ. Press, 1997).

98. John Engstrom, "ABC Condemns 3 Shows to 'Hiatus' Status," *Seattle Post-Intelligencer,* Dec. 17, 1992.

99. Ibid.

100. Ibid.

101. Matt Roush, "'Homefront' in for an Untimely Demise," *USA Today,* Dec. 7, 1992.

102. John Kiesewetter, "Talk Back to Your TV," *Cincinnati Enquirer,* Nov. 29, 1992.

103. Ibid.

104. Mimi Kennedy, VQT newsletter, Jan. 1993.

105. Ibid.

106. Ibid.

107. John Engstrom, "ABC Condemns 3 Shows to 'Hiatus' Status."

108. VQT Conference on Quality Television, Sept. 24, 1994.

109. VQT panel discussion, Sept. 1994.

110. Marvin Kitman, "'50s 'Bridge' down the River," *Newsday,* Nov. 23, 1992.

111. Ibid.

112. John Kiesewetter, "Talk Back to Your TV."

113. Greg Dawson, "'Brooklyn Bridge' Is Falling: Are Fans Strong Enough to Lift It?" *Arizona Republic,* Nov. 25, 1992.

114. Steve Bornfeld, "'Brooklyn Bridge' Needs Support," *Albany Times Union,* Nov. 18, 1992.

115. Peter Johnson, "Inside TV," *USA Today,* Nov. 23, 1992.

116. Ibid.

117. Ibid.

118. Greg Dawson, "'Brooklyn Bridge' Is Falling."

119. Ibid.

120. Ruth Butler, "Lack of Support Kills 'Bridge'," *Grand Rapids Press,* Nov. 29, 1992.

121. Ibid.

122. Tom Shales, "'Brooklyn Bridge' Is Falling Down," *Washington Post,* Nov. 24, 1992.

123. Ibid.

124. Ibid.

125. Ibid.

126. Rick DuBrow, *Los Angeles Times,* "Support for 'Bridge' Spans Country," Dec. 6, 1992.

127. Tom Shales,"'Brooklyn Bridge' Is Falling Down.".

128. Frances Katz, "Cancellations Irk Viewers," *Boston Herald,* Dec. 7, 1992.

129. Marvin Kitman, "'50's 'Bridge' down the River."

130. Ibid.
131. Ibid.
132. Ibid.
133. Steve Bornfeld, "'Brooklyn Bridge' Needs Support."
134. Ibid.
135. Ibid.
136. Ibid.
137. Letter from Gary David Goldberg, Jan. 26, 1993.
138. Ibid.
139. Ibid.
140. Ibid.
141. Steve Bornfeld, "'Brooklyn Bridge' Returns to CBS," *Albany Times Union,* Mar. 30, 1993.
142. Ibid.
143. VQT newsletter, May/June 1993.
144. Ibid.
145. Katherine Phillips, "It's the Time of Year When Viewers of 'Quality' TV Get Hearts Broken," *Richmond-Times Dispatch,* Apr. 24, 1993.
146. VQT newsletter, Nov. 1992.
147. Ibid.
148. Matt Roush, "Season of Discontent: A Tough Year for Fans of Quality TV," *USA Today,* June 1, 1993.
149. VQT newsletter, July 1993.
150. Steve Bornfeld, "Groups Battle over 'Blue'," *New York Post,* Apr. 7, 1994.
151. Joe Mandese, "Quality-TV Group Comes to Defense of 'NYPD Blue'," *Advertising Age,* Apr. 11, 1994.
152. Ibid.
153. "The Morning Report," *Los Angeles Times,* Apr. 8, 1994.
154. Jefferson Graham, "Winning Over Affiliates and Viewers."
155. Robert J. Thompson, *Television's Second Golden Age.*
156. David Zurawik, "'Homicide' Loses Spot on NBC's Fall Schedule," *Baltimore Sun,* May 15, 1993.
157. Ibid.
158. Joanne Ostrow, "Playing It Safe, Networks Unwrap 40 New Series," *Denver Post,* Sept. 8, 1996.
159. VQT newsletter, Nov. 1996.
160. VQT newsletter, Dec. 1996.
161. VQT newsletter, Jan. 1997.
162. Marvin Kitman, "'EZ Streets,' Rough Road," *Newsday,* Oct. 27, 1996.
163. Ibid.
164. VQT panel discussion, Conference on Quality Television, Sept. 28, 1996.
165. Alan Bash, "Kelley Gives Religion Role in 'Practice'," *USA Today,* Apr. 8, 1997.
166. Ibid.
167. Marvin Kitman, "Objection, Your Honor!" *Newsday,* Apr. 7, 1997.
168. Ibid.

169. Ibid.
170. Ibid.

Unconventional Ideas

1. Diana Lundin, "VQT Gathering Has Star Quality," *Los Angeles Daily News,* Oct. 16, 1990.
2. Ibid.
3. Ibid.
4. Ibid.
5. Ed Bark, "Tuning In to the Viewers."
6. Ibid.
7. Ibid.
8. Patricia Wettig, VQT newsletter, Apr. 1996.
9. Ed Bark, "Tuning In to the Viewers."
10. Ibid.
11. Ibid.
12. Brian Lowry, "Net Execs, VQT Debate Quality," *Daily Variety,* Sept. 23, 1991.
13. VQT Conference on Quality Television, Sept. 25, 1995.
14. Ibid.
15. Ibid.
16. Ibid.
17. Ibid.
18. Ibid.
19. Ibid.
20. Ibid.
21. VQT Conference on Quality Television, Sept. 24, 1994.
22. Ibid.

The Sincerest Form of Flattery

1. Dorothy Swanson, quoted in Jo Griffin, *Jackson* (Mich.) *Citizen Patriot,* Apr. 25, 1984.
2. Sharon Rhode, quoted in Nan Bialek, "Local Group Voices Opinion in TV Land," *West Allis* (Wis.) *Star,* Sept. 26, 1996.
3. Karla Johnson, report to VQT.
4. Stewart Wilke, "Oasis for Quality Springs Up in 'Vast Wasteland'," *New Berlin/Greenfield Observer/West Allis* (Wis.) *Star*, Nov. 2, 1989.
5. Ibid.
6. VQT newsletter, Milwaukee, Wis. Affiliate Program, July/Aug. 1990.
7. Duane Dudek, "Dispute Reveals Quality TV Is in Eye of the Beholder," *Milwaukee Sentinel,* Mar. 19, 1991.
8. Ibid.
9. Ibid
10. Joel McNally, "Local Leader of TV Lobbying Group Fired," *Milwaukee Journal,* Apr. 7, 1991.

11. Ibid.

12. Ibid.

13. Duane Dudek, "Dispute Reveals Quality TV Is in Eye of the Beholder."

14. Viewers Voice flyer, Apr. 1991.

15. Ibid.

16. Mary Balistreri, "Cancel Quality Shows? Viewers Voice Says No," *West Allis* (Wis.) *Star*, July 25, 1991.

17. Ibid.

18. Ibid.

19. Barb Falk, "Television Viewers Voice Concerns Regarding Network Programming," *West Allis* (Wis.) *Enterprise*, Sept. 22–28, 1991.

20. Ibid.

21. Ibid.

22. Ibid.

23. Ibid.

24. Joanne Weintraub, "Write Stuff: Your Letter Could Help Save a Show," *Milwaukee Journal Sentinel*, May 4, 1997.

25. Joanne Weintraub, "Woman's Efforts Have Helped Keep TV Shows on the Screen," *Milwaukee Journal Sentinel*, July 1, 1997.

26. Greg Dawson, "Whine-o-grams Won't Save Shows," *Orlando Sentinel*, Apr., 1992.

27. Viewers Voice newsletter, Nov./Dec. 1995.

28. Viewers Voice newsletter, Aug./Sept. 1992.

29. Nan Bialek, "Local group Voices Opinion in TV Land."

30. Ibid.

31. Ibid.

Misconceptions, Misunderstandings, and Manipulations

1. Stephen Lenius, VQT newsletter, Mar. 1991.

2. Timothy Carlson, "TV News Update, The Buzz about 'Rosie'," *TV Guide*, Dec. 14–20, 1991.

3. Ibid.

4. Jefferson Graham, "Fans' Support Could Save Borderline Shows," *USA Today*, Feb. 18, 1991.

5. Jefferson Graham, "'Rosie' on Ratings Trial," *USA Today*, Mar. 6, 1991.

6. Jefferson Graham, "The Scheduling Trials of 'Rosie O'Neill'," *USA Today*, July 11, 1991.

7. Matt Roush, "Keeping 'Rosie' Intriguing May Be Its Toughest Trial," *USA Today*, Apr. 10, 1992.

8. Monica Collins, "The Bloom Is off This Long-Fading 'Rosie'," *TV Guide*, Mar. 28, 1992.

9. Ibid.

10. Ibid.

11. Ibid.

12. Ibid.

13. Barney Rosenzweig, presentation at the Television Critics Association, Los Angeles, July 21, 1994.

14. Lori Medigovich and Katie Cotter, "Sharon Gless," *Lesbian News,* July 1996.

15. Ibid.

16. Linda Bloodworth-Thomason, Quality Awards banquet, Sept. 1989.

17. Susan Littwin, "The Delta Factor," *TV Guide,* Oct. 26, 1991.

18. Ibid.

19. Ibid.

20. Ibid.

21. VQT newsletter, Mar. 1995.

22. VQT newsletter, Nov. 1994.

23. Elizabeth Kastor, "Giving Thumbs Down to 'Valerie'," *Washington Post,* Sept. 2, 1987.

24. Ibid.

25. Ibid.

26. John Carmody, "The TV Column," *Washington Post,* June 4, 1990.

27. Ibid.

28. Peter Johnson, "Inside TV," *USA Today,* June 4, 1990.

29. Ibid.

30. Ibid.

31. Michele Greppi, "'Wiseguy' Wahl's No Fall Guy," *New York Post,* June 4, 1990.

32. Interview with Terri Corigliano, May 5, 1997.

"Family" Television

1. Susan Spillman, "Life of the 'Party'," *TV Guide,* Dec. 9, 1995.

2. Mike Antonucci, "Family Dramas Fail to Impress Watchdog Group," *Orange County Register,* Mar. 23, 1994.

3. Ibid.

4. John Levesque, "Groups Lobby to Keep 'Second Noah' and 'EZ Streets' on TV," *Seattle Post-Intelligencer,* Nov. 19, 1996.

5. Monica Yant, "Where's the Flood for 'Second Noah'?" *St. Petersburg Times,* Apr. 21, 1996.

6. Ibid.

7. Ibid.

8. Ibid.

9. Ibid.

10. Ibid.

11. Ibid.

What's Wrong with the System?

1. Matt Roush, "Followers Stay Faithful to the End," *USA Today,* Feb. 2, 1993.

2. Mimi Kennedy, VQT newsletter, Jan. 1993.

3. Ibid.

4. VQT newsletter, Dec. 1996.

5. Interview with Lee Ann Gradwell, May 4, 1997.

6. Interview with Susan Lempke, May 3, 1997.

7. Interview with Trish Elliott, May 3, 1997.

8. Ibid.

9. Dorothy Swanson, "Don't Kill Off New TV Shows So Quickly," *USA Today,* Dec. 13, 1988.

10. Ibid.

11. Ibid.

12. Interview with John Doucette, May 4, 1997.

13. Ibid.

14. Interview with Heidi Sanchez, May 5, 1997.

15. Ibid.

16. Interview with Rhea Baldino, May 21, 1997.

17. Ibid.

18. Interview with Laurie Strollo, May 8, 1997.

19. Ibid.

20. Ibid.

21. Interview with Leon Czikowsky, May 4, 1997.

22. Ibid.

23. Interview with Robert Black, May 21, 1997.

24. Ibid.

25. J. Max Robins, "NBC's Lineup: Familiar Faces, Formats," *TV Guide,* May 24–30, 1997.

26. Verne Gay, "The Eve of Self-Destruction," *Newsday*, July 7, 1998.

27. Jeff Jarvis, "The Couch Critic," *TV Guide,* Apr. 13–19, 1996.

28. Interview with Sue Chapman, May 11, 1997.

29. Conference on Quality Television, Sept. 22, 1995.

30. Ron Cowen and Daniel Lipman, VQT newsletter, Apr. 1993.

31. Ron Koslow, VQT newsletter, Sept. 1989.

32. Kim LeMasters, VQT convention, Sept. 1989.

33. Robert Singer, VQT newsletter, Feb./Mar. 1994.

34. Ibid.

35. Ted Harbert, VQT newsletter Feb./Mar. 1994.

36. Marvin Kitman, "Nielsen Made 'em Do It!" *Newsday,* Apr. 2, 1997.

37. Ibid.

38. Stuart Elliott, "Networks Deliver Smorgasbord to Fill Order for Young Viewers," *New York Times,* June 21, 1999.

39. Ibid.

40. Ibid.

41. Ibid.

42. Michele Greppi, "Too Old at 50 for TV's Party," *New York Post,* June 9, 1999.

43. Rick Kushman, "The Ratings Game Is a Guessing Game," *Sacramento Bee,* Apr. 20, 1997.

44. Rick Kushman, "How Nielsen Selects the Families That Rate TV," *Sacramento Bee,* Apr. 20, 1997.

45. Ibid.

46. Ibid.

47. Marvin Kitman, "Nielsen Made 'em Do It!"

48. Ibid.

49. Ibid.

50. Ibid.

51. Matt Roush, "Followers Stay Faithful to the End," *USA Today,* Feb. 2, 1993.

52. David Bianculli, *Teleliteracy: Taking Television Seriously.*

53. Matt Roush, "Followers Stay Faithful to the End."

Epilogue

1. David Bianculli, *Teleliteracy: Taking Television Seriously.*

INDEX OF TELEVISION TITLES

247

INDEX OF NAMES

THE TELEVISION SERIES
Robert J. Thompson, Series Editor

Bonfire of the Humanities: Television, Subliteracy, and Long-Term Memory Loss. David Marc

Cue the Bunny on the Rainbow: Tales from TV's Most Prolific Sitcom Director. Alan Rafkin

"Deny All Knowledge": Reading the X-Files. David Lavery, Angela Hague, and Marla Cartwright, eds.

Dictionary of Teleliteracy: Television's 500 Biggest Hits, Misses, and Events. David Bianculli

Gen X TV: The Brady Bunch *to* Melrose Place. Rob Owen

Laughs, Luck . . . and Lucy: How I Came to Create the Most Popular Sitcom of All Time. Jess Oppenheimer, with Gregg Oppenheimer

Living Room War: The Making of TV's Top Newspaper Drama. Michael J. Arlen

Lou Grant: *The Making of TV's Top Newspaper Drama.* Douglass K. Daniel

Prime Time, Prime Movers: From I Love Lucy *to* L.A. Law—*America's Greatest TV Shows and the
People Who Created Them.* David Marc and Robert J. Thompson

Rod Serling's Night Gallery: *An After Hours Tour.* Scott Skelton and Jim Benson

Storytellers to the Nation: A History of American Television Writing. Tom Stempel

Television's Second Golden Age: From Hill Street Blues *to* ER. Robert J. Thompson

The View from Highway 1: Essays on Television. Michael J. Arlen

DATE DUE